Getting Around
in China

Notes from an American Traveler

Fred Richardson

Tips and Tales

A Practical Handbook for Anyone Traveling,
Living, or Doing Business
How to do what YOU want or need to do

FOREIGN LANGUAGES PRESS

First Edition   2007

<http://www.gettingaroundinchina.com>

Home Page:
  http://www.flp.com.cn
E-mail Addresses:
  info@flp.com.cn
  sales@flp.com.cn

ISBN 978-7-119-04793-5

Published by Foreign Languages Press
24 Baiwanzhuang Road, Beijing 100037, China

Distributed by China International Book Trading Corporation
35 Chegongzhuang Xilu, Beijing 100044, China
P.O. Box 399, Beijing, China

Printed in the People's Republic of China

Dedicated to the memory of my sister
Betty Richardson
who inspired me to go to China the first time.

Acknowledgments

Many friends have assisted with the information in this book, far too many to list here, and I thank them all. However much help I've had, the errors are all mine.

Special thanks to Sun Weihua, Dr. Kevin Stuart, Litaiji, Tillie Scruton, Dana Pope, Alix Fortson, Shelly Sutton, my late sister Betty Richardson, Cai Zisheng, Lun Xin, Lobsang Tsering, Prof. Yingting Zhang, Ilse Huntley, Marv Vickers, Frans Hoenderken, Dave Zeretzke, Gretchen Wagner, Tan Jingyun, Dr. Stan Williams, Prof. Tao Renchuan, Carson Sprenger, Millie Thorson, Ollie Wilgress, Jim Lovering, Anita Anderson, Gerald Roche, Josie Scruton, Mark Minkler, Anthony Robinson, Sam and Sally Green, Sybil Wong, Jared Roach, Nurse Yan Aili, Niu Xiaojun, and many, many more.

Preface

The Book of Changes

China is changing at a breakneck pace. Nearly all aspects are changing, no matter where, no matter how poor or remote the area. For at least twenty years, China has continuously been the world's most rapidly growing economy. Some observers say China is the most rapidly changing country in the history of the world, and most Chinese citizens see this change as "better, better, better".

Some say this growth and change is closely controlled by central planning. Others argue it has long since flown entirely out of control, with the organs of central policy barely hanging on to their hats and seats. There are as many different guesses as there are "experts", and over the past quarter century many, perhaps most predictions about China have either completely failed to materialize or have occurred much earlier than anticipated. Some of the regularly repeated predictions have become stale, such as "the coming collapse" (this seems a common theme in the USA).

Some China specialists argue that the Soviet system had stability through the 1980s, but still collapsed suddenly and completely, and that the Chinese system is sure to follow this year. Well, okay, then next year.... Okay, okay, certainly the year after that. It doesn't look likely to me, but who knows? I sure don't claim to know, but I am curious and completely fascinated.

Where is it all going? Is it planned? Is it as stable as it seems? *Tianzhidao* (heaven knows).

My self-description as I watch China with amazement is "walking around with my mouth hanging open", as I ponder the changes day by day and year by year. Nothing in my life gives me the mental tools to fully comprehend this rate and scope of change. I often find it hard to believe what I'm seeing with my own eyes. It's impossible....

One thing is certain: tomorrow will be different, just as today is different from yesterday and last year was different from the year before. Dreams, too, are fluid.

Modern China is a fascinating and welcoming place. I feel honored to hear the hopes and dreams of some of the people there, and to know and share a little of their lives. It's wonderful that many of my best friends live in the middle of this great change. It is their country, their lives, and our shared future.

Notes on Language, Romanization, and Names

Hanyu pinyin (the Chinese Phonetic Alphabet) and simplified Chinese characters, standard in the PRC, the People's Republic of China, are used throughout. *Pinyin* is the standard Romanized spellings of *Putonghua,* or MSC (Modern Standard Chinese). For simplicity, I have omitted the *pinyin* tone signs in the body of the book. The glossary includes characters and the *pinyin* with tone signs.

Romanization of place names can be difficult, especially in autonomous regions and minority areas. A good example is "Nei Menggu" (Inner Mongolia). Official Chinese maps and many good dictionaries give the spelling as "Nei Mongol", but the correct *pinyin* for the Chinese characters is "Nei Menggu". The spelling "Mongol" more closely represents the Mongolian pronunciation, but I choose to use the *pinyin*. Similarly, "Bose" is the spelling officially used for a small city in Guangxi: I use the *pinyin*, "Baise". I use "Huhhot" for Huhehaote, the capital of Nei Menggu, and "Urumqi" for Wulumuqi, the capital of Xinjiang Autonomous Region.

"Uyghur" is the spelling I choose to use for the large Muslim minority group in Xinjiang. Of at least four common Romanizations, this one is preferred by many of my Uyghur friends, and seems the most correct.

I use the English words "China" to refer to the country and "Chinese" to refer to the people, and to the national language, which is correctly called *Putonghua*. I also use the English words, "Tibet" and "Tibetan", instead of Xizang and *Zangzu*, because they are more familiar to readers.

Pinyin spellings are italicized except when they are proper names; for example, Xizang, in the line above. Locations are given in conventional Western order (city, province) for the ease of readers, rather than the Chinese "big to small" (country, province, city, person) ordering.

I use 元, the Chinese character for *yuan*, the basic unit of *RMB* or *Renminbi*, China's currency. (A little less than 8元/US$1 in 2007.)

I have changed people's names and occasionally adjusted places in all my stories.

Contents

Introduction: Why China?

CHINA is important, and changing fast. This book is about China and about getting along, taking things as they come. It provides the information you need to get around on your own, to get to places not mentioned in your guidebook. It's not about famous sights, great villages, or the best hotels, but it will help you find those things for yourself, whether it's your first or fifteenth time in China. I hope it will help you accept your experiences calmly and help you see more, to be aware and appreciative of the differences, and help you to reduce your impact on the places you go and the people you encounter. Keeping the mutual negative impacts to a minimum is good for us all.

Maybe you are a businessman, and having problems with a supplier or factory in a more remote area: this book gives you the tools you need to drop in unexpectedly and see what's happening with your own eyes. Perhaps you won't enjoy the "getting there" as much as I do, but tools are tools; you use computers and probably don't like them very much, either.

Perhaps you are an "ordinary" tourist, happy with your tour: I've never met a tourist who didn't dream of stepping away from the group. Here is the information you need to do that, for a half-day or for a week, with comfort and safety.

Living or working in China? There's a lot here for you, too.

The "getting around" part of traveling — just getting to places, going somewhere, wandering, and all that involves — is what I focus on in this book. I won't tell you where to go or even in any detail the places I've especially liked. Rather, I offer broad information about gallivanting around China, and provide an authentic "feel" of it. I greatly enjoy this getting around process, with all its frustrations, and you can too. What I remember are the surprises, adventures, and people I meet, but to whet your appetite and prepare you, or maybe make you glad it happened to me and not you, I promise to tell a few terrible stories. I've carefully preserved a thread of complaint: I whine a bit. Expect some hard work and travails when you get off the beaten track.

Traveling in China is the most exciting thing in my life. I've met many people from all over the world in both China and in the USA as a result of my travels, but mostly I meet citizens of China. I go back again and again, to see my old friends and the changes in their lives, to learn something of new places, and to gain new thoughts and insights. I make the most of opportunities to see how Chinese live. Simply trying to absorb the extremely rapid transformations happening everywhere in China keeps me fully occupied. What will the situation be tomorrow? Next year?

Famous sights and places, the "must sees", hold little interest for me. I want to know who lives out back. I'm pretty ordinary and interested in ordinary things. Daily life, work, schools, construction, in the cities and in the countryside: it all attracts me. I want to know what's different and what's the same. Sometimes it's hard to discover, as people in the middle of their "ordinary" lives often tend not to notice the details that stimulate my curiosity. I ask and they say, "What?"

I travel by myself, *yige ren* (one person). As I have no one traveling with me for company and support, I have little choice but to deal with the people around me. One of my American friends tells me I'm eccentric, but you don't have to travel the way I do to use the information in this book. Do it your own way and seek out your own interests. Use the knowledge and information I've gathered as a starting point and build on it.

You too are interested in China or you wouldn't be reading this; if you've never been there, perhaps you will travel to China and gain a firsthand feel for the country and the people. I hope you will glimpse some of my fascination and see that you too can get around in a very different and interesting culture, and enjoy yourself while you are doing it. If you've spent time in China, perhaps my notes will convey useful and interesting tips and make you want to return, or write your own stories.

Guides

Most travelers want to know something about their destinations and usually carry some kind of guidebook. Getting Around in China won't replace your guide, but it will provide more detailed and up-to-date information. Use it as a companion to your favorite guidebook, or read it before you go. I offer some guidebook recommendations in the third chapter.

I try to not repeat information that is commonly available, but rather, to add to it. Unless I have something additional to offer, I don't waste space on subjects covered adequately in the better guides, or easily available from other sources. Topics such as toilets, tipping, foods and special food needs, seasons and weather in different areas, cultural and social etiquette, and common mistakes and misunderstandings are covered well in many books. Look through the background sections in your guide; read the useful parts. Seek out other information relevant to your interests: the Internet is a good place to start, and you can access the Internet easily everywhere in China; you don't need to carry it, or do all your research in advance.

Warning: Nothing you read or hear about China is up-to-date, including the latest you find on the Internet or in this book; everything is changing too rapidly. Visit this book's website for occasional updates and additional information <http://www.gettingaroundinchina.com>.

Organization

I've sifted through more than thirty notebooks containing my travel journals, looking for the pieces that may help while you pursue your own interests. Some sections of this book you may never need or read, while other parts may be useful as a continual reference.

The first seven chapters contain background and information about resources such as maps and dictionaries, travel in general, and common modes of transport. The next ten chapters are about safety, hotels, food, telephones, Internet, being sick, standing in line, and similar kinds of topics that are a part of the fun and reality of being on the road. The appendix contains a glossary of Chinese words used in this book.

I've assembled some stories as a second section, and include a suggested reading list. If you plan to carry this book with you as you travel, you can tear out the stories to make it smaller and lighter. Like most travelers, I'm always carrying too much; less is more freedom. This book is intended as a practical reference; you can skip parts that don't interest you without losing the flow. Read the chapters that interest you, and as much or as little of the stories as you like.

The stories and travel fragments come from my journals and are roughly organized by the same topics as the practical chapters, and dated. They contain examples of the usual, and the odd, special, and

3

crazy things that have happened to me while getting around. The full stories and the people that fill them are too long, too many, and too complex to be included here. The most recent three or four years of stories are possibly the most useful, but the older stories add some depth and a greater sense of the rapid change. China is a big and diverse country; even the oldest things I describe still exist somewhere.

Is China So Important?

What is it that has me so hooked, as I hitch a ride on the back of this dragon? What am I: A visitor, a guest? A nuisance? A traveler? An observer? A learner? How can I possibly presume to make observations, much less judgments? Is China being Westernized, or, heaven help us, Americanized? Or will China Sinicize the rest of the world? Is China being changed by the Internet? Or are the huge numbers of Chinese *wangchong* (net worms) changing the Internet, and thereby the rest of the world? China is already the world's largest broadband market, and as a first language, more people in the world use Chinese than any other.

Obviously China is a huge and powerful country, dynamic and complex, and engaged with the USA and the world in an unbelievably swiftly evolving relationship. If China's growth keeps on at the present rate, it will have the world's largest economy in less than twenty years, perhaps much sooner. A broadly cooperative relationship with the rest of the world is essential, but problems caused by misunderstandings and lack of current knowledge are rife. The Chinese view of the USA has long been positive: a golden land of dreams, riches, and freedoms, although recently this view has been shifting and becoming more realistic and balanced. Americans for their part are poorly informed about China, now the USA's biggest trading partner (replacing Canada in mid-2005). The American view of China seems able to switch alarmingly easily from positive to negative and back again. I see little reason for the Americans to be afraid of China, but it is easy to fear the unknown. Lack of understanding can lead to dangerous misjudgments and hostility.

Technology and Telecommunications

Where is China heading and where are they today? The mobile (cell) phone system is by far the world's largest, and considerably lower-cost than in the USA or Europe. It works better, too. Some industry experts say China's telecommunications system as a whole is now the most advanced in the world. Government policy seems to be that communication is important and everybody must use it; therefore, anything that lowers the price or improves service is good. Wow, what a concept! (Look at the chapters on telephones and Internet).

Education and Minority Culture

China's education policies and performance: excellent, or mediocre? A huge plan is under way; China is rapidly expanding schools, colleges, and universities across the country. Teachers must be created, prepared, and educated years before classrooms are built, and classrooms, indeed whole new campuses, are being built at a great rate everywhere in China. The percentage of high school graduates who can attend a college of some sort is increasing steadily, and China's literacy rate is similar to that of the USA, according to United Nations statistics. Literacy in China may in fact be substantially higher than that of the US, but literacy is difficult to measure and many different standards are used, making comparisons problematic.

China has chosen English as a required foreign language that all students must study, and a test of English competence is a part of college entrance exams. Is China becoming bilingual, in English and Chinese? Are some of the minorities therefore trilingual? Are native minority cultures being preserved, or subsumed? How about the dominant *Han* culture? Are people preserving their identities and strengths in the face of globalization and Westernization, as I think and hope they are? Why do I care? Why should you care? Do answers to these questions shed some light on China's intentions toward the rest of the world?

Social and Sexual Revolution

How about changing sexual mores? China's current sexual revolution has spread fast to all corners, coastal cities and remote places alike, pushed or assisted by mobile phones and the Internet. What will be the result of the increasing numbers of pregnancies and secret abortions among students and other young women, and what about the spread of sexually transmitted diseases, given the common male reluctance to use condoms? Will sex education in China be improved? The central government recognizes that this is important, but it is difficult. How can teachers be required to teach about something that embarrasses them? If new teachers must be trained for this, how quickly can enough teachers be created for the huge number of schools in China? What about the young people who are putting off marrying, or have married but are putting off having children? Who's going to take care of the previous generation when so many young people suddenly don't want to live with their parents, or want to live a great distance away? And who will take care of the kids if the grandparents aren't in the home and both parents are working? Life expectancy has increased substantially during the past generation, so the next twenty years will also see a huge increase in China's elderly population.

2

Background: So ... 中国, China

THERE are many ways to experience life in China: time spent walking or biking around anywhere is worthwhile. Meet some locals, find some new friends (even if they are only five or six years old). Try eating in local noodle shops. Find a teahouse and sit around for half a day; explore the local parks; go out for a walk early in the morning at first light, or even earlier, in the wee hours of the morning (see how clean the streets are!). You'll be perfectly safe. Wander off at right angles from the places mentioned in your guidebook: only a few blocks away, you probably won't see any other foreign visitors, and the locals will be surprised to see you. Spend time in places that have no tourist attractions and aren't mentioned in your guide. Visit some schools and universities; walk in as though you belong there. Go into small shops, hospitals, or factories you pass that attract your interest. You'll often be welcomed and only occasionally asked to leave. The main rules seem obvious: be polite, be open, and make yourself available.

I'm sometimes able to make the step "off the track" to small places because someone I meet (on the street, perhaps on the train, or at an English corner) invites me to go with them to their hometown, or on a business trip or something. Grab the chance. Go! It will rarely be boring and occasionally it will be supremely special.

Personally, I prefer "quests" to goals. It doesn't really matter whether I make it or not; instead, my quests give me direction, and I'm never finished. Of course, goals are mixed in continuously: buying a train ticket, getting to a particular place to see an old friend, or buying a new pair of socks....

The Dirt

Is China dirty? Many books tell you so, and standards are certainly different. Chinese toilets are honest: they tend to smell like toilets, not like artificial forests. The ground may seem dirty to you, but you — your body and your clothing — can seem equally dirty to the Chinese around you. I try to keep myself a little cleaner than I do at home, and I've worked to develop a tolerance for things that seem dirty to me. I try to shower daily, especially in the south, and I carry and use some good unscented deodorant. The reason dogs bark at you in the countryside while they don't bark at anyone else: they smell you. (That's in the south and east; working dogs in the north and west bark at everything.)

Habits are also different. Blow your nose on a handkerchief and stuff it back into your pocket: if you catch the unguarded face of someone watching you, you may note an expression of extreme disgust. In Chinese culture and traditional Chinese medicine, mucus (phlegm and snot) is something to get away from yourself, expel: spit. Don't put your bag down on the ground or on the floor, and then put it on a chair. Someone who saw it on the ground might see you put it on the chair. Don't put your feet on a chair without first taking off your shoes. The ground or floor is considered dirty. Fields are fertilized with night soil. You wouldn't spit on the chair....

As with any generalities, these things vary from region to region and among different ethnic groups. Don't use your foreign eye when you make judgments. Try to adopt a Chinese eye and see what the people around you see. Adapt to the local standards where you are.

Staring

You will be stared at; find a way to take it in stride. The staring, people studying you, is often open and brazen, frank curiosity and astonishment. If you can't accept this, you won't like traveling in China. The staring isn't hostile (it's not!). I like to meet the starer's eyes and greet him or her politely (*Ni hao*). That often breaks the stare, except when I'm the object of twenty or fifty starers: I can't say "Hi" to each of them. Ten years ago, there wasn't much staring in the major cities but it has become common again, as huge numbers of economic migrants flood into the cities from the countryside — probably the biggest migration in human history. There are many people in the countryside who have yet to see a foreigner (other than on television).

The first time I was able to watch the starers without being their object, I was wandering around with a man from Ghana. Samuel was as black as it's possible to be and an experienced welder (I also weld). We were inspecting iron gates, auto body repairs, and any other weldments we could see, as well as examining all the welding equipment around, such as arc welders and torches. It was as though I had become invisible. Samuel was so different that no one noticed me, a long-haired white foreigner. The country people wanted to touch his skin and hair to see how it felt. They crowded around to touch first him, and then their neighbor's skin, trying to see if black skin felt somehow different. He had been in China for several months and was good-natured about it. Later, he told me that some country people were afraid of him. He accepted that in children, who sometimes cried, but it made him a little angry when adults were fearful. He said "They are adults, they should know better".

Like Samuel, anything that makes you stand out will attract even more than the normal amount of attention. A flashy foreign bike, wearing Spandex or a helmet, having very blond hair or dreadlocks, or long hair and a white beard like me.... If you are a woman with large breasts, expect extra attention. One such woman I met told me old ladies out in the countryside sometimes walked directly up to her and put their hands on her breasts, saying "*Hao!*" (nice!). She was offended and upset, and was leaving China in a rush.

Name Calling

All foreign visitors are officially referred to as "foreign friends", and you will meet a fund of genuine friendliness wherever you go. With few exceptions you won't find hostility, no matter what your country or race. However, the ancient view of all outsiders as strange and unnatural barbarians or demons remains a deep underpinning of Chinese culture. When you surprise someone on the street, you'll often hear "*Laowai!*" Understand it as an identification, "foreigner". Literally, it means "old outside" and is rarely derogatory. You may hear other terms such as "*laogui*" (old devil), "*yangguizi*" (foreign devil; devil from across the sea), "*yanggou*" (foreign dog), "*da bizi*" (big nose), and there are many variations in local dialects. I take them all as expressions of surprise rather than hostility. Although if a small child calls me "*yanggou*" and spits on the ground near my feet, I'm quite certain the locals haven't been impressed by the tourism they've seen! (That's only happened once in the more than four years I've spent in China, but I try to avoid day-trip destinations.)

Foreign Terms

"China" is an English language name: 中国 *Zhongguo* (central country, or middle kingdom) is the proper short name for the country.

9

Students have asked me many times "Where does the name 'China' come from?" I get lost trying to explain about ceramics, porcelain, dishes and bowls.

There are, equally, Chinese names for foreign countries: USA, America = 美国 *Meiguo*, this short name means literally "Beautiful Country"; the UK, England = 英国 *Yingguo*, lit. "Heroic Country"; France = 法国 *Faguo*, lit. "Law Country". These short names were chosen for the sounds, not the meanings.

"Chinese" (also an English word) often refers to the dominant ethnic group, the *Han*, or *Hanzu* (about 90% of China's population). 中国人 *Zhongguoren* is a person or citizen of China. A *shaoshu minzu* (minority nationality) person will probably be happy to be called *Zhongguoren*, but in some areas may be a bit sour about being referred to as "Chinese". "Chinese" also refers to the language, *Zhongwen*. The national language (standard pronunciation) is properly *Putonghua* (common tongue). "Mandarin" is the incorrect but commonly used English language term for *Putonghua*.

I use the terms "China", and "Chinese", as do Chinese people when they are speaking English. There are many other foreign terms Chinese will use when speaking English, and some have entered into the Chinese language. But if you need to be understood by someone who doesn't speak much English, try to use the Chinese terms and names, maybe pointing at the characters in your phrase book or dictionary. There'll be less confusion.

Dates and Addresses

In China, dates are ordered big to small: year, month, day. Addresses and many other things are also ordered big to small, or nonspecific to specific: first comes the country, then province, city, street, apartment, and last, the person's name.

Other Foreigners

Away from the guidebook track I rarely meet other foreign visitors — maybe an occasional teacher — and I find I prefer it that way, as do many other travelers. But in hub cities (where I may be passing through to get to somewhere else) I meet many; and I always run into more foreigners in western minority areas (for example, Xinjiang, Nei Menggu, Qinghai, and some parts of Yunnan) than in the populous and economically booming eastern areas. If you are one who wants to avoid other travelers, just picking a random spot off the map in the eastern Han core areas is more likely to put you well out of the path of other tourists. Their density on the ground may be about the same, but their presence is overwhelmed, so the foreign visitors simply vanish into the vast Chinese population.

Most of the foreigners in China are non-American, and it's both useful and fun to compare notes with them about China, and to learn a little about their own countries, which I'll probably never visit. Their viewpoints can open my eyes to things I'd otherwise never notice. And those living, working, or doing business in China have very different experiences from a traveler like me.

Taken as individuals, these other foreigners can be interesting; in groups, though, I often find they spend their time complaining about the country they are in — the people, the culture, the lack of familiar amenities — and so I tend to avoid groups. Some of the complaints come from people who simply aren't travelers; some come from those who are unable to reconcile the China in which they find themselves with the China of their imagination. I guess if you have to complain, it's better to find other foreigners; but don't blame me if you get depressed. Students occasionally tell me of foreign teachers who complain about China in the classroom — that's definitely bad behavior.

A friend who is a drug chemist and researcher once told me a story about the only foreign teacher he had at his university in the mid-'80s. He described her as beautiful; a very young blond American woman. She began every class by writing on the board "America is great because..." and then added a new phrase. He said he and all his fellow students would put their heads down on their desks, and then sit up and try to learn something from her.

Another time, inside a major university in Beijing I needed to find a telephone, so I stepped into a residence building for foreign experts and graduate students. While I was waiting for the phone, I spoke with a professor from Manhattan who had just arrived to work on a Ford Foundation grant, something about setting up community colleges in China. She was convinced she had answers for China, and knew the way. Although she told me she loved it in China, she seemed to love only her fantasy, and believed she could save China, if only "they" would do it her way. She was annoyed "they" had changed the airport because it confused her. And although she had only been in her room in the residence for half a day, she was angry and wanted the construction noise outside the building stopped. She said she lived in Manhattan and expected to get away from noise when she came to China!

After I made my phone call, I talked with a student from Hungary who had been in Beijing for eight months. He told me he was sick of China and the Chinese. He said his country was socialist before, so he understood the system, but that people were nice to each other back home. He told me all the foreign students and teachers said the same thing, and were angry at China for the same reasons. Boy, listening to them was pretty depressing, and a good reason not to meet or hang around with other foreigners. All they seemed able to do was complain. I got quite an earful in just fifteen minutes.

Me (I'm a foreign visitor too), I often get angry about smoking and drinking, when I can't get away from it. This angers me at home, too, but I feel freer to show my ire in my own country, my own culture. In China I'm a guest, so when I get worked up and act rudely, I'm always embarrassed by my actions later. One of my most embarrassing memories is of a time I was on a trip with friends, a newly married couple. We were visiting her family, and her grandparents who had never met her new husband. Her father held a fairly powerful position in the local government, so our time there was a nearly continuous round of banquets in smoke-filled rooms. With all the required toasting (normal in China), I got very cranky and acted rudely. I should have left a few days earlier, while I was still in control of my crankiness, but that also would have been rude. It was a special occasion, a special trip, and I was lucky to be invited. My face gets hot when I recall my rudeness.

There are also many evangelical missionaries who seem unable to understand any other reason than their own for being in China. I've been asked what I'm doing in China, and when I speak of my various interests and activities, been met with a puzzled look and sometimes asked if I was "called" to be in China. I feel as though I'm speaking in a foreign language. Some appear to care nothing about the local people they meet, their beliefs and culture, but seem concerned only with whether they can change them. These are the folks John Hersey refers to as "stupid enthusiasts" in his 1985 novel, The Call, based on his missionary boyhood in China. Mabel Cabot calls them "the mishes" in her 2003 book Vanished Kingdoms: A Woman Explorer in Tibet, China, and Mongolia, 1921-25. It seems sad and limited to me, to be missing out on so many wonderful things about China.

It is possible that currently more than half of all foreign visitors in China are Christian missionaries. They are not restricted to Americans; many come from South Korea, Canada, Australia, New Zealand, the UK, Germany, and other countries. The numbers shouldn't be surprising: missionaries have long viewed China as a land of potential converts. Imagine a land of 1.4 billion people where only 1-4% of the population (depending on whose figures you accept) are already Christians. It's hard to know the numbers: in a village in southern Guangxi, I once met a very old man who said he was 108 and a Christian. He told me a story about having met an American man, a sailor, I think, when he was a young man. The American "saved" him. I asked if this was important to him, this Christianity. He replied that at his age it couldn't hurt, but that he was a Buddhist too, and also believed in demons!

These missionaries include foreign students, teachers, and travelers, and are most visible in minority areas. It is a fact that most Chinese are wary of missionaries for all sorts of reasons, and until they know I'm not one, can be reticent. Some reasons are clear: for example, many Chinese students, especially college students (once they determine that I'm not on a mission) will not only complain to me about unwelcome advances, but will ask my advice: "He (a student missionary) comes to my dormitory room in the evening and wants to talk about Jesus. I need to study and he won't leave. I don't want to be impolite, but it's driving me crazy. What can I do?" And what can one say? I tell them to be as polite as they can, and to use the opportunity to practice their English; or to simply say they aren't interested. I tell them they must be direct. Many young Chinese don't feel polite being direct, but the missionaries are also impolite when they insist on talking about religion. Under Chinese law, a teacher is not allowed to talk about these things at all in the classroom. I tell students they should feel free to complain to their school leaders if it happens and bothers them.

I bring up this phenomenon not to comment on the rightness or the foolishness of the missionary enterprise, but because it can affect your travels. I'm a bit wary of other foreigners, and they for the most part are wary of me. Proselytizing (of any sort) is frowned on in China, often strictly forbidden, so missionaries can't be very open about their goals. Other foreigners I meet, and many young Chinese, especially among the national minorities, are wary of me until they determine whether or not I'm religious. Of course, not all religious people are Christians, not all Christians are missionaries who force their faith on others, and there are many strong Christians who focus on good works.

In China, people can be Muslim, Christian, Buddhist, anything or nothing, and are free to worship as they choose as long as they keep it private. They can't fight, proselytize, or even argue very loudly about their beliefs in public, as it simply isn't allowed to try to impose your beliefs on others. I have deeply religious friends of many faiths in China who don't seem to consider this a problem for them. Sometimes I think America has too much religious "freedom"; maybe the Middle East, too, in its way. This "freedom" can allow the rise of fundamentalism. It seems to me that part of what is allowed is religious zealotry, not truly freedom of belief. The fundamentalists (of whatever stripe) call it freedom, but see it as freedom to try to impose their views on others. My country seems to export this in a big way, along with McDonald's and other fast foods.[1] Real freedom shouldn't impose on others.

If you want to understand more about Chinese culture in general, and their historical view of the Christian religion, look at the cultural guides mentioned in the next chapter, especially <u>Encountering the Chinese</u>, and <u>Culture Shock! China</u>. It is useful to understand that from the Chinese perspective, Christian missionaries and the opium traders arrived hand-in-hand, and are a part of imperialism and unequal treaties.

If you are not a missionary, I suggest you should figure out how to let people know this as soon as you can in ways that make you and others comfortable, and learn to avoid the company of those whose activities might not agree with your own.

For the most part, I try to spend as little of my time in China as I can with other foreigners, largely because I'm there to experience and learn about the country and the people on their own terms, and I want as few distractions as possible. There are already tremendous economic and cultural pressures from the outside world subtly affecting the ways in which China is changing.

Women

I frequently refer to younger Chinese women as "girls" in English, attempting to be correct within the China context as I've learned it. Most of my female friends in China prefer to be called girls. If I call one of my young friends a woman, I'd better be prepared to duck! And age is significant: unless they are OLD, younger is better. Two girls, a month apart in age, will usually be very clear about who is younger. If they aren't married, or are married but haven't yet had a baby, it may make them feel old to be called "women", or even "young women".

---

[1] See, for example, The Wall Street Journal, May 26, 2004, Page 1, "Diplomatic Mission: Evangelicals Give U.S. Foreign Policy an Activist Tinge", by Peter Waldman.

Many don't like it. Even among those who have a child but are still under forty or so, "girl" is often the preferred term, although "lady" also seems okay. But like all things in China, this is changing.

Chinese men sometimes make a joke, a bit dated now, saying "Liberation was for women". The English word "Liberation" of course refers to the Communist revolution of 1949, when women were declared equal under Chinese law.

Jobs and Leaders

Women are well represented throughout the professions in China. Top engineers, scientists, doctors, professors, skilled labor, and workers of all sorts are commonly women. The place where women's position falls below the rather poor North American standard is in top leadership and management. Those positions are filled mostly by men. Statistically, even there China is a bit ahead of the USA: according to the UN Inter-Parliamentary Union, China's national parliament has 20% women, while the USA manages about 15% in its congress. Still, many bosses are "traditional" and try to hire men, especially in technical fields. Legally, employers are not allowed to discriminate because of sex, ethnicity, or religion, but there are always ways: "I'm sorry, but he is better qualified...." Then there are others, especially in service industries, who want to hire only tall and pretty young women, believing they better attract customers. For example, tall and pretty nurses easily find work in the higher-ranking hospitals, even with minimal qualifications. Toll booth operators on the expressways are also often tall and pretty young women. In some areas, they are seen as the province's "window on the world."

Before about 1995, college and university graduates were assigned jobs by the government. This was phased out in many parts of the country during the '90s, and most graduates now must find their own jobs. For young men graduating from top schools, this is mostly good. For the young women, it is a mixed blessing. When a woman was assigned to a job by the government, the bosses had no choice, but the woman had no choice, either.

Students graduating from so-so colleges, male or female, often find job-hunting back home difficult and may be put on long waiting lists. Only unusual *guanxi* (relationship, connections) enables them to jump the queue and get a job fast. Waiting for a government job — often the only jobs available in more remote areas — can last years. This situation may get worse as colleges and universities open their doors to earn more revenue from their "paying customers", students. Of course, that's got two sides: it also means many more young people are able to attend college. And away from home areas, there are increasing numbers of less traditional jobs. Many of these offer little security, but provide more opportunities for the adventurous and industrious.

Many Chinese see their country as ruled by a gerontocracy, based on a presumption of age having intrinsic value. Leadership positions are filled mostly by old men (old *and* male); success and promotions have often come with age instead of with ability, in business (especially state-owned enterprises) as well as in government. During the last ten years or so, policy has been slowly rectifying this, but nothing about it changes fast enough for most of my friends in China, male or female.

Practicing English

Often people approach me to try using their English, sometimes asking politely, "May I practice my English with you?" Unless I'm in a great rush, I answer, "Sure, what do you do, where are you from?" I can usually control the topic, avoiding the standard conversation starters such as "What's your favorite sport? Do you like to watch NBA?" I bring up subjects interesting to me. I frequently find I'm talking with interesting people and having interesting conversations. And I may have help for whatever I'm having trouble with at the moment, whether it might be buying a ticket, finding a particular office or bus station, doing my laundry, or whatever.

Nearly as often, or so it seems, other travelers have said to me, "All 'they' want to do is to practice English with me." I always want to respond tartly "What the heck are you in China for?", but I mostly manage to politely restrain myself.

I often go to **English corners** to seek out these interactions, especially at universities. It's how I've met many of my friends. The people at English corners aren't all students, and they're mostly well-educated, intelligent, curious, and open-minded. An English corner is usually an informal gathering where everybody speaks English to each other. There are often no native speakers of English, and the corners usually occur at a set time and place. Ask students; somebody will know and they will show you where.

Is learning English so important? I don't know, and it wasn't my decision or choice, but these people are studying my language. As a native English speaker, I think I ought to be helpful, and anyway it's fun. Although I'm in their country a lot, I haven't learned nearly as much Chinese as they have English. Nearly all students in China study English. By senior middle school (high school) graduation, most have had six, eight, or more years of English, but foreign language is studied in the same way Chinese is mastered: by memorization. Many know more English grammar than I ever learned.

Oral ability, speaking and listening, lags. Older teachers often have poor speaking ability and can't effectively teach oral English; big class sizes also make it difficult. Many English teachers essentially lecture about English grammar in Chinese. There are many reasons for this, the most important being that English exams concentrate heavily on grammar and not on oral ability. It's easy to make up questions about grammar for examinations and easy to grade them. And the examinations are national and should be fair to all students, regardless of the ability of their teachers. So teachers must spend much of their classroom time teaching students to pass the examinations. Reading and writing skills and vocabulary will be far ahead of spoken ability. Carry pen and paper always; you'll be able to communicate a lot in English by writing back and forth, and you'll often solve communications problems by writing (or reading) a misunderstood word or two. It's not unusual for someone to use their mobile phone to type a word or short message to show you.

Schools and teaching methods are changing quickly, as is everything else in China. You will meet many young children with some oral ability, especially in the cities. But most adults and older students will have been taught the old way.

Take care to speak more slowly, enunciate carefully, and use short sentences. It's polite. You don't need to speak more loudly, or ridiculously slowly. Your efforts will be appreciated.

Chinglish

There are many common errors in written and spoken English in China. Most have their roots in the different structures of the two languages. These errors are commonly called "Chinglish" (Chinese-English). Foreign visitors are often amused or annoyed by Chinglish, but I see it as one of the ways Chinese students have fun with the English they are studying so hard, a language many will never use. Literal translations can be funny between almost any languages, and

Chinese and English make fertile ground, as they share little foundation.

"Good good study, day day up" is a simple (and popular) literal translation of a Chinese idiom "*Hao hao xuexi, tian tian xiangshang*", meaning something like, "Study hard, and you will make great progress".

I greatly enjoy looking for Chinglish printed on shirts. I never know whether it is bad English, or has been written that way for fun. *Tianzhidao...* On a bus, a girl who's the conductor was wearing a nice blouse decorated with printed stylized US$50 bills and a lot of phrases in English. One read "The United Anerica of States is such a thing in the 2006 of then". On the back of the shirt of a young guy working at a restaurant where I'd eaten dinner several times, "To inform is our duty. To know is your right." On a sweatshirt: "PEPSI ME". A pretty girl with "What's Now" written across her breasts. None of this "what's new?" — Get with it in the present!

Travel Costs

I've removed most prices and costs from my stories as useless and uninteresting. I'm a budget traveler, and my last half-dozen trips have averaged US$9-$12 per day for everything I spend inside China, including Hong Kong (high), my visa, buying a bicycle (which isn't necessary but I like one for getting around, for exercise, and the ease of exploring wherever I am), and everything else I buy, including gifts, and medical and dental care. I spend nearly every night in a hotel and eat most meals in restaurants. Some cities can easily cost me three or four times more (I try to leave quickly) and I spend less than half in smaller places. I don't like to stop anywhere for less than a week, which reduces my transportation expenses. Consumer price inflation in China has been low from 1998 to 2007, so my costs in US dollars have not changed much. However, it's been getting harder to find budget hotels, as they've been going upscale fast, especially in larger cities. Any major revaluation of the *RMB yuan* could change my costs significantly.

My round-trip **airfare** from the USA west coast to Hong Kong adds about US$4-$6 a day, depending on the length of my stay. I shop for a bargain ticket, the best price I can find. Best airfare prices were fairly constant over the previous ten years, but rose sharply in '05, and again in '06. Between 1996 and 2004, my round-trip ticket varied from US$420 to $720, depending on the season. I paid $800 in '05, and $880 in '06. I usually fly into Hong Kong because the tickets are cheaper and it's convenient to arrange my visa there.

Every kind of housing imaginable can be seen in China, from Tibetan tents to the beautiful Miao house above, located in an isolated mountain spot in south-western Hunan.

Increasingly common today, in cities and towns, are new housing estates, such as the above picture, in Huhhot, Inner Mongolia. Suburbs are growing quickly around cities, even small ones. New streets are built and the buildings go up. Tower cranes dominate the skyline.

19

Your standards may be different: my preferred hotels are *zhaodaisuo* (hostels), certainly not tourist hotels; my preferred restaurants are *dapaidang* (street restaurants); and I rarely travel by airplane inside China. I adopt a Chinese budget, so amounts that would matter little at home become important. Balancing all that, I usually get a private room, and for dinner, I eat two- or three-dish meals with a beer. I get a sleeper on the train whenever possible, and I often travel by deluxe express bus. I'm frugal so I don't like to spend much, but still, I could spend a lot less by avoiding big cities, getting shared rooms in hotels, eating more often in less interesting noodle shops, skipping the beer, and traveling by hard seat on the train. Or by **camping**: a few travelers I've met do, but it's rare in China and I've never tried it.

Your costs will depend on your preferred level (or idea) of comfort, the places where you choose to spend your time, and your interest and experience in finding the budget options. There are plenty of more expensive options: it is easy to spend US$100/day without going first-class, and I think it would be possible to spend $1,000/day with fancy rooms in five-star hotels.

There is no need to travel as I do to use the information in this book, but if you are seriously tightfisted like me, plan to spend US$25/day, excluding airfare. You should do fine and have money left over to take home with you. Just make your stay in Hong Kong and other eastern cities short, and don't expect to stay in any tourist hotels. Don't plan to go often to the coffee shops, or to the bars for nighttime entertainment. If you enjoy the bar, disco, and karaoke/KTV scene, or like to drop in at the increasingly common coffee shops for a cappuccino, you can quickly up your costs to more than US$30/day.

As you travel in China, when you travel in China, I hope you enjoy it as much as I do. Go for it!

3

Maps, Dictionaries, and Other Resources

Maps

Many Chinese seem to prefer asking directions to poring over *ditu* (maps), but good maps are essential for visitors with limited language skills. It's best to buy them after you are in China, where they are easy to find, better, newer, and much cheaper. Hong Kong, even though it's a part of China, is not a good place to buy maps of China; certainly, they'll be more expensive. Maps available outside of China will rarely have Chinese characters; don't waste your money.

You will want the newest map you can find. Many economists believe transportation infrastructure is developing faster in China, now and for the past eight or nine years, than it ever has at any time or place in the history of the world. A map with a publishing date of six months or a year earlier will already be outdated. A map more than three or four years old is nearly useless. New expressways, ring roads, and whole new districts in a city can confuse your navigation if they aren't on your map. No matter how new your map, don't be surprised when it doesn't show a new road.

To be useful, maps you buy **must have Chinese characters** on them. Otherwise few Chinese will be able to read your map and help you. My main criteria for a good map are:

— A recent publishing date.

— Chinese characters (*pinyin* on major streets is nice if you can find it).

— Lines indicating bus routes. Spotting the number of a passing bus or the numbers at a bus stop can often aid in locating your position on the map, in addition to helping find the right bus.

21

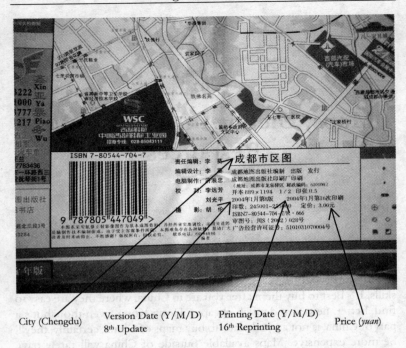

City (Chengdu)

Version Date (Y/M/D)
8th Update

Printing Date (Y/M/D)
16th Reprinting

Price (*yuan*)

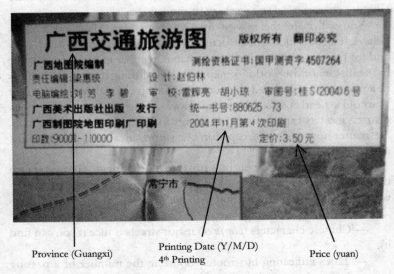

Province (Guangxi)

Printing Date (Y/M/D)
4th Printing

Price (yuan)

These are typical; there are many variations.

— If it's a **tourist map**, it shouldn't have English substitutions for common words in street and place names (such as *road* instead of *lu*, *avenue* instead of *dadao* or *dajie*, or *bridge* instead of *qiao*). These confuse directions you may try to give to a taxi driver or others.

At **Xinhua Shudian**, the government bookstore in any town or city in China, you can find an assortment of maps: local, county, prefecture, province, or the whole country. Maps of the rest of the world, in Chinese, are also available — useful if you need to know the Chinese names and official transliterations of places outside China. The map selection varies in different shops as you move from place to place even within a city, so it's worthwhile to keep looking. The Foreign Language bookshops will have yet a different selection. On the whole, each shop has a good selection.

A few years ago, bookshops weren't profitable, and the government ran them as a service so that every place had one. Nowadays, private bookshops are common. They tend to have fewer maps, but not always. Some of the big new ones are better than the biggest government shop. *Da Shudian* (The Big Bookstore) in Guangzhou's Tianhe District is a good example of a huge private one, and worth a visit. It's one of the earliest big ones, but there are similar shops in many cities now. If you ask students and teachers, they'll know where to find the best bookshops.

One of the **first** things I do when I arrive in a new place is to **look for a good local map**. I generally find them in shops near the bus and train stations, and vendors often wander around outside such terminals with an arm full of maps. Sometimes these street vendors have a bigger selection of local maps than the bookshops. Newspaper stands on the street are also a good bet, as are bookshops.

City maps will often be flat and unfolded. Some will have a decent province map on the back. Every map has a **publishing block** (see illustration). Boxed advertising often surrounds the edges of city maps, and somewhere in those boxes there will be a publishing block. Sometimes you can spot it by a bar code. It won't be flashy like the ads, but once you find it, you will see the price, usually near the bottom of the block, and a date. Sellers who have watched you find the publishing block will rarely ask more; they usually assume you were checking the price. On other (non-city) maps, the price and date will usually appear in the bottom margin, or on the back if the map is folded.

Often, no single map has all the desired features. You may need to buy a couple and work back and forth. Sometimes you'll see **tourist maps** that have some English on them (which can be very helpful!) and the names of the larger streets written in *pinyin* as well as characters. These tourist maps are often old and haven't been updated — although that is changing as the 2008 Olympics approach. Even an old tourist map supplemented with the newest one in Chinese can make a good set.

Many local maps are commercial. The hotels and restaurants they show may not be the biggest or most important, but rather businesses that have paid the map company to be marked.

I slice off all the advertising (I can't read most of it, anyway) and fold the map so it fits in my back pocket and shows the central district or the area that interests me without unfolding. I'm often able to do this paring and custom folding on a glass counter in the shop where I buy the map. They usually have scissors I can use. Don't worry about the crowd you attract; they are watching out of amusement and curiosity (*Wa!* Look at this *laowai* [foreigner]. Some *laowai* have brains!).

In the last few years, new maps have gotten better about showing roads that are planned or under construction, so I'm less frequently confused by finding a big road that does not appear on a map I thought was up-to-date. Different departments and bureaus don't seem to communicate well, and this no doubt impedes the production of good maps: "This is my business. Why do you want to know?" and "That's their business. It doesn't have anything to do with me." It must make the job of mapmaker hard; the planners are over there, the builders somewhere else, and neither considers their business the mapmaker's business. Policy makers may be addressing this problem, recognizing that up-to-date maps, and information in general, are important to continuing economic progress. The Internet is wide open, bookstores are proliferating....

Detailed topographical maps and marine charts are hard to find. Most I've seen are prominently labeled 内部 "*neibu*" (inside) which roughly means "Restricted" or "Classified"; i.e., not for outsiders, foreign visitors.

The best **map of the whole country** for a traveler is from the China Cartographic Publishing House (also called SinoMaps Press), with *pinyin* and Chinese characters. It's big — nearly a meter square — so it comes folded. Other outfits, such as the Chengdu Cartographic Publishing House, produce similar maps. The current one costs 13 元, about US$1.60. It's easy to spot, in a paper sleeve or an attractive cardboard folder with English and Chinese titles that both say <u>Map of the People's Republic of China.</u> Since the cost is low, I often clip out the section I need and discard the rest, buying another when necessary. A version with only English in the title is available, but it has only *pinyin*, lacking Chinese characters.

This map shows political boundaries. Others in the series show different information. The landform map is the most interesting to me, but I've never found *pinyin* on any versions except the political map, so this is the best one for a traveler. It is available in most *Xinhua* bookshops. Check the date, because you don't want one more than about a year old, and the shop may be selling old stock.

Along with maps, bookshops have a shelf or two of **small atlases** of the world, country, province, and maybe (but less commonly) prefecture. Other small atlases show airline routes, train routes, demographics, and climate. Road atlases for drivers are available, but they may be in a different section of the bookstore. Some show the whole country and others only the cities in simplified detail. It's easy to spend half a day just glancing through all of them.

The best **whole-country road atlas** is tall, with a brown plastic cover and a gold steering wheel symbol on the front (Bus Driver Road Maps). It is updated yearly and shows nearly every road in China, but has no landform information at all. It's easy to use even though it has no *pinyin* or English, as it has a numbered grid laid over a simplified map of the country in the front. Each map in this atlas has numbers around the edges showing the page of the adjoining map. A few other driver's atlases also use a grid indexing system.

If your interest in maps goes beyond practical travel needs, check out the large-format ones from the China Cartographic Publishing House (SinoMaps Press). They are commonly about one by two meters in size, but even larger ones are available. You can find political maps, landform maps, and specialized ones like my favorite, <u>Map of the Glaciers, Frozen Ground, and Deserts in China</u>. The <u>Metalogenic</u> map is likewise fascinating for those with a taste for geological details. These two maps come with books of explanations, in English and Chinese. There are many more, such as <u>Desertification</u>, <u>Historical Earthquakes</u>, and <u>Pollution and Ground Water Flows</u>. The only large-format map I've seen with Chinese characters and *pinyin* is the one with political boundaries titled in English and Chinese, <u>Map of the People's Republic of China</u>. It has more detail than the smaller one of the same title described above, and costs 15 元, an even better bargain if you plan to cut it up.

Map enthusiasts will like the new **Sinomaps Press shop** in the SW part of central Beijing, where they can immerse themselves in vast piles of maps. It's located at #50 Sanlihe Lu, a little northeast of the Military Museum on Fuxingmenwai Dajie.

If you carry a laptop with a CD drive, you may wish to check out the *dianzi ditu* (**electric maps**). They look interesting, but navigating the ones I've seen requires users to read and input Chinese. They are found in the CD/DVD section of bookshops. Cheaper versions may be available on the street, but they are usually illegal pirate copies.

An excellent free **map of Hong Kong**, the <u>A-O-A Street Map</u>, is available from any HKTA (Hong Kong Tourist Association) office. It is also available at information stands as you leave the airport. This map shows downtown Kowloon and Central and may be all you'll need. If you plan to stay in Hong Kong longer, or if you just like maps, visit the Hong Kong Survey and Mapping Office, Lands Department, 382 Nathan Rd., Kowloon. It's a fifteen-minute fast walk from Chungking Mansions. They have a fine set of large-scale hiking maps, among many other interesting items.

Sadly, many, perhaps most young students in China can't use maps at all. A college girl told me she knew of no reason to learn to use a map; there weren't any questions on the examinations about map reading. We were riding bikes together in her home city near the neighborhood where she had grown up. I wanted to go to a place she wasn't familiar with and I had the route plotted out on my map. She said it wouldn't work, she'd ask somebody, but I insisted and we found our way without problems. She told me it was the first time she'd seen any value in being able to read maps and maybe she'd have to learn. Many Chinese prefer the "mouth" way to the "map" way in any case, preferring to ask locals rather than look at a map, unless they are in an area where there are almost no people around. For the foreign visitor with limited language, a good map is necessary to even try using the "mouth" way.

Dictionaries and Phrase Books

A good two-way dictionary, excellent for travelers, is readily available in most *Xinhua* bookstores. It is small, fat, red, about six inches tall, three inches wide, and an inch and a half thick. The spine and front cover say <u>CONCISE English-Chinese Chinese-English Dictionary</u> in white lettering in both English and Chinese, and in smaller print, <u>Third Edition</u>, <u>The Commercial Press,</u> and <u>Oxford University Press</u>. The color, size, and English on the spine make it easy to spot, but if you don't see it, write out the English title on a scrap of paper and show it to a clerk. It has about 650 pages in each section, and, as of December 2006, costs 36 元, US$4.50. It's also available outside China and in Hong Kong, but you'll pay a lot more.

This dictionary provides *pinyin* Romanized spellings of Chinese characters in both sections, important for foreign visitors. The third edition is fairly new, published in October 2004. It is printed on thin but tough paper, making it smaller and easier to carry, and has been updated to include Internet and computer terms. You can also find a slightly larger version that weighs twice as much but is easier to read, for 42元 (US$5).

The <u>Lonely Planet Mandarin Phrasebook</u>, the old 4th edition which you can find second hand, is useful although it's too big. Its dictionary is inadequate so I tore mine off. This phrase book doesn't always give the Chinese characters, and I find the font used for the Chinese hard to read and copy. At least two-thirds of the phrases I've never used as they have nothing to do with the way I travel or what I want to do. The 5th ed. (9/04) is useless as it doesn't use *pinyin*; instead it uses its own "intuitive" pronunciation system. *Pinyin* is necessary and I like it, but like it or not, it's the official Romanization and it's what you'll see everywhere. There is a new 6th ed. (9/06) which has gone back to *pinyin*; I haven't had a chance to review it yet. The previous editions have been useful, but have had many errors and bad choices of words; I hope the new one is better.

Another phrase book, <u>The Pocket Interpreter: Chinese</u>, published by the Foreign Languages Press in Beijing, has never led me astray. It's available in English and several other languages, but it lacks phrases necessary for the budget traveler and backpacker (which the Lonely Planet has), and is out of date. It was originally published in 1988, and reprinted in 2002 with minor updates. It has a red and white cover with a couple of blue stripes and is available in many bookstores. Its dictionary is more useful, and its sidebars (for example, "What You'll Hear", and "Signs") are especially useful. Foreign Languages Press is revising and updating it, and an entirely redesigned new edition should be available in early 2007.

I have carried both of these phrase books and the dictionary for many years. It makes for a bulky set, but each has advantages, and I use them all regularly.

Chinese books, like the maps, have a publishing block, either in the front or the back. The last line is the price. The block includes printing dates, the ISBN number, and other information.

Guidebooks

Most travelers carry a guidebook: I've found <u>Lonely Planet — China</u> (the newest edition available) a reasonable guide for the backpacker, and it's the most popular. It has helped me in major cities and in travel hubs, sometimes taking the work out of finding hotels, banks, and other things. On occasion I find the hotels they recommend entirely satisfactory. Other times I look for something more to my taste in the next day or two.

The new <u>Let's Go China</u> (2005) and the latest <u>Rough Guide</u> (2005) also look useful. Like the Lonely Planet, they have some Chinese characters on their maps. If your guide has no Chinese characters on the maps and you try to use it on the street, no one will be able to help you. You'll also have less ability to figure out street signs.

There are many other guides, and a different one may suit you better, but the three above are the only ones I've seen with any Chinese on the maps. Preparing for a trip, look at what is available and choose one that pleases you and reflects your interests. If you don't want to carry a guide, you'll meet others who have one and will let you look at it for information about your next city, or loan it to you so your can photocopy a few pages.

However, no guidebook will help you much in places it doesn't mention. China probably has more than 150 cities of over a million population, and at least half of even those big cities are not mentioned. Small places? Probably 95% of China is not mentioned in any guide. Going only to places mentioned in guidebooks is the best way to ensure you meet other foreign visitors, if that is what you want, but it will greatly limit you.

The various guidebooks cover many common things adequately, such as toilets, insect problems, and seasons, so I don't write much about this kind of stuff unless I think I have something new to say. With any guide, don't waste weight and space by carrying anything but the latest edition. If you are traveling light, tear out and carry only the pages you think you'll need. Abandon or pass on the pages as you finish with them.

If you are new to traveling, or new to traveling in Asia, take a look at Rough Guide's <u>First-Time Asia</u>. For a general **introduction to economical traveling**, <u>Europe Through the Back Door</u> in the Rick Steves series contains information that is useful for travel to any foreign destinations.

Other Books and Culture Guides

There are many books about China: a few are wonderful, others are bad or outdated, and some popular travel books are straight from the ego and imagination. I suggest a few of my favorites in the back. We each travel in our own way with our own goals; what is a useless book for me may be perfect and delightful for someone else.

Numerous books provide an introduction to Chinese culture, customs, and etiquette. <u>Culture Shock! China</u>, by Kevin Sinclair and Iris Wong Po-yee covers a lot of territory. Many details are out of date, but the book is useful and entertaining. <u>Culture Smart! China</u>, by Kathy Flower is also a good resource. For those planning to stay longer in China, perhaps working, living, or doing business, check out the excellent <u>Encountering the Chinese, A Guide for Americans</u> by Hu Wenzhong and Cornelius Grove.

Business Cards

A two-sided Chinese-English business card is useful even for recreational travelers. I use one to help me introduce myself, communicate basic information about my background, and give people my email address. As much of my experience and interests lie in the area of engineering, I can often hand my card to an engineer at a construction site and be welcomed and given a hard hat, if one is required. You'll receive red-carpet treatment nearly anywhere that is related to the work or interests on your card. It's better not to present it at immigrations, or put this information on your visa application. Keep it simple — Call yourself a tourist or traveler.

You don't need to track down a printer with Chinese fonts. Better photocopy shops can produce acceptable double-sided cards cheaply. The most difficult part is preparing the Chinese side once you have decided what the English side will say. Look for a Chinese student at a local college or university: You can probably find somebody who would like to earn a bit of money and can do the translation and produce the Chinese copy on a computer for the photocopy shop to work with. Make the same edge of the card the top for both sides. 200-500 cards is probably a reasonable supply. You can have them made in China, but it takes more effort and the price is only a little less.

My current card has a translation I have refined over several trips. My first one had a translation done by a foreign student in China. Everyone was too polite to tell me "Richardson Marine Electric" had been translated as "Richardson Electricity on the Water." It was useful even so. I have never taken a Chinese name, instead using a transliteration of my name on the card. Some foreign visitors take a Chinese name and have fun with it, choosing names like "Big Dog" or "Gorgeous Lily." With help from a Chinese friend, you can choose a name that tells something about you — or you can emulate Chinese custom by picking a name that reflects your parents' hope for you, or special events around the date or place of your birth.

When you hand someone your card, be sure to give it to them Chinese-side up. It is also more polite to give it with two hands, and to receive a card with both hands. Don't quickly put a card you are given in your pocket. Study it politely for a few moments, even if you can't read it.

An Album about Home

Nearly every person you meet will be curious about you. It's nice to be able to tell people something about yourself, and photos work well when you have limited Chinese language skills. My solution, suggested by a friend before my first trip to China, was a collection of photos and maps about where I live.

My album started with a series of maps: North America, then the Northwest, and finally a detailed map of where I live in the San Juan Islands in northern Puget Sound. I marked the North American map to show the area of the regional map, and I marked the regional map to show the area of the most detailed map. Photos followed, mostly borrowed from friends' collections: what the islands look like, what I can see from there, what houses are like, shops and the post office, boats, old people, young people, parties, children, the school, farms and gardens, produce, and myself doing a typical day's work. Altogether, it had eleven double-sided pages. The ordinary things of daily life interest people most. Nearly everyone has already seen tourist shots, so don't use picture postcards.

In Seattle, I located a Chinese exchange student at the University of Washington whom I paid to make simple Chinese titles for the maps and photos. I told him why I felt each photo was important and then let him make a short title for each using his own words. I believe this album was critical to the quality of my early travels. I carried and used it for more than ten years, with a few revisions, until I lost it and the bag it was in. It was studied by hundreds of people and sometimes passed hand-to-hand in a park or on a boat deck. I often lost sight of the album but soon learned to stop worrying, as it was always returned respectfully, sometimes hours later.

4

Getting Around

T HE actual "getting from here to there" part of traveling in China is often frustrating, exhausting, and occasionally infuriating: like life, it is also an adventure and wonderful. Plan on some stress and hard work. Most of the time nothing much will be familiar when you get where you are going even if you've been there before. I try to never let this diminish my experience or make it less important or real. When I'm relaxed I find I can communicate, even if it's just a quick smile.

Whatever you do, don't set an overly ambitious or rigid itinerary. Most travelers I meet who hate China have set themselves unrealistic itineraries and find all their time and energy spent trying to stay on schedule. Maybe you want to be able to tell friends about all the places you visited, but if your trip is for pleasure and for what you can learn, make it that. How much energy do you have and what are your personal interests and goals? I try to take myself into account and not force myself into the kind of trip I or others assume I should be making. Indulge yourself; whatever your true interests, seek them out. I like to think I'm smart enough by now to scrap my plans and slow down when I catch a cold.

It helps me if I keep my plans flexible, stay in places longer, learn something about the daily life of the people who live there, and find friends. I like to become a "regular" in a *dapaidang* (small street restaurant), visit some schools and colleges, find an English corner, find somebody who does the kind of work I do and see how they do it. I try to relax and take it easy. The longer I stay in places the longer my money lasts. I try to never take too seriously decisions about where to go or what to do. If something comes up that seems better, I want to be able to drop "Plan A" happily. If it doesn't work out I move on, secure in the knowledge that something better is around the corner.

Try using your guidebook in reverse fashion sometimes: don't go to the places it says are best. There you'll mostly meet other foreign visitors, and locals who are used to dealing with foreigners (although that can be okay). I like to go to places that aren't mentioned at all. That's easy as China is a big country, and the beaten track is limited. If you gathered all the books available, most places in the country would still not be mentioned.

Try a place your book says is terrible. (But don't expect the locals there to be friendly at first. Most foreign visitors they've met arrived expecting to hate the place and to be cheated, and many also left promptly after sneering at everyone. Guidebooks can and do create what they write.)

If you travel in ordinary ways, the ways used by most working Chinese (for example, not by plane, soft class on trains, or in tour groups), your fellow travelers will mostly be going about their lives. I use the opportunity to ask why they are traveling: Where are they from? Where are they going? Do they do it often? Maps facilitate communication and are an integral part of the conversations I have in transit. Your maps must have Chinese characters to work for this, even with Chinese who speak English.

The transportation system is overloaded, so it is often hard to get tickets, especially for the train. The wait can easily be three or four days for sleeper class, so buy your tickets a few days early. Tickets are usually available the same day for buses, and are easy to get for boats, which are slow but comfortable (if you are lucky enough to find a passenger boat still running). Watch out for the holiday periods when all forms of transport will be jammed.

If you stay on the guidebook track you'll find the process of buying tickets fairly easy, as the ticket sellers see many foreigners and have experience with the language problems. Politely ask "Does anybody speak English?", or point at the characters in your phrase book or on a map. (Be sure to point at the characters, not at the *pinyin*, especially don't point at the English words.) The seller will usually then write times; point at the one you want. Less-touristed areas will be more difficult.

When I have a hard time getting a ticket, I try to remember that it's a taste of the ordinary for all the people around me. I'm in China to see and taste a bit of Chinese life, aren't I? I try to slow down, take a deep breath, and look around for something else to do. **Don't get angry** or upset; it certainly won't help.

Roads and Infrastructure

There is a slogan currently popular in China: "To get rich, first build a road." As the economy has been unfolding, all aspects of the transportation system and infrastructure have been growing and changing with it at breakneck speed and on a massive scale. In 2003 China was the world's largest producer of cement. In 2004 China also became the world's largest importer of cement. A large part of this cement is used building new roads, expressways, and other parts of infrastructure.

According to <u>The Economist</u> (June 4, 2005), China has the third longest highway network in the world, at 1.8 million km (1.1 million miles), and 44% of it had been built in the past fifteen years. 34,000 km (21,000 miles) of that was expressways, all built in the previous seventeen years. The rate of construction is continuing to accelerate.

However, the system's not growing fast enough to keep up with increasing demand. Chinese citizens have more money, can travel, and must travel more. Any information you have, including this, is already outdated. Some aspects will be more modern than anything you have ever seen, and other parts ramshackle. Expect differences from what I write and differences from what you've read and heard elsewhere. Immediate local information is best, but most locals (even tourist offices) won't know of the recent changes. Only the truck drivers will know, and they only know about the roads they use. New maps are outdated as soon as they are published.

The public transportation system as a whole is superior. It's just packed full. This seems almost a constant over the eighteen years I've been visiting China, although the system is expanding and modernizing unbelievably fast. It's still jammed (though not as badly). Since there are more trains and buses than before, the wait isn't as long to the next one, your next chance.

The coverage of plane, train, and bus routes is excellent. I don't think there is a road anywhere in China that doesn't have a bus on it at least once a week, or more likely, daily. Bigger roads have several buses a day, and, on major roads, a bus will go by every minute or two. However, service may be spotty and roads poor in remote and sparsely populated areas.

Times to Avoid

Don't travel long distances, if avoidable, in the month before and the month after *Chunjie* (Spring Festival, or Chinese New Year). *Chunjie* occurs each year sometime between January 20 and February 20, following the lunar calendar. The exact date is easy to find with Google. This two-month period is called *Chunyun* (*Chunjie* transportation). Crowding gets progressively worse and in previous years, most ticket prices got higher closer to the day. In 2007, a new national regulation forbids price increases. On the actual day of *Chunjie* no one wants to travel, so you may be able to get any ticket you want, but only for that day.

China has become increasingly migrant, and workers want to get back to their family homes for *Chunjie*. If you are in Guangzhou, Shanghai, or other major coastal cities, be wary of trying to get out until the day of *Chunjie* (unless you like to suffer). If you are heading for Guangzhou or other coastal cities, by contrast, it can be easy. You may be able to bargain, as everybody else is going the other direction. Expect the reverse, leaving Guangzhou and the coastal cities after the day of *Chunjie*. However, in most of China, the system is plugged for the entire period, going any direction. If you need to get somewhere, you can usually buy a plane ticket as they are too expensive for most people.

National Day (**October 1**), and **Labor Day** (**May 1**, International Workers' Day), and the week following each, are also crowded times to travel. Most workers and students have week-long holidays. These are called 黄金周 *huangjin zhou* (the "golden weeks"). In September, 1999, the government extended these holidays from one day to a week and began strongly encouraging everyone to travel, to take money out of their savings and spend it. Many hotels will be full and rates up. During *Chunjie*, however, the hotels aren't so full, as most people are visiting their families.

Avoid the **school rush** when students are heading to their colleges and universities for the start of the school year. From about **August 10-September 15**, students from all over China are moving toward the major cities. The last week of August is the worst.[1] Traveling is difficult during that time period toward big cities like Beijing, Shanghai, Chongqing, Chengdu, Guangzhou, and, to a lesser extent, toward any provincial capital. It may be close to impossible to get any kind of ticket. Don't fight it. Go the other direction, away from the cities. You'll find it's easy.

I try to keep my itinerary flexible. If all else fails and you can't get a

---

[1] To relieve the pressure on the transportation system, schools have been staggering their starting dates, so this period has been steadily growing longer. At the same time the colleges and universities are also expanding rapidly, so every year many more students can attend, making the situation worse.

ticket, try going somewhere else, to some place for which tickets are available. Just buy a ticket and figure out where it goes later. Chances are it will be at least as interesting as where you had planned to go.

Long-Distance Buses

There are many long-distance buses, and most of all types now run only partly full, often only a third full. A few years ago almost every bus was completely full. They are still packed during seasonal peak travel times.

New express buses, the *Kuaike* (sometimes called *Kuaiche,* and often *Kuaiba,* or *Kuaiban,* in the south), have become common. They are too new to have a very standard name. You'll see coaches by Daewoo, Volvo, Iveco, Nissan, and Benz, all joint-venture and built in China. (GM [General Motors] now owns a chunk of Daewoo. I've read they bought it to get into the Chinese bus market.) There are also several Chinese brands. These *Kuaike* are all modern, comfortable, and clean (usually even the windows). Most run on schedule, full or empty, with no stops allowed to pick up more passengers along the way. A few unregulated ones will make many stops. On longer routes, some are sleeper buses.

When these *Kuaike* first appeared a few years ago, they only ran on the new expressways. Soon they began to appear on provincial highways. Now, they are in use everywhere, it seems, even on roads that haven't been improved much. The tickets cost a bit more. Smoking is forbidden and many people seem willing to pay extra for that. There are also many smokers on these buses who wait eagerly for a toilet or meal stop, so they can have a smoke. Some sleeper buses allow smoking in the front alongside the driver, but not in the beds. When entering a sleeper bus you must remove your shoes and put them in a bag, which you carry to your berth.

Where the *Kuaike* run in parallel with rail lines, they generally cost half to two-thirds of train hard sleeper price (a lot more than hard seat), and can be considerably faster. I don't find them as comfortable as hard sleeper because I can't walk around and I lose the chance of meeting others. They are fine for rides of up to ten, or occasionally fifteen, hours. Longer, I opt for the train if possible.

There are slightly older kinds of sleeper buses, at about two/thirds the ticket price of an express bus. They are a much lower number two in comfort and speed. And there are "special route" buses that are about

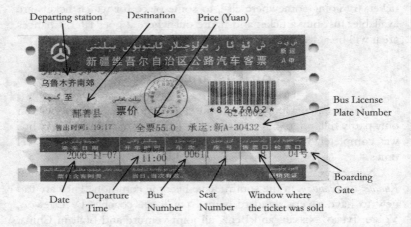

Departing station   Destination   Price (Yuan)

Bus License Plate Number

Date   Departure Time   Bus Number   Seat Number   Window where the ticket was sold

Boarding Gate

This ticket is from Urumqi, Xinjiang to Shanshan. Unlike train tickets, which are national, bus companies are provincial or regional, leading to variation in tickets. Some are similar to train tickets, while others are more like this one.

Xinjiang is the Uyghur Autonomous Region, so this ticket has words in the Uyghur language, as well as Chinese.

Fellow passengers on a bus in Hunan.

36

as fast as the *Kuaike*, but smaller and less comfortable. Next, at about half the price, come the older common buses. There are only a few left running now as most have been worn out. Some of the old rattletraps still run on back roads, and they stop everywhere.

I see almost no buses with luggage tied on the roof anymore, although the older buses (and a few of the new ones) still have roof racks. This is a new safety regulation, but enforcement varies from area to area.

For tips on buying tickets, see the next chapter, "Trains". The techniques described there work equally well for buses.

City Buses

In cities and larger towns, the buses on main streets will start around 5:00 or 6:00 A.M. and run until 10:00 or 12:00 P.M., often ten-to twenty minutes apart. In big cities, a few routes may have buses running all night. They are jammed at rush hour. Most no longer have conductors, so you need to carry the correct change, board at the front, and get off at the rear. The price is often prominently displayed on the side of the bus near the front door. If you tell the driver (or conductor, if there is one) where you want to get off, usually he or she will call or catch your eye to make sure you get off at the right stop. Disabled people can ride city buses for free, but unless the disability is obvious, they are required to show a "disabled" card.

At bus stops, the small sign with the bus number will commonly list the stops (in Chinese, of course) and the hours the bus runs. The price is often also on the sign, but may be hard to read, as it is usually stenciled on so it can be changed. Any good city map will show the routes with the beginning and end points marked, usually by a small circle with the bus number inside.

The Pocket Interpreter has a good explanation of bus stop signs, with the characters you need to know. (See Phrase Books, in Chapter 3.)

Planes

I don't fly much in China, as I find plane travel boring and expensive. I'm in China to learn about China, not to spend my money getting from place to place efficiently, and planes seem too expensive for ordinary people and are also outside my budget. However, since the cost is high, plane tickets are usually available when nothing else is.

Prices are coming down and discounts are possible. Ask for a discount, bargain for your plane ticket. You can get a 20/35/50% (sometimes 75%) discount from agents or the airline. A certain portion of seats are discounted, and the further in advance you book, the bigger the discount. Four days in advance may well get you 50% off, and two days, 20%. Check baggage allowances: an excess baggage charge can reduce or eliminate your savings. Try to carry on as much as possible. Airport tax is now included in the ticket price, it used to be separate.

Pedestrians

Some pedestrians walk freely wherever they want: down the bicycle lanes four abreast; down the sides of streets; and across streets at will. Sidewalks may almost be ignored on smaller streets. They are commonly used for other things, such as stacking freight, parking bikes and cars, and by vendors of all sorts. I was reminded how strange this seems to the average foreign visitor when an American friend who was in China for the first time kept grabbing my arm to jerk me back onto the sidewalk.

The variety of vehicles is amazing. Every kind of vehicle possible can be seen on the streets and roads. The mix of human-powered vehicles such as bikes, trikes, and carts particularly impresses me. Traffic in China seems chaotic, but I see few accidents, and walk and bicycle with impunity on most streets, except the fast ones.

Right-of-way: As best I've been able to understand it, pedestrians come first; human- or animal-powered vehicles second; and trucks, buses, and cars last. Liability also seems organized the same way. If a bike hits a person, it's the bike's fault no matter what. And if a motor vehicle hits a pedestrian or bike, it's the motor vehicle's fault. I like it. It fits and seems suitable and fair.

I must admit that I sometimes find this right-of-way scheme infuriating: when someone steps directly in front of my bike, when the bike lane is plugged with people walking slowly.... As a visitor, I'm embarrassed when I react this way, but I have to believe many Chinese are also angered by this kind of inconsiderate carelessness, though I see little outward sign. In 2005, I heard there was a move afoot to change this rigid liability progression and determine fault in accidents between pedestrians and vehicles in an attempt to keep traffic moving efficiently.

Traffic lights: They are fairly new except in the major cities, so most of the ones you see are modern, using the latest technology. Some are bright LED arrays which are low-power and reliable.

Traffic lights and pedestrian crossing lights often have countdown timer displays. These show the seconds until the signal changes. I've seen a few that use a bar graph showing the relative time left. The timers have interesting effects: drivers know when to shut off their engines to save fuel and reduce air pollution. They also know when it is time to restart their engines. (This may be wishful thinking on my part.) And few drivers jump or run the lights. They know exactly what to expect, so anxiety is reduced. They can think about something else, or make calls on their mobile phones.

Hitchhiking

It's not common, but you can hitch; it works as a way to get around on small roads where buses aren't frequent. Trucks pick up riders all the time, but usually locals and people they know. Often the first truck going by that has space will pick you up. Be prepared to pay; many riders will be paying the driver about the same as the express bus fare. Know the rough fare in advance so you have an idea how much to offer; fares are based on distance. When you offer the money at the end of the ride, it will probably be refused the first time; offer it again, and a third time. If it is refused the third time, put your money away and thank the driver. The third refusal really means "No!". A Chinese person usually must pay, but you're a foreign visitor and may get to ride for free. If you smoke, give the driver a couple of packs of cigarettes. Give him your business card if you have one, or some other small foreign souvenir, whatever you've got. A pack of matches from your home country works well and is fun.

Don't raise your thumb to ask for a lift; it won't be understood. A raised thumb means "very good", so the driver will think you are telling him "Wow! Nice truck!" and he'll wave happily. Raise your whole arm and gesture with your palm downward like you are trying to stop a taxi. Watch others flagging down taxis and trucks and do it the way they do. You can stop some buses the same way.

Be prepared with a good local map that has Chinese characters on it. Show the driver on the map where you want to go, and he can show you where he is going. And as you whiz along, you can use your map to keep track of where you are by spotting the place names on signs, often on the signs of businesses.

Hitching is somewhat risky anywhere, so be cautious and use good judgment.

Cars

Don't plan on doing any driving, as it really isn't an option. If you want a car, you can hire one with a driver anywhere easily. Then it's the driver's problem to find a parking place, and you can get out anywhere you want. However, as car ownership becomes more common, this is changing. In some big cities, if you have a Chinese driving license and a local guarantor, it is possible to rent a car. Give it another few years, maybe it will become easy to drive around.

Private car ownership is increasing rapidly, so the percentage of new drivers is high, bringing many added problems. For a Chinese citizen, getting a driver's license requires a comprehensive training course, which isn't cheap. Still, many people are getting their licenses, although they as yet only dream of having a car. Some drive cars belonging to their *danwei* (work unit), and access to a company car is becoming an expected perk in many jobs.

Until recently, traffic fines were paid directly to the policeman at the time of the infraction. This gave instant pain, and seemed to change drivers' habits quickly. Horn-honking, which has been flatly prohibited in some cities, is a good (and wonderful) example. To try to reduce the chance for corruption, a policeman was required to give a receipt for the money he received. A driver could go to the police station the next day and show their receipt, to make sure the fine wasn't pocketed.

I've been told the rule was changed in most of China in late 2004. Policemen now give tickets (called "Decision Papers"), which the driver must sign and pay at the bank within fifteen days. This change was to avoid corruption, following the policy, "Penalty and enforcement must be separated". The amounts of the fines have been raised to keep the pain factor high.

When there is a traffic accident, the vehicles stop right where it happened. That might well be in the middle of a busy road, blocking traffic. They often stay in position, not moved until the police arrive. After the cops look over the situation and make any necessary determinations, they may have the vehicles moved to the side of the road while they write up their report. The vehicles involved in the accident are rarely moved before the police get there, no matter how big a traffic jam they are creating and no matter how small the accident.

Most drivers seem to want the police involved, even though they are officially encouraged to work it out between themselves.

In May 2004, a new national law about drunk driving was implemented. A driver caught driving while drunk now faces fifteen days in jail and a moderate fine, first offense. A seriously drunk driver will probably also lose his license for two or three years. Jail for first-time drunk drivers (at least for those who don't have the political connections to get out of hot water): I like it.

Look at the chapter on "License Plates": the vehicles belonging to officials, the army, and other of the high rank are clearly marked by the coding on the plates. Local traffic police almost never stop an important car for anything; they simply don't have the power.

A *motuo* (motorcycle) taxi equipped for rain.

5

Trains

CHINA has the largest passenger railway system in the world, and its safety record is excellent. Much of it is thoroughly modern, and the whole system is being continuously expanded and improved at a great rate, contrary to what has happened to rail systems in most "developed" countries. Many lines are electric, speeds are being steadily increased, major new lines have been opened in the past ten years (such as the one to Lhasa), other new lines are currently being built, and existing lines are being doubled-tracked and upgraded. But no matter how fast the system is expanding, no matter how modern the cars or trains, it can still be hard to get a ticket, especially a sleeper ticket.

Although road and air links — which are already quite good — are improving fast, the railways remain by far the most widely used long-distance transportation in China, for both freight and passengers. I don't expect this to change, and see no signs of stagnation in China's rail system.

The trains run frequently and there are many **different categories**, varying from locals that stop at every station to nonstop expresses. The faster trains have a letter prefix indicating category before the train number: "**Z**", a new nonstop express running between a few cities, about 10% faster than a "T"; the standard "**T**" express; the slightly slower "**K**" express that makes more stops; the fairly new "**N**" trains that are like "K", but run in limited regions (many are double-deckers); and several slower categories. The slower ones have no letter prefix and are numbered from 1000 up to 9000. The larger the number, the slower and older the train. The faster the train, the higher the price.

My preference is for the "T" trains, if they stop at the station I want, if I can get a ticket. They are modern and all are air-conditioned (*kongtiao*). Most "K" and "N" trains are also air-conditioned, but stop at more stations. Above 2999, few trains are air-conditioned. It's been years since I have been on a train above this number. Check them out if you want to see what trains were like fifteen years ago. Maybe in the 8000s, you can find a train somewhere, maybe on a branch line, pulled by a steam locomotive. If you are interested in these, there are web sites devoted to steam in China.

The trains nearly always run on schedule. If you are at the starting point of the train, the gates in the waiting room will open and loading will start about half an hour before departure. If you are boarding at a small midpoint station, the train may be stopped for only a few minutes. I like to be at the gate at least 45 minutes before departure.

Nearly everyone, especially railway staff, will help you find your car and seat: show your ticket and they will point. You probably won't be allowed to board the wrong car.

Once the train is moving and everybody is settled, the conductor will come through the car checking and collecting tickets (occasionally the conductor will collect the tickets as you board the car). In sleeper and soft class, you'll be given a plastic or metal card showing your berth or seat number in exchange for your ticket. Before the train arrives at your stop, the conductor will collect the card and return your ticket. This makes it very easy for the conductor to wake passengers before their stop, if it is in the night. Don't trade berths with someone without telling the conductor, if you plan to get off at an intermediate stop.

You'll need your ticket to exit the station, so don't lose it. If you do lose it, there will be a little trouble, and you may have to pay a little money. Foreign visitors are sometimes forgiven.

Ticket Classes

There are four basic ticket classes on the longer distance trains: hard seat; hard sleeper; soft seat; and soft sleeper. I ignore the "soft" class, as it is more expensive and I find my fellow passengers less interesting. The compartments in the soft sleepers have doors, so there are fewer chances for interaction.

"Hard" class is the way most "ordinary" people (professors, engineers, doctors, students, researchers, farmers, horse traders, and the like) travel. "Soft" class seems full of rich entrepreneurs, their families, and government officials. They don't associate much with the likes of me, a long-haired backpacker.

Hard seat, YZ (硬座, *yingzuo*) has two kinds of tickets. One has an assigned seat. The other, called *wuzuo* (no seat) or *cheng piao* (ride ticket), has no seat assignment and is best avoided if at all possible. You may have to stand, or do as some do and try to find a place to sleep, under a seat or in the aisle, first spreading papers on the floor. You'll want to bring newspapers with you if you are so unlucky or tough. There are 118 seats per car, three on one side, two on the other, and it can be quite comfortable if not too crowded. For me, *yingzuo* is adequate for trips up to eight hours or so but not much longer if I can avoid it. There is a lot of smoking.

There are no thermoses, so you have to walk (climbing across all the people in the aisle, if it's crowded), to the hot water boiler to fill your teacup. In the older cars, hard seat usually consists of sets of padded seats facing each other, with small tables between. The seats are narrow, have vertical backs, and often have blue velour covers. Newer types of cars with the same layout appear all the time and conditions steadily improve, although you will still find these old cars on slower trains, occasionally even some really old ones with wooden slat seats.

Hard sleeper, YW (硬卧, *yingwo*) is my favorite for longer trips, occasionally as long as fifty hours or more when I'm crossing the country. Most Chinese also prefer *yingwo*, if they can afford it and can get a ticket. These days, smoking is banned in the sleeper class, and the ban is fairly well enforced on the faster trains. and on any train with *kongtiao* (air conditioning). Smoking is allowed in the connecting ends of the cars where the exit doors are. Enforcement of the ban depends on the conductor and the train policeman, and seems to get better every year.

The *yingwo* cars have an aisle down one side and rows of triple-deck bunks down the other, in eleven compartments of six beds each, 66 beds per car. The two upper bunks have a rail or a couple of vertically connected straps to prevent people from falling out. The compartments are open, and the middle and upper bunks are accessed by climbing a ladder in the aisle, or in some of the newer cars, by steps inside the compartments. The steps make for less congestion in the aisles.

The aisles have small tables with fold-down seats, and there is a larger table under the window in each compartment. They are communal. You can leave things, such as food and your teacup, on the tables, but each two are shared by six people if the car is full. (If you are traveling in hard seat without a seat, sometimes late at night it is possible to move into a hard sleeper car and sit on one of these fold-down seats for a while, until you are caught by the conductor, who'll make you move back. If you try this, you'll have to leave your luggage unattended in the hard seat car, a little risky unless you can get someone to watch it for you.)

Luggage is stowed on overhead racks, under the table between the berths, and under the bottom bunks. In some new cars, access to the overhead rack is from inside the compartments, reducing aisle congestion and improving safety, as luggage can't fall into the aisle. Only about a third can fall at all, as the rest of the space opens onto the top bunks, but it is harder to get your stuff up there.

I pack everything I expect to need during the trip, such as a towel, soap, toothbrush, maps, dictionary, and reading matter in a small bag I keep on my berth. It is inconvenient for me and for everyone else if I need to get into my luggage. However, if I do need to get into my bags, others will usually cooperate and help.

I prefer 中铺 *zhongpu*, the middle bunk. With the middle berth, my junk is at eye level and I can lie down any time I want. 上铺 *shangpu*, the upper bunk, is a little lower-priced but has more difficult access. Neither have enough head room to sit up comfortably. The lower bunk, 下铺 *xiapu*, has plenty of head room. It is a bit more expensive, and communal; everyone sits on it. You can politely ask people to move when you want to stretch out, it's your bed, but....

Berths 1 and 2, and 21 and 22 are somewhat undesirable, as they are at the ends of the car, closest to the toilets and smoking areas which are lighted all night.

In hard sleeper, I move around freely from one compartment to the next, and from car to car down the aisles. I can always find interesting people. Even ordinarily busy people have little to do on the train other than eating and pursuing conversation. It is fun, and I have made good friends on the trains. I also play with little kids, usually appreciated by their parents, unless I get them all wound up right before bedtime.

Music may start playing loudly around 6:30 A.M. (less likely now than a few years ago), and lights-out can be as early as 9:30 P.M. It's variable from train to train, and individual conductors seem to have a lot of control over this. If you are lucky, you may find a control on the wall or behind a curtain near the speaker to shut the thing off or reduce the volume. There is a speaker about every three compartments, which is bad if it happens to be centered on your compartment and the volume is high.

Hot water for drinking is available from a boiler at one end of the car (or every other car on older or partially filled trains), and there is a thermos or two in every sleeper compartment which you fill yourself. Every self-respecting traveler carries a small bag of tea and a *pingzi* (traveling tea jar, usually with a tight sealing screw-on lid). Many kinds of *pingzi* are available in shops around the stations and in any department store. There are fancy and expensive stainless steel thermos cups, simple plastic ones with good lids, and cheap ones. Check the gasket and the quality of the screw-on lid. Some of the simple ones have better gaskets and lids than the expensive ones.

The other end of the car has a couple of toilets and sinks. Toilet paper is not provided; carry your own. The newer cars have LED signs that indicate when the toilets are occupied, and the toilet door locks also change a small mechanical sign on the door from green (unoccupied) to red (occupied) when locked. Some new cars also have continuous reading signs that give information such as time, next stop, outside temperature, and current speed. Part of this is sometimes displayed alternately in Chinese and in English.

Soft Seat, RZ (软座, *ruanzuo*) is available on some trains. The seats are comfortable, even luxurious, and it is less crowded. Passengers without seats aren't allowed in the cars. It is considerably more expensive than hard seat.

Soft Sleeper, RW (软卧, *ruanwo*) has compartments of four berths with doors that can be locked from the inside, usually 36 berths per car. It is nearly as expensive as a bargain airplane ticket. A few long-distance trains do not have a soft sleeper car; they are luxury travel for the rich.

Food

On most trains except short-distance ones, there is a restaurant car. Some passengers like this service, but I don't use it often, as I find the price excessive and the boxed meals nearly as good. The restaurant car is more comfortable; you have a lot of space and elbow room.

Carts are pushed down the aisles frequently offering snacks, instant noodles, bottled drinks, and at meal times boxed hot food. I like to get off the train for a few minutes at stops to stretch and sometimes buy food from vendors on the platforms. There is usually a schedule posted at one end of the car, so it's easy to find the time of the next stop.

Most passengers carry bags of fruit, hard-boiled eggs, sometimes a roasted chicken, and containers of instant noodles. Everything is lower-cost outside the stations, and some Chinese complain that the food in the stations and on the trains is poor quality. I'm always carrying too much so I pay the higher prices, and I find the quality okay.

Schedules

Train schedules (in Chinese) are posted in every station and ticket office, in most train cars, and at many hotels. There are also various schedules for sale in stations. The smallest is a single sheet, showing trains from that city, or in the area. Next is a small book showing more trains in the region.

I buy the biggest schedule, *quanguo lieche shikebiao*, the "whole country train schedule" book, 320 pages (in 2006). It lists most passenger trains in the country, and all the stops. (There is a smaller *quanguo* [whole country] version that shows only the main stops, or only the beginning and the end cities.) Many smaller branch lines are not included in the big book; information on these is often only available locally (or in Duncan Peattie's English schedule; see below).

If you hunt, you can find the big schedule book in three formats: a small-print one I find difficult to read; the middle-sized common one, which I find reasonably easy to carry (after I thin it down by tearing out all the advertising at the ends); and a much bigger large-print version. The middle-sized one currently costs 8 元 (about a US dollar) and they are updated twice a year, in April and October. Smaller local-area schedules may be updated more frequently. The year and month is clearly printed on all of them in Arabic numerals, year first, i.e. 2006/10. Be sure you have a current one; you'll be happier. Look for the schedule book in train stations, at shops and booths outside the station, and in book shops.

These schedules are all in Chinese characters (no *pinyin*), but I find them usable with some effort. I start by **finding the characters** for where I am and where I want to go, usually from a map. Then I scan down the index pages until I find the two cities, and turn to that page. Most trains making the route are on that page. I can then work out the entire route of the trains with a good map, a quiet room, and patience, although the full route of the train may be continued on several pages. (There will be a page number at the top or bottom of the column for the particular train.) I have not managed to use the Ministry of Railways web site schedule. It's all in Chinese, and the menus and commands buffalo me. Maybe someday they will post one in English.

I find it actually quite easy to **read place name**s (my maps come in handy for reference). I look for something a little different in the characters of the place name I'm interested in, something I can try to find and recognize, and then scan down the columns. I managed to do this the first time I visited China. Now, most of the Chinese I can read are words common in place names; it doesn't help with a newspaper! I also get some practice writing (copying) these few characters when I make notes to help with buying tickets.

English Schedule: If you find the Chinese train schedules intimidating and plan to do a lot of train travel or live in China, you may want more. Duncan Peattie has compiled and maintains an excellent translated train timetable for all China. This English timetable also includes information on some local lines not included in the big Chinese schedule book. Notes and information he provides have helped me understand many details that were incomprehensible before, for example trains that don't run daily. It is available in PDF (if you carry a notebook computer) for US$18, and in printed form, A5 size (5 7/8" x 8 1/4"), US$30, or in a larger and easier to read, but harder to carry, A4 size (8 1/4" x 11 3/4"), US$36. Both prices including airmail postage to anywhere in the world. Order from his web site, <http://www.chinatt.org>.

The full version of this schedule includes a **printable ticket booking form**. It can help, but I find the simple printed notes I make adequate. This booking form does allow the ticket seller to explain many more complex things to you, and may help when you encounter difficulties.

Duncan's English schedule is arranged differently from the Chinese one, by route instead of by train, and you may find it easier to use. China's railway system is huge, and any schedule for the whole country is guaranteed to be intimidating and complex. He also produces a free **Quick Reference Timetable** which you can download from his site. It covers popular trains between major cities, but doesn't show all stops. Download or print it: it may be all you need, and certainly will help you understand the Chinese schedules described above, where you'll be able to find additional information, if you need it.

Internet: There are web sites that offer train schedule information, but the ones I've looked at often don't give the date or source of their information. One I tried allowed me to type in the names of two cities, the start and where I wanted to go, with the option of adding the name of a city in the middle if there was a choice of routes. It worked well enough, but didn't show the whole route and all stops, and there was no date. When I checked, the information was current for the train number I tried. Find these sites by googling subjects such as "China train schedule" and "China railway timetable". These sites do provide train numbers which are then easy to look up in a schedule book. Other sites offer information for railway buffs and are fun to look at, but useless for average travelers. New and better web sites appear all the time, and Internet cafes are everywhere in China.

Electronic notice boards are becoming common in larger stations. These show the train number, and may show the kinds of tickets available for that train over the next few days. These boards switch through different trains a little too quickly for me to read, but once I figure out which column is 硬卧 *yingwo* (hard sleeper), I can catch whether that column says 无 (*wu*, don't have) or 有 (*you*, have) for my train. I may have to watch the display roll around several times, but it works.

Tickets

The train station ticket office sells same-day tickets and tickets for up to about a week in advance, and maybe for as much as twenty days in advance before *Chunjie* (Chinese New Year). Before going to buy a ticket, I prepare a simple note consisting of an arrow pointing to the name of the city (in Chinese characters) where I'm going, and below that the train number (or numbers, in order of my preference), then the date I want to travel, and the ticket class I want. All this is in Chinese, copying the few characters needed from a phrase book and map.

I try to tell the ticket seller all this in Chinese, but the note helps her (or occasionally him) understand and to be happy she is selling me the ticket I want. I managed to prepare these notes the first time I was in China, and you can, too. Even as my minimal Chinese improves, I still prepare the notes. It can be noisy in the ticket office, crazy and crowded. Anything that helps the clerk gets me better service. It seems everyone else is yelling at her. Duncan's printable booking form (see English schedule above) can help, if you need more information.

A few larger stations, such as the main Beijing station, may have a special ticket window for foreign visitors. Other than these, don't expect any English from the clerks, as most young people with good English can find better jobs. However, as the 2008 Olympics approach, the use of English at service counters all over China is increasing.

Someone at the information desk may know some English and be able to help you understand your ticket. They might help you write a note for the ticket seller, or even help you buy your ticket.

There are often others buying tickets who speak some English, and they may offer to help you. Just stand around looking confused (that's easy!). After a bit, someone will probably approach you. A few are scalpers who will get you a ticket for a price. If you look as if you know what you are doing, you'll usually be left alone.

When buying a ticket at a small intermediate station for a train that starts somewhere else, the seller may tell you the only ticket is 站票 *zhan piao*, with no seat or bed. This doesn't necessarily mean the train is crowded, only that the station cannot sell a ticket with reserved seat or bed. (If you are told this at the starting point of the train, it's bad news; try for a later date.) When you board the train, you can 补票 *bupiao* (upgrade) and get a bed if the train isn't crowded, but there is no guarantee one will be available. Boarding a train with *zhan piao*, tell the conductors you want to *bupiao*, and they will direct you to the car with the office.

On your ticket (see picture) in the upper right corner is the name of the city where the ticket was sold; on the line below that, the name of the departure city, an arrow to the name of the city where you are heading, and the train number; on the next line, the date (year-month-day), time of departure (24-hour Beijing time), and the car number, followed by your seat or berth number; below that in about the middle of the ticket is the price. If it is a sleeper ticket, the berth number is followed by characters for upper (上, *shang*), middle (中, *zhong*), or lower (下, *xia*). Soft sleep has only upper and lower berths.[1]

It's possible to buy **connecting tickets**: about 1999, train tickets became computer-printed all over China. By 2001, the computers were networked. Now, it is possible to buy a ticket from anywhere to anywhere at almost any railway ticket office in China, with some advance purchase limits.

At the beginning it was difficult to do this, as the seller had never done it before and didn't really believe it was possible. If I had the train number and could get the clerk to type it into the computer: *Wa*! It works! There is no commission charged if you buy your ticket at the station, and most clerks are now familiar with selling connecting tickets.

---

[1] This is the layout used in 2000-2006. It may change. For example, tickets increasingly have the origin and destination city names also in *pinyin*.

HOW TO READ A CHINESE RAILWAY TICKET

This is an example of the most common Chinese railway ticket.

The background color is pink, although the shade may vary. On most tickets issued since mid-2006, station names are shown in both *Hanzi* (Chinese characters) and *pinyin*. This ticket is for a *yingwo* (hard sleeper) from Chengdu to Xining.

Thanks to Duncan Peattie, <http://www.chinatt.org> (English Schedule) for helping with this ticket page.

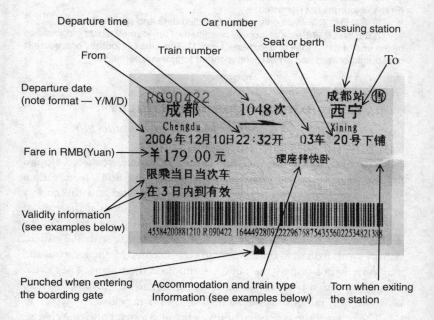

Departure time — Car number — Issuing station

Seat or berth number

From — Train number — To

Departure date (note format — Y/M/D)

Fare in RMB(Yuan)

Validity information (see examples below)

Punched when entering the boarding gate — Accommodation and train type Information (see examples below) — Torn when exiting the station

上(upper), 中(middle), 下(lower) may appear after the berth number. In the case of seat numbers 上 or 下 refers to the upper or lower deck of a double deck car. If the characters 无座 are shown instead of a car or seat number this indicates "no reserved seat".

Examples of accommodation/train type information:

硬座 Hard class [seat]	新 New (higher standard accommodation)
软座 Soft class [seat]	准高速 Quasi-high-speed train (Guang-Shen line only)
硬座卧 Hard class sleeping berth	特快 Express train
软座卧 Soft class sleeping berth	快速 Fast train
空调 Air-conditioned	普快 Ordinary train

Characters are combined as appropriate, for example:

硬座普快 Hard class [seat], ordinary train.
硬座普快卧 Hard class [sleeper], ordinary train (the example ticket above).
新空调硬座特快 New air-conditioned hard class [seat], express train.
新空调硬座特快卧 New air-conditioned hard class, express train, sleeping berth.

Examples of validity information:

当日使用一次有效 Valid on the specified date on any train - one use only (Break of journey not permitted).

限乘当日当次车 Valid only on the specified date and specified train.

在3日内到有效 Break of journey permitted — the journey must be completed by the end of day 3 (day of departure is day 1). The break of journey procedure is not straightforward and is not recommended for the inexperienced.

Advance Purchase Offices
火车代售票处 (*Huoche daishoupiaochu*)

There are railway advance purchase ticket offices scattered around most cities, even small ones, including some that don't have a train station. The first were operated by the railroad, and had the railway symbol (an inverted C over the shape of a track, shown at the start of this chapter) on the sign. In these, the clerks usually wore railway uniforms, and there was a plaque on the wall inside with the official railway symbol on it. Many are private now, licensed by the railroad, and may or may not display the railway symbol on their signs. They often have signs with a blue background saying 代售票处 (*Daishoupiaochu*). Most sell only rail tickets, but some also sell plane tickets.

They charge the face price of the ticket plus a small booking charge, currently 5元 (≈US60¢) and print your ticket immediately. There are advance purchase limits, although they seem variable. Generally, you cannot buy a same-day ticket, or one for more than five, or maybe eight days in advance. You can probably buy a ticket from anywhere to anywhere, although this also is variable. Think about the next leg of your travels. The advance purchase limit may be longer before *Chunjie*, possible up to twenty days. The rules are usually the same as at the station ticket office.

These agent ticket offices can be hard to find. The train stations won't tell you where the offices are located, as the station's ticket office wants the business. They may be huge, as big as the ticket office at the station with many windows and lines, or more often tiny, with one or two clerks and one window. Some are only a window opening onto the sidewalk. However, they are worth finding as it makes getting rail tickets easy. Only people who travel will know of the advance purchase offices, but even they won't if their *danwei* (work unit) gets their tickets for them. Frequent travelers such as businessmen and some students may be able to tell you where one is located. Sometimes a friendly travel agent or the *fuwutai* (receptionist) at your hotel will tell you. As you wander around, keep your eye open for the railway symbol, or something that looks like a tiny ticket office with posted railway schedules. It might be a freight office, or *Wa!*, a ticket office. There are usually offices somewhere around universities.

Other booking agents such as the many private travel offices, hotel travel desks, or CITS (China International Travel Service) and its counterparts charge much higher fees, usually at least 20 元 (≈US$2.50), possibly as much as 50 元 (≈US$6.25) and you seldom get your ticket immediately. You pay, receive a receipt, and must return later, maybe after a few days, to pick up the ticket. (They may deliver the ticket to you if you have an address and someone is there to receive it.) If my departure time is important, this makes me nervous. I like to have the ticket in my hand, and of course I also hate to pay the higher commissions. These agents are allowed to add a maximum 5 or 10 元 commission, but they can always find ways to add services charges.

Lunch with a nurse and a teacher.

53

College students on their way home.

A retired engineer tells a story about building a hospital in a remote part of Qinghai Province.

6

Boats

TRAVELING by boat has been my favorite since I first came to China in 1988. I live on an island; I like boats. Back then, passenger boats ran several times a day on most rivers and canals, and coastal steamers were still common. Now, most have disappeared. I'm including this information as passenger boats still run on some rivers, and are occasionally put back in service on other rivers for a few runs in peak travel times around Chinese New Year, but you'll have to hunt a bit to find them. The new infrastructure, including rail lines, expressways, and greatly expanded and improved trains and buses, has displaced them. Water transport, even for freight, is all but gone. If you come across a passenger boat, grab your chance and take it wherever it's going. The descriptions here are close to what you'll still find.

Boat transportation is too slow, and freight must be specially packaged to protect it from moisture. Delivery of goods is necessarily from dock to dock, requiring extra handling and usually a warehouse on each end. In contrast, truck freight requires no special packaging, and the truck can go directly from business to business with little warehousing required. Roads are unbelievably better than they were only eighteen years ago, and newer, faster ones are opening daily. It's the death of river freight, and for passengers there are speedier ways to travel. The new buses are fast, comfortable, air-conditioned, plying good roads, and have VCD or DVD movies, so why take a boat?

In 1988 on the Zhujiang (Pearl River) system, traveling by boat was nearly the best way. Now, the overnight steamers from Hong Kong to Guangzhou (a lower-class berth cost about the same as a cheap bed in Hong Kong) are gone. The only passenger boats now from Hong Kong are a few fast catamarans and hovercraft. They are more expensive, charge extra for baggage, often have darkly tinted windows so you can't see much, and don't allow passengers to go out on deck.

On the river above Guangzhou, the old inland riverboats were slow but wonderful (to me) and inexpensive. A trip that back then might have taken eight or ten miserable hours by bus on bad roads took twenty hours or more by boat, but was comfortable and easy on the body. Many of the boats were fairly large, carrying up to 500 passengers. A middle-class ticket included a bunk in an open dormitory. There were cheaper and less comfortable classes available, including lower-deck dorms with no ports, *cheng piao* (ride ticket) with no bed, and higher classes with more or less private cabins, four times the price of the upper-deck dormitory. On the boat, people moved around, gathered in groups, talked, and played cards. It was a great place for me to make friends, learn some Chinese, share food, and hit the toilet anytime, which allowed drinking a great deal of tea. Food was served on the boat but cost extra, about twice as much as a noodle shop in a town. Or you brought your own. There were endless supplies of boiling water for tea, and I could visit the engine room and sometimes go up on the bridge. I could lean on the rail in the fresh air, enjoying the river and a multitude of boats of all types. If you find an old boat running, it will probably still be similar to this. Hard sleeper on a train, my preferred way of travel these days, is similar in some aspects but less free, and you can't go out in the fresh air.

On a bus in 1988, I got a narrow, thinly padded seat with luggage piled in my lap and in the aisles. It was hard to even move. The bus made a toilet and food stop every four hours or so. Not much fun, hard to talk over the noise, and hard to make friends. The cigarette smoke could be overwhelming. Today's modern buses are comfortable, fast, and frequently nonsmoking, but contact is limited to immediate seat mates. I'll still take a boat any time I can find one.

I've taken the passenger boats from Guangzhou to Wuzhou many times. These boat commonly carried 400-500 passengers, had three decks, and were about 100-125' overall. Usually there were seven classes. Fifth class, which I liked, was the upper deck dormitory. Each bunk had a port, actually a window, at its head. In 1988, this eighteen-hour trip cost about US$2.50. In 2004 during *chunyun*, I got a fifth-class ticket for about US$8.

In January 2006 before *Chunjie* (Spring Festival), newspaper advertisements in Guangzhou papers announced that there would be passenger boats to Wuzhou during *Chunyun* (the travel rush). There was little more information other than that tickets would be available at the Dashatou Wharf in Guangzhou.

I liked the sounds, the splash and slap of the bow, the steady thrum of the engine, and the motion of the boat. The engine was a big ($\approx7'$ long) six-cylinder diesel. It usually looked beautifully maintained, all painted and polished, with open rocker arms.

The riverboats sometimes met small boats in mid-channel to take on or let off passengers where there was no dock. Occasionally modern-day pirates (swindlers and gamblers) quietly boarded the boat, out to fleece a few simple passengers with some kind of confidence game, and then slip away into the night. The games I've watched were sucker guessing games of the "Heads I win, tails you lose" variety, with money wagered on the outcome. There were usually police on the boats, but these con men were clever at blending in with the passengers and avoiding them.

The vast Zhujiang system changes its name with each major stretch of the river, and only the locals seem to know exactly the point where the name changes. The part from Guangzhou out to the sea between Hong Kong and Macao is properly the Zhujiang. This is the stretch the translated foreign name, Pearl River, comes from. The stretch between Guangzhou and Wuzhou is the *Xijiang* (West River), and the next stretch in Guangxi going toward Guiping is the Xunjiang. Each branch has a different name, but the locals at each confluence tend to refer to the rivers by the compass, for example, *Beijiang* (North River), and *Nanjiang* (South River), adding to the confusion.

Most other rivers in China use the more conventional naming system, where the main river has the same name from the mouth to the headwaters.

On the Xunjiang above Wuzhou, the now long gone passenger boats were a bit smaller, 200-400 passengers, and more powerful with twin engines, perhaps because of stronger currents and narrower channels in this stretch.

I've also taken passenger boats on the Changjiang (Yangtze River). A few still run, and there are many expensive tourist boats. A lot of people want to sight-see, and tour boats are popular. The ordinary passenger boats are less common, harder to find.

It is still possible to find small boats that carry passengers short distances on every river. There are also ferry boats, crossing rivers where there are no bridges. Often, there are market-day boats between small towns along rivers. They are low-cost, and it's interesting to visit the small towns on a market day, places that are difficult to reach by road. The market days alternate between the towns, so sellers can get to them all. These boats leave early in the morning, and return late. They often cost less than 5元 each way. Hop on one early in the morning and see where it goes. Just don't miss the return trip in the evening! Although if you do miss it, local people will help you find a place to sleep, even if there are no hotels.

These small passenger boats are at Jiankou, a market town on the Xijiang River in Guangxi.

7

Bicycles

CHINA may have more bikes than anywhere else in the world. They are being displaced rapidly by motorbikes, electric bikes, and by small cars, but there are still a lot of bikes. It's much safer riding a bike in traffic in China than in the US, as bikes are common so drivers watch out for them. And the liability system gives the bike right-of-way, adding to the safety. (See the next chapter, "Safety", and the sections on pedestrians and traffic.)

I like exploring on a bike. I feel I fit in, and it is much better than riding a bus as I can easily stop any time something interesting catches my eye. I can make sudden decisions and prowl at my own pace. And I find places I don't find any other way. Driving a car is something you probably won't find possible, although it's easy to get a car *with* a driver. A bike gives you more ability to make spur-of-the-moment decisions and wander around. It cost a lot less and has few parking problems. However, when I take a bus or taxi, I realize how much of my attention goes into riding the bike and how much more I see if someone else is driving. I just can't stop as readily, for a minute or a day, or quickly get away from an annoying person or smoker.

Renting or Borrowing: Ten or fifteen years ago, it was easy to find bikes to rent. It's more difficult these days, but bikes can still be rented in some tourist areas and hotels. You may be able to borrow a bike but it's likely to be old, too small, and in bad condition. Most bikes I've rented, although sometimes new, were also in bad condition. I've usually had to repair my rented bikes to make them rideable. I'm happy to do repairs on a bike I borrow from a friend, as I can return it in better condition, but it annoys me to do repairs on a bike I paid to rent.

Buying: If you plan to stay in a place more than a couple of weeks, buy a bike if you can't find one to rent or borrow. When you move on, dump it, give it to a friend, or sell. US$25 (even as little as US$13) will get a cheap but serviceable new single-speed bike, and with careful shopping US$50 will buy a decent quality one with gears. Used bikes (often stolen) can be found for about US$10 or less. Good-quality locks and other things can add US$20 or so, but you can keep the locks for the next one you buy, borrow, or rent.

Customizing: I like an upright riding posture for better sightseeing. I get a tall seat post and handlebar riser installed when I buy the bike. The dealer will often do this at no additional cost. I walk around the shop and point at the parts I want that are on other bikes: these wheels, those tires, this seat. I always want fenders, reflectors, a kick-stand, and a good rear rack. These make the bike more practical.

Locks and Security: I usually carry two rigid motorcycle-style U-locks on my bike. They are a bit heavy and inconvenient, but secure. I spent 25% of the cost of my Giant bike on the locks, but the best Chinese locks cost less than a third of what comparable ones cost in the USA. Sometimes I've carried a less-secure cable lock that allows me to lock the bike to small trees. Most Chinese lock the rear wheel of their bikes. I usually lock the front wheel, or both wheels, so standard theft methods (hopefully) don't work easily.

I also put serious effort into making my new bike look unattractive, believing this will help me keep it longer. I buy a can of black spray paint and give it a splotchy paint job, partially covering any fancy paint and chrome. I scratch up the new paint and put dents in the fenders by whacking them with a wrench. After looking it over, if I think it is necessary I buy a small file and scratch up the wheels and brake levers. Then I let it get dirty. I replace it when *xiaotou* (a thief) forces me to do so, or when I decide it's time for some new wheels.

Safety Equipment: I don't use a helmet (rare in China, except on foreign visitors), or have any lights on my bike. I do have reflectors front and rear and in both wheels. I used to carry a flashing LED tail lamp but never actually used it. I like having a small bell, but rarely use it. Instead I click a brake lever or do something such as pedaling backward to make a little low-key noise, or call out "*Wei*" (hello, hey), or "*Jie guang*" (excuse me, lit. lend some light) to alert pedestrians in front of me.

Rain: A bicycle rain cover (poncho rain coat designed to work on a bicycle) is important and available everywhere. The cover is long in the front, so it covers the handlebars and a basket, and long enough in the back to partially cover the rack. There are often straps sewn or glued about where the bike hand grips are, so you can hold the cover down in front as you ride. The air circulates underneath, so these covers are much more comfortable than a rain coat, unless it is cold. There are very light low-priced ones, or better quality but bulkier ones. Some have two hoods, to also cover a child you are carrying. The second hood may be in front of you or behind you, your choice.

Like an umbrella, a rain cover will cost you more if you wait until it's raining to buy it, so plan ahead. I carry both an umbrella and a rain cover. If it's warm or only raining lightly, the umbrella is often best. Some people have a flexible mount on the handlebars for an umbrella to clip to so it works hand-free. I've also seen umbrella hats: a headband that holds a small umbrella a few inches above your head.

Bike Parking: Parking areas with attendants who watch the bikes used to be common, but are getting harder to find. A motorbike takes up as much room as two or three bikes but pays five to ten times more, so many lots have converted to motorbikes; less effort, more profit. There is still bike parking to be found, but you must hunt more, and walk farther. These parking areas cost a few pennies, two to five *mao*. In my experience, they are completely safe places to leave a bike. If you expect to come back late, be sure you understand what time the keeper goes home. All the bikes still there may be taken somewhere secure and you may not be able to recover your bike until the next morning when the attendant returns. The cost for overnight may be 1元, but this depends on the place.

These days, I often must park my bike without an attendant. I try to find something to lock it to, such as a small tree, a sign post, or a fence.

Bike Lanes and Ramps: Most pedestrian stairways have bicycle ramps built in. This is a ten to fifteen inch wide strip up the center of the stairs, and up the right side going up, and center and left (looking up) for coming down. The center ramp works both ways, and some stairways only have the left and the right. Many major city streets have heavy movable barriers that separate motor vehicles from bicycles, and sometimes have abrupt speed bumps where motor vehicle accesses cross the bicycle lanes. But more and more, taxis have access to the bike lanes, and often block them.

Repairs: Bicycle repair shops are easy to find, although less common than a few years ago. They are often in small stands or permanent booths along the streets, and do everything from minor to major repairs, sell tires and tubes, seats, and all manner of parts and accessories. They often have several tire pumps, and for a small fee you can use one to pump up your own tires. These days, many have air compressors. If the repairer has time, he will pump up your tire for two *mao* or so. Few Chinese pump up their own tires when the fee is so small. I've also been able to use the shop's tools, often for free. It's small money; drop it into a can if you see one.

If you buy a bike, find a repairman to take it apart and put grease in all the bearings. It won't cost much. This is important if you want the bike to be nice to use and want it to last for awhile. I service mine myself, but I'm a mechanic and don't mind getting greasy. Most middle and lower-priced bikes come with little or no lubrication in the bearings. I guess it's so they look cleaner on the showroom floor, and the sales people don't get their hands dirty. Because of this, most one-year-old bikes you see in both the USA and China already have rust leaking out of the bearings. The shops also get to sell more bikes that way. Rust (iron oxide) is a wonderful abrasive!

License: In most towns and cities, bicycles are supposed to be registered and licensed. As a foreign visitor, the police won't bother you for not having a license, and anyway the license is local, not good in the next place. In the case of a stolen bike, the police probably won't accept a report unless it is licensed. If you are living or working in China, register your bike.

Camping: I haven't tried it; I've never carried a tent or sleeping bag while traveling in China. I occasionally meet travelers who do camp successfully, but in more than four years spent on the road, I've only wished I had a sleeping bag a few times (usually because I was too cold in a hotel). Most of the time I'm glad I'm not carrying one.

Camping attracts a lot of attention: bike travelers I've talked to say they like to spot a good place a little before dark, scout it out and ride on, returning to the spot about dark to set up camp. Wake up a little late in the morning, they tell me, and you may find ten or fifteen people standing around you in a circle to see what will crawl out. Others have told me they wished they weren't carrying camping equipment, as they had always found hotels. Prowl Google if you're thinking about this; find camping stories.

Longer Trips: On the worst day of my most challenging trip to date, I made only 25 km, and had four flats (narrow tires on a rough rock road). Three quarters of the time, I was sweating like a pig (I know pigs don't sweat, but I favor the phrase), pushing my bike loaded with all my stuff up steep hills. One percent of the time, I was riding down the other side praying that my brakes wouldn't fail and wondering if I loved danger. That kind of day doesn't make me enthusiastic. At 60, I feel too old.

Riding through the countryside in gentle terrain at an easy pace on a good road, being stopped by the locals who are curious about who is passing by and why, now that is a lot of fun! Being able to stop anywhere to visit, to eat, to look at construction or farming. Riding into a small town at the end of the day looking for a hotel, collecting (like the Pied Piper) thirty kids who have never seen a foreigner before (except on TV), and are so excited: it can be overwhelming, but I mostly enjoy it. I always manage to find a bed.

Carrying a Bike: In 2000, I started carrying a bike with me as I traveled. It's a bit crazy and few do it, but I'm hooked. I was urged to do so by an Italian friend who lives in China. He convinced me, helped me choose and buy one, and showed me how to pack it in a bag. I initially did it to get him off my back. Before then, I always tried to find a bike to borrow or rent. This allowed me to ride around a lot and I loved it. However, it's wonderful to have a bike that is the right size for me and in good mechanical condition with all the features I want. I use it mostly for local travel around a city, or around the area for day trips. Occasionally, if the weather is good and I'm feeling strong, I will travel between places carrying all my stuff. 200-500 km is my personal limit, depending on the terrain.

I had the bag made in a canvas shop. All the explanations involved in ordering it were easily solved by taking the bike apart in the shop and packing it up on an unrolled piece of canvas. The canvas worker and I then drew an outline around the pile and marked the positions of the grommets for tying it closed. When I returned the next day, I again dismantled and packed the bike, lacing the new bag closed and tying it up tight. We then marked places to add reinforcement patches and handles for carrying it. I reassembled my bike while the man finished the bag. Cost: less than US$20. The material is heavy cotton canvas, bulkier than I like for carrying, but I wasn't able to find any suitable nylon material. I had the bag made a bit larger than necessary, so it has worked with several different bikes. I'm on my second bag now, wore out the first one.

To pack the bike, I remove the pedals, seat and seat post, handlebars and riser, and the front wheel and fender (see pictures). My current bike requires only two tools for this, a 6" adjustable wrench and a hex key. I manage to cram a lot of other stuff in the bag along with the bike, such as my rain cover and umbrella, the locks, the pannier that carries the bag and all my bike-related stuff (it folds pretty flat when it doesn't have the bag in it), and the homemade pannier with hooks to hang on the rack that holds my backpack and keeps it clean. I have a small set of luggage wheels I strap under the rear wheel of the bagged bike, so I only have to carry one end, and it rolls along behind me.

On the train in hard sleeper, the packed bike will just fit under the lower berth, but it sticks out 15-20 cm. near the table. That's really not allowed, luggage is supposed to fit entirely underneath, or on the luggage rack. I always apologize to my compartment mates for it. I've been told by conductors several time that it's not allowed, and have been required to pay a small charge for excess baggage once. Mostly, it's just hard work, getting it on and off. I try to get on the train as early as possible, when the gate first opens. Getting on at intermediate stations is harder, often there is already luggage under the berths.

It is a serious pain in the butt, packing it and unpacking it and dragging it around. Packing takes about half an hour at either end. I must find a relatively clean and quiet corner near the station entrance to do the packing and unpacking. I must lug it on and off trains, on and off buses, and drag it around in its bag while carrying all my other stuff, but once I put it together, it carries everything for me. I can go much farther, looking for a hotel in a new place. Once I have a hotel and dump my stuff, I have a bike that is in excellent condition, suits me, and fits me. It's a mixed bag — I keep questioning the wisdom of carrying a bike, but I continue.

I've tried putting the bike fully assembled in the train luggage car a few times, but it hasn't always arrived at the same time as me. Sometimes riding buses, I'm able to put my bike in the luggage compartment mostly assembled, only the handlebars and pedals off and the seat lowered. This only works with the bigger buses, but it sure is nice.

I'm now riding my fifth bike, each one bought in China. My last one was a Giant brand fifteen-speed road bike with medium-width tires, and I paid less than US$100 for it. Those tires aren't great on rough rock roads, but most of my riding in China is on pavement where it's nearly perfect. My latest bike has the same tires, is an eighteen-speed *Yongjiu* (Forever) brand, and cost only $45 new! It's adequate, but not a great piece of machinery. I'm careful with it but unconcerned about leaving it locked on the street.

Travelers who bring high-quality foreign bikes with them have much lighter and nicer wheels than mine. However, their bikes are expensive so they must be overly protective toward them. Many leave their bikes locked up in their hotel, and walk around. They often only use their bikes for long distances. My use is opposite to that.

Bicycle disassembled for packing.

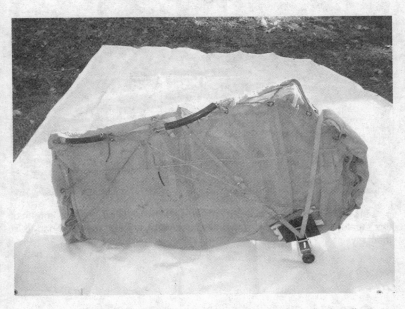

Packed and ready to go. My latest bag is better, with sewn-on handles, instead of rubber hose over rope.

My lucky day: I had a blowout on a small highway, almost directly in front of this repairman. The next day, I had several flats on a rough road and had to fix them myself.

8

Safety and Security

DON'T worry much about danger while traveling in China; just use normal caution and common sense. Don't make yourself an attractive target: appear alert, look people in the eye, and be aware of those near you. If you've been careless, don't expect the police to be able to do much to help you. If I see a fight, or some other sort of trouble, as I occasionally do, I avoid it; I don't go over to watch.

Walking down dark streets at night anywhere in China, maybe in a strange city the locals consider rough: I do it by myself frequently and feel safe. I meet solo women travelers who tell me they also feel safe walking alone on dark streets. All in all, I feel safer anywhere in China than I do in many parts of the USA.

Personal violence is rare in China. You can always meet a crazy person, it's possible anywhere in the world. However, don't worry about someone in China attacking you or pulling a knife or a gun on you. It's not a culture of personal violence and **few people have guns**, as the penalties for possession are severe. Nonviolent crime, the skilled pickpocket, a thief snatching your bag when your attention isn't on it: it's possible, but not common, in my experience. You are more likely to have something lifted by a broke fellow traveler in a shared room.

Pickpockets have attempted (unsuccessfully) to take something from me five times in all the time I've spent in China. Recently, I had a small camera stolen out of a belt pouch; I wasn't able to figure out how it was done, the thief was good! I've had a bike I parked on the street stolen, and a small day pack stolen from beside my chair when my attention wasn't on it and I had neglected to put my foot through the strap (so if someone tried to move the bag, I'd feel it). I was careless. I've also had a sneak thief break into my hotel room while I was sleeping, and lift my wallet out of the pocket of my pants, which were folded on a chair. I spent half a day with the police making a report, and the hotel gave me my room free for a week, as an apology.

This is all that has happened to me, in more than 4 1/2 years on the road in China.

If you carry something expensive, such as a **notebook computer** or a fancy camera, avoid displaying it unless you keep it with you all the time. I keep my computer buried in my bag and if I do show it, I stay a little closer to my bag. I update a couple of sets of flash memory backups of my important work regularly, carry one set with me at all times and keep the other in a different bag from my computer. I find I can easily carry flash cards in my neck pouch, and I use the same kind of cards for backups as my camera takes. My computer is a secondhand one about two years old, so it's not too valuable and is less attractive to thieves, and would be less of a disaster to me if it was stolen.

Money Belt and Neck Pouch: Use standard procedures for travelers anywhere: carry most of your money in a concealed inside pocket or pouch. I use a simple homemade money belt which I wear above my hips inside my pants; no one ever sees it. I carry the money I need for a week, my passport, and other important things (such as credit cards and the flash memory backup for my computer) in a standard small documents pouch I wear around my neck under my shirt. I don't worry about people seeing it when I need to pull it out. I keep my daily money in my pockets.

Day Bag: If you are carrying a day pack or fanny pack in a crowded situation such as a busy train station or on a city bus at rush hour, pull it around in front of you and wrap your arms around it. There are stories of thieves with razors who can slit open a bag in a flash without you noticing a thing. In any case, it's plain impolite to push through a crowded bus with your bag on your back, smacking it into everyone else. I prefer a day bag with a single strap worn diagonally across my chest. It's easy to pull around in front, or carry behind me where it's more comfortable and out of my way. I don't regularly carry things I can't bear to lose in such a bag, and I never put my passport or money in it.

Locks: I carry small Chinese padlocks I hook through the zipper pulls to lock my bags. The lock or the zipper pulls could be broken easily with a pair of pliers, or the bag readily cut open, but the lock is like a sign, "Keep Out", and seems to be respected.

I often put this "sign" on bags I leave in my hotel room or on the luggage rack in a train or bus, although I'm a bit casual about it. I don't worry about most hotels. I don't bother locking my bags to the rack in trains, although some travelers, both foreign and Chinese, do. I've seen evidence that curious hotel workers have looked through stuff I haven't locked, and one time removed a small amount of money I had carelessly left with papers in a drawer, but I've never seen any indication that one of my locked bags has been tampered with. This "sign" also makes any tampering obvious.

In workplaces, many Chinese keep their desk drawers locked with small locks and flimsy hasps that would be easy to pop off with a screwdriver or pocket knife. I don't think this approach would stop a thief or nosy coworker in the USA. Many things, from gates to drawers on desks, are ostentatiously locked, but often in the flimsiest manner imaginable. With a decent screwdriver I could break into almost anything. Newer bikes and the doors on private shops and houses tend to be stoutly locked.

Warnings: Chinese friends frequently warn me to be careful and to watch out for thieves and robbers, but they seldom have experience in other countries. I frequently meet skeptical disbelief when I try to explain that compared to the USA, China is remarkably safe.

Under close and repeated questioning, I've never been able to get any of my Chinese friends to admit any fear of being unjustly accused of a crime by the police. This might be why America has so many lawyers, while China has few.

Guns: In 2001, at the end of a three-month national "Strike Hard" campaign against crime, the *China Police Daily* proudly reported that 330,000 guns and 1.5 million bullets had been unearthed and confiscated nationwide. To put these numbers in perspective, that's less than five bullets per gun, and the number of guns found was one tenth of one percent of the number of mobile phones in China in 2005. In a special campaign in 2005, Guangdong Province police reported crushing 475 criminal gangs and confiscating 106 cars, 440 motorcycles, 47 guns, and 74 bullets. That's one gun for ten gangs, and less than two bullets per gun! There are guns in China, but the number is small.

I see few police officers carrying guns, not even the *Wujing* (Armed Police, the civil arm of the Chinese army). Somehow, this all makes me feel a lot safer. As in other countries, I do see security guards with shotguns around armored truck delivering money to banks.

Police: Chinese police say they don't have enough manpower, that there are too few policemen. Chinese people say there are too many police. My friends say the people's attitude comes from seeing what they think is a luxury life for the police. Many police drive around in big and expensive SUVs, police can be seen sitting around with their uniforms unbuttoned, not acting as police should, and there is a general feeling that police have too much power and there isn't enough oversight. However, when somebody wants a policeman, they want him there right away. These attitudes don't seem much different from those in the USA, on both sides of the question.

Pedestrian Hazards: Don't get me wrong, keep your eyes open. Pedestrian hazards abound; safety barriers around open manholes, or warnings at other kinds of hazards are rare. I occasionally whack my head or catch my hair on branches. Trees on the streets are pruned for slightly shorter people. Watch out for guy wires and various hanging loose wires. Watch out for open holes and ditches; China doesn't have so many lawyers.

A bicycle rider must also be careful of hazards such as unmarked open manholes, cables, loose lids, drains with missing grates, and the odd brick lying on the street, in addition to the obvious dangers from aggressive taxi drivers and the like. Mostly, though, it's the inanimate dangers you must watch for.

Traffic: Being run down by a taxi or private car, or being in a bus wreck: now those are real dangers. However, traffic safety records are fairly good by world standards, and railroad safety records are excellent. According to WHO (the World Health Organization), China's per-capita road accident rate is slightly higher than the USA's. Since the car ownership rate is much lower in China, the roads are probably more dangerous. In spite of this, I feel safer riding a bicycle in heavy Chinese traffic than I do when driving or riding in a car during rush hour on Interstate Five north of Seattle in the USA, which I think is about average for American freeways.

I ride a bicycle all the time on city streets in China, and on highways and small roads. I ride in heavy city traffic with great freedom. I went over the handlebars once in rush hour traffic in Beijing, when somebody pulled in front of me. I was knocked down once by a taxi when it turned abruptly in front of me, clipping my front wheel. Both times, pedestrians and other bike riders were around me immediately to see if I was hurt, and to offer assistance.

With the taxi, I was glad to have them around. I was angry and had kicked the cab after I jumped up, yelling at the driver that he was a tortoise egg (*Wangba dan!*, bastard). He jumped out of his cab with his fists up, wanting to punch me in his rage. Seeing all the pedestrians laughing at him (*Wa!* The foreigner can speak! Did you hear him call that man "tortoise egg"?), he cut his losses and left quickly. I rarely yell insults like that, and felt I had been both foolish and lucky.

If you enjoy danger, go swimming in a polluted river, run across a street right in front of a bus, or find one of the new climbing "rocks" that have suddenly appeared on some college campuses. Show off a little! Or travel in a more dangerous country.

The Great Wall: Fear as a National Policy

One weekend in Beijing in 1988, a group of adult students in a special English-polishing program hired a bus for an outing to *Changcheng* (the Great Wall). Most were from other parts of China and had never been to the wall before. They invited me along, altogether more than thirty of us in the bus. The wall is important in Chinese history, and something nearly all Chinese want to visit at least once in their lives.

When we reached the wall one of the students, a boisterous young man, hurried forward to be the first to put his foot on the steps. He raised his hand above his head dramatically and intoned "We are all true men, for we have been to the Great Wall!".

I said "Hey, hey, hey, that should be "We are all true persons..." because half of this group are women." The women around me all growled "Yeah!". The man, a senior engineer, wilted a little and again raised his arm but less dramatically, "We are all true persons, for we have been to the Great Wall." He made a face and added "But, the saying is 'We are all true men...'." (*Bu dao changcheng fei hao han.*)

We wandered on the wall for a few hours and had a picnic lunch. What a group of guides I had, making a rare and special event. Among them were structural engineers, historians, a philosophy professor, a couple of doctors, and others with specialized knowledge, all top working professionals in their fields.

We talked about the wall, its construction and history, and its place in Chinese history. At the end of the day I asked the philosophy professor, a very tall woman in her late 30s, if the wall had ever worked, if it had ever served a real function: with all that we had been talking about, the huge costs both in people and materials, the strategic planning, the centuries spent in construction, had it worked?

She replied brightly and quickly "Oh, about as well as your President Reagan's Star Wars."

(This professor was on her way to Scotland to study the Scottish poets. She was constantly hopeful when she met English-speaking foreigners such as me: she wanted to talk about the Scottish poets.)

9

Hotels

FINDING a satisfactory hotel takes some effort, unless you are in a city mentioned in your guidebook. If you don't mind spending money, it's easier, but it can take some time if you are frugal like me. In a hotel recommended by a guidebook, the price may be satisfactory but you'll often find other foreign visitors and a staff that is used to dealing with foreigners. If that's not what you want, then you must do it for yourself. In any case, most towns and cities in China aren't mentioned in any guide: unless you stay on the beaten track, you have to find your own hotel because you have no information. And most places you can save money, sometimes a lot of money. The lack of a star rating doesn't indicate a bad hotel; some hotels with stars are terrible. No-star places just aren't on any list, which means they are usually less expensive.

In a new place, I start by asking someone on the street "Please, where's a *zhaodaisuo* or *lüguan*?" You can use your phrase book. A *zhaodaisuo* is a budget hotel or hostel, usually government-run or formerly government-run, and a *lüguan* is a smaller private hotel, possibly new. Most don't have a license to have foreign guests, and may never have had a foreign guest before. (This licensing rule has been relaxed in most areas. Your visa and its expiration date are supposed to be checked when you register, and a form sent to the PSB [Public Security Bureau]. Small hotels often don't have the forms, and haven't been instructed in correct procedures. These days, most hotels have the right to receive foreign visitors, but it may still be a new experience for them.) In a small place, that's not a problem; but in a town or little city, the old rule may be kept even if it has changed. If the *zhaodaisuo* has been warned by the police before, it can mean trouble for them to let you stay. If they haven't been warned, they can pretend they don't know the rules. If a hotel doesn't ask for your passport and doesn't have you fill out a form for foreign visitors when you register, it's reasonable to assume they have little experience with foreigners.

Zhaodaisuo (hostel) in Nei Menggu (Inner Mongolia).

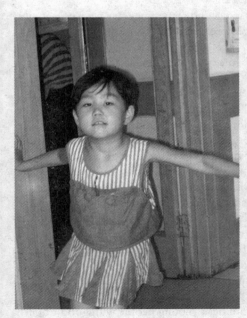

Small *fuwutai* (receptionist) in the *zhaodaisuo* telling me I can't go to my room.

Don't make trouble for the small place. (They may be fined if the old rule is being enforced, and you'll make it hard for the next traveler. Don't crap in your own nest.) If you stay in a *zhaodaisuo* or other small hotel, don't tell any officials where you are living. Be polite (always be polite when dealing with officials), but be creative: maybe say you are staying with a foreign teacher at the university, catching the next bus, or that you just arrived and don't have a hotel yet. Don't outright lie; it's best to be politely vague.

In a small town, often the first person I ask will

73

guide me to a place and, if I like it, even help me to check in. Most *zhaodaisuo* have dorm rooms, but rarely put a foreigner in a room with a Chinese person (imagine having to share a room with a barbarian, a foreign devil). So if you ask for a bed (一个床位 *yige chuangwei*, a berth or bed) you may effectively get a private room with two or three beds.

If another foreign visitor comes by, they will dump him (or her) into your room. Sometimes I get a private room by paying for all the beds. Most of the time, there is no toilet or shower in the room. Instead, there is a public one down the hall. That has the advantage of keeping the room drier and smelling better. Hot water in the shower may be limited to a few hours a day, maybe in the morning or in the evening (energy saving). Ask about the hours or go check before you get ready to shower.

Your room may have a telephone and almost always color TV, probably with cable. The beds have sheets and the sheets will be clean. (If they aren't fresh, ask for clean ones.) If you have a phone, you may be able to make local calls for free. If not, you may need to buy a telephone card of some sort to call out, commonly a "201" card. Or make your calls on the street. Ask for the telephone number; you will be able to receive calls in your room.

I like many of these *zhaodaisuo*, and sometimes stay for weeks in one that pleases me. I rarely pay more than 50元 for a private room, and occasionally less than 20元. The sheets are changed weekly in most places, or whenever you ask. In east coast cities, and Beijing, the prices may be considerably higher.

Bargain politely for the price. You may get a 10-20% discount. I usually only ask once for a discount and when I hesitate, sometimes the price comes down a little more. The words and phrases you need are likely in your phrase book, or just move your hand down a little with a smile. If you plan to stay for five days or more and are willing to pay in advance, 30-40% is often possible. In a fancier hotel in the off-season, you may get a 50% or more discount just by asking. The more expensive the room, the bigger the discount. You can usually pay less than the posted rate unless the hotel is full. Don't pay too much attention to the posted price in private hotels; the real price may be less. In some government-owned hotels, there's no bargaining from the posted price. Try anyway, as a matter of form.

If your comfort level requires a staff that speaks English, expect to pay a lot more, but even in "real" hotels with stars, the English rarely extends much beyond the front desk. Young people with good English find better jobs, the same as at ticket counters. You'll be happier if you don't expect English to be spoken.

10

Food

FOOD in China is wonderful. That's about the only thing most travelers in China agree on, while they may disagree about nearly everything else. I like the food in the south best, where there are many kinds of fresh green vegetables all year round. In the far northwest, I eat a lot mutton, *nang*, kebab, and pilau (*zhuafan*, a steamed rice, carrot, and mutton dish). I'm willing to eat almost anything and find healthy and tasty food nearly everywhere I go. I try to eat as the local people do; it can be wonderful, and certainly it will be inexpensive, even in the coastal cities.

Getting the food you want sometimes is a problem. Even if you can read the menu, as most Japanese travelers can, it doesn't seem to help much. The name of a dish often has nothing obvious to do with the ingredients or the way it's cooked. However, it's easy to order by looking at what others are eating and pointing at something that looks good to you. If a Chinese person does this it's a little rude, but a foreign visitor can do it freely. The person whose food I point at will often be pleased I choose to eat the same. If I order by speaking the names of dishes I know, I end up eating the same things over and over. You can also order by pointing at the names of dishes or ingredients in your phrase book and dictionary.

If no one else is eating, walk into the kitchen to see what they have to cook. Point at what you want, and point at the way you want it cooked. The restaurant people will be happiest if they feel they truly understand what you want and can prepare it. Anything you do to help them understand what you want won't be seen as terribly rude.

When you want the bill, call out "*Maidan*" or make a writing motion with your finger. (*Maidan* is originally Cantonese, but the phrase is now in use almost everywhere.) Usually when several people are eating together, one person pays the bill. Don't figure your share of the bill at the table unless you want to look like a barbarian. If you are eating with

Chinese friends, it can be hard to pay the bill even though you have much more money. There are ways: head off to the toilet toward the end of the meal and detour by the cashier, say you want to pay for the meal. (Say "*maidan*" and circle your finger indicating the whole table.) If the bill isn't ready, it will be by the time you come out of the toilet. Pay it quietly. If one of my friends sees what I'm doing and rushes to pay, I say I'm first, *diyi* (number one). If that doesn't work, I give in gracefully and let my friend pay. I've gotten fairly good at winning this game but it doesn't break my budget, and it's a heck of a lot easier on my friends' budgets. Tipping is unnecessary, and many Chinese will be insulted if you try to tip them.

It's never really hard getting good food at a fair price, but I sometimes have problems getting up the gumption to go out and find it. Merely the process of getting a meal frequently intimidates me, especially if I am feeling under the weather. When I get hungry enough, I always find I can get good food easily. I walk in anywhere and they feed me.

I do miss brown rice: in the west, quality is often compared to snow, "As pure as the driven snow". In China, it's rice, "As fine as the whitest rice." Brown rice is hard to find, and most Chinese consider it dirty.

Tap Water: I brush my teeth, and wash fruit and vegetables with it everywhere, but I don't drink it unless it's been boiled. I drink hot water or tea, as most Chinese do, and occasionally bottled water. Hotel rooms provide boiled water in thermos bottles. Reliably safe bottled water is readily available, but often costs more by volume than gasoline, same as in the USA. (I've never understood why, as it isn't carried in tankers half way around the world, isn't dangerously flammable, and doesn't need refineries.)

Street Food: I like to eat in *dapaidang*. These are street restaurants that are set up on sidewalks and the sides of streets, especially in the evening. Sometimes I find a "food street" with many *dapaidang*. Everything they have to prepare is out on display, and it's cooked where you can watch. All this makes it easy for me to get what I want and to try new things, vegetables I've never seen before, or whatever. The price is good, too, better than any inside restaurant. If the weather is bad, awnings and umbrellas are set up over the tables. If you are in a colder area, there may be an inside place to sit and eat and the cooking may be done inside.

Street food **snacks** are available everywhere, especially in markets or anywhere there are many people. You might smell the aroma of roasting

Lunch at a *dapaidang* (small street restaurant).

Kids at the *dapaidang* watching me eat. The boy in front took the upper picture for me. His mother ran the place.

sweet potatoes; follow your nose until you spot the oil-drum oven. Or maybe it will be big slices of fried spiced potato, or roasted ears of sweet corn, or... chocolate-coated popcorn! There are local specialties everywhere. You don't know what it is? Try it.

Yogurt: *Suannai* is widely available. I like the fresh live-culture stuff that comes in small glass bottles, although it's getting harder to find in many places. It's fresh and must be sold quickly so it's harder to handle. You can buy it sweet, or less sweet. I find the processed packaged stuff available in every shop a poor substitute. In the north and northwest, sometimes fresh yogurt is available on the street and in restaurants in small bowls, completely unsweetened. You may need to learn the local name. It's wonderful, and there is sugar if you want it. In the summer it might be mixed with shaved ice. I love it.

11

Internet, *Wangba*

W ANT to check your email, look something up, or read news? It's easy in most places bigger than small villages. *Wangba* (net bar, net cafe) are common all over China. Since 2000, they have been easy to find, and the cost is typically 2元 an hour to sit at a good computer with a fast connection, these days often broadband or a still respectable ISDN or DSL connection. That price is affordable, even for a Chinese student. (A city bus ride costs 1-2元.) For a while the price was lower, but now seems to have stabilized at a level that allows the owners to make a profit.

The characters for *wangba* are used in the title of this chapter. *Wang* (net) is especially easy to recognize, 网, an open-bottom box with xx inside it, making a nice picture of a net. Watch for this character on signs or on doors. This usually indicates an Internet cafe, but occasionally it will be a shop selling fencing, fishing equipment, or maybe an IP (Internet phone) place.

Once you train your eye to spot the character 网, you'll start seeing *wangba* everywhere. The signs commonly say 网吧 *wangba*, but also can say 上网 *shangwang* (on the net), or other variations around the word *wang*. A few signs don't use this character, so you'll miss those, but there are plenty more.

There are places for foreign visitors in or around hotels. They are expensive, five or more times the common price, and often offer older equipment and slower connections (they have fewer customers). If you don't want to use them, walk around a bit with your eyes open. In a few cities, *wangba* are hidden out of sight, hard to spot, with nonexistent or small signs. Some may not be registered; local policies vary. Ask young people if you need help finding one. Students, and especially young men, the game players, know all the places.

Wang 网 is pronounced with a falling-rising third tone. *Ba* 吧 with a high tone is a sound used for "bar". It's a bit tricky, but if you gesture with your hands as if you're typing on a keyboard, nearly everyone will understand. *Wangba* is a common usage term, but be careful: if pronounced with the wrong tones it can easily be offensive or funny, being mistaken for tortoise, a common word for "bastard" or "cuckold". This wrong *wang* has a rising second tone, and its *ba* a neutral tone.

When you find one, go in and tell them you want to "*shangwang*" (go on the net). Some places require a deposit but you'll often just be pointed to an available computer. If a password has to be typed in, they'll help you. The first time, you may be surprised to find you're facing a Chinese OS (operating system) with all the menus in Chinese characters. It's Windows and usually Internet Explorer. Try to remember where the commands are located in the menus you are used to: everything is arranged the same, the commands are in the same places as in the English OS. The keyboard shortcuts (commands) are the same, and the menus show the same letter combinations. If you are familiar with Windows, you won't have much trouble.

Part of the job of the *wangba* staff is to assist users, and sort out their problems. I often have had to call for help to figure out which button to click. As I look around trying to catch the eye of a staff person, someone near me often reaches over and fixes the problem or tries to help me.

In smaller towns, the owners seem to be mostly men in their twenties who often use the ground floor of the family house. These are typically small operations with eight to fifteen computers. Most places, however, now have rules forbidding *wangba* with fewer than twenty computers.

In larger cities, by contrast, it's a big business. You can find *wangba* with well over 1,000 computers. It is common to find *wangba* with more than 100 computers all over China. However in Guangzhou, said to have the highest per-capita home computer ownership in China, it can be difficult to find any *wangba*, as there are few customers, maybe only kids avoiding parental rules forbidding playing games.

When all this was new back in 2000, in smaller, out-of-the-way towns in Guangxi Zhuang Autonomous Region, I might have found one *wangba* that was not too busy and run by China Telecom. By 2002, in those same places I easily found thirty or more private ones, all busy. Interestingly, Guangxi, a relatively poor province, seems to have had an open and free policy relating to the Internet, especially *wangba*. A few provinces have been more restrictive. These days, I think it is impossible to count the *wangba*.

Beginning in 1998, the Chinese government has actively pushed people to use the Internet. The users are still mostly students and people under thirty, although it is possible to see every kind of person in *wangba*. Game playing, chat, watching movies (and smoking) seem to be the main activities, but you can see everything.

The authorities keep track of the *wangba* and sometimes raid them looking for illegal activity. The operator is supposed to watch the users to make sure they do not visit illegal sites such as gambling and pornography. There is probably also some political supervision, but it is not obvious to me. Rules (which vary from place to place) may require saving browser history for a week or more, maybe sixty days. This allows the authorities to see if there has been "improper" use, however that's defined at the moment. A place found allowing illegal activity can be ordered closed and the owner fined. The punishment will depend on the seriousness of what the authorities found.

Internet regulations come from Beijing, but each province has a significant amount of control, and leaders in each city also have some local autonomy. Consequently in different places there are variations in policy, regulations, service, and price.

Everything changes daily in China — especially things related to the Internet. Disregard nearly everything you've read in the Western media about *wangba*. Whatever is described — a crackdown and closures; that Google can't be used; invasive filtering or whatever — probably actually happened somewhere at some time in some particular city (would a journalist lie?). Whatever it was you read, you may never see it or find anyone who has experienced it.

During the eighteen years I've been traveling in China, my main impression is change. Everything changes, and at a rate that constantly befuddles me. Of all the changes, I think the opening of the Internet will turn out to be one of the biggest. In 1997, only ten years ago, almost no one in China except academics and business people had ever used the net. Now it is open and cheap (cheap even by Chinese standards) for everyone.

A growing but still relatively small part of the population have their own computers, but the Chinese government National Network Information Center (CNNIC) counts 137 million users of the net, two thirds broadband (January 2007), and says only 32.3% of those use the Internet at *wangba*. I believe this number to be grossly inaccurate, wildly undercounting the Internet users, especially at *wangba*. (For the latest full reports, go to their web site < http://www.cnnic.net.cn> and click on the "English" button on the upper right, then click on the "Survey Reports" button on the right.)

It's so hard to know the validity of statistics, and so easy to state them as fact. I don't believe there is any reliable way to count either the number of *wangba*, or the number of Internet users in China. Everywhere, these numbers seem understated. (To keep hard-liners from getting scared, possibly?) In Beijing, after a terrible arson fire in a *wangba* in June 2002 where more than twenty students died, the city government said it had closed 2,400 *wangba*, all of the *wangba* in the city. I was sure there were many more than that in Beijing.

When I arrived in Beijing about a week after the fire, I found that all *wangba* I knew about were closed. I had no trouble accessing the Internet in libraries: the Internet was open, just *wangba* shut. I had visited something around fifty *wangba* the year before, in just a part of the *Haidian* district (the main university area of Beijing), doing research for an article.[1] These were all closed; I could find none open. Friends in other parts of the city told me that none were open in their areas either. Some students laughed at the Beijing government numbers, guessing around 20,000 had actually been closed.

Most of those students also believed *wangba* had been closed in all other cities in China at the same time. I actually heard few knowledgeable reports of *wangba* closures in any cities other than Beijing, and I had no trouble in other places I visited. A year later *wangba* were again easy to find in Beijing.

A professor told me he believed the *wangba* had been closed after the fire because the government was afraid of student rage if they did nothing. Sounds possible, but I sure don't know.

China is the world's largest market for computers, and in late 2004, also became the world's largest broadband Internet market. In 2005 China became the world leader in PC production. China may already have far more Internet users than any other country, but they are officially called number two, behind the USA.

In 2001, the number of mobile phones passed the USA, and China became the world's biggest mobile phone market. By 2004, they had nearly three times as many as the USA, and in 2006, nearly five times as many. These things are hard to measure, and change fast. China's

---

[1] "A Growing Click: Net Cafes' Popularity Soaring," *China Online News*, 2001, June 1.

mobile phone networks, service levels, and prices are now the best in the world. (See Chapter 15, Telephones.)

What I'm curious about isn't so much how the Internet will change China, though it surely will, but rather how China will change the Internet. Soon, maybe already, Chinese will probably be the biggest language on the Internet. Only a few years ago, English was said to be 98% of content. Research ICANN (Internet Corporation for Assigned Names and Numbers) and ITU (International Telecommunications Union) statistics, if you're curious.

In any case, finding a good and low-cost place to check your email isn't a problem in China.

Internet Terms and Slang

Diannao: Computer, lit. Electric Brain.
Heike: Hacker, lit. Dark Guest.
Heiwang: Blocked site, lit. Black Net, or Dark Net.
Shangwang de difang: Place to get on the net.
Wangchong: Net Worm, someone with a lot of knowledge, or someone who is on the net a lot, perhaps for chat or to play network games.

Typical signs outside *wangba* (Internet cafes). The traveler needs to train the eye to see and recognize the character *wang* ('net') repeated in all these signs. The *wangba* on the left is in Nei Menggu (Inner Mongolia), so features Mongolian script. The top left *wangba* has the name, "*Wang Chong*", or Net Worm. The one right below it, a nice hand-painted sign.

12

Sick on the Road

BEING sick is something most travel books don't talk about, but it's an all-too-frequent problem. In reviewing the notebooks containing my travel journals, I find that notes related to health problems make up about 7% of the content. It's a part I like to forget, but it sure stands out when I look back at my journals. I may get sick more than average, but in China where people are much closer together, it's easy for travelers to catch bugs. Small illnesses tend to have a bigger impact on anyone who is away from home and a network of friends. I catch *ganmao* (colds or flu) more in China, especially in the south, than at home. *Ganmao* is a big problem for the locals in the subtropical south, too, especially during the monsoon season.

Chinese doctors have always taken good care of me, even when we don't share a language. I have been treated for minor and severe infections of various sorts, and have had minor surgery. I've also had work done on my teeth. Excellent medical care is available all around China, and it is inexpensive by Western standards, a small fraction of the cost of care in America.

If you are sick and want to see a doctor, go to a hospital. When an American says, "I'm going to the hospital," it's serious. In China, it simply means, "I'm going to see a doctor." Most doctors in China have their offices inside hospitals. If you have a choice, bigger hospitals are more likely to have a few doctors who speak some English. If a specialist you're seeing doesn't speak or read English, and it's important, the staff will look for another doctor who can help with communication. A hospital associated with a medical college or university is best of all, as there will be many young, recently trained doctors who have, at a minimum, a good command of written English. Chinese doctors (inside hospitals, at least) are well trained, and the treatments are effective and safe.

The doctors may seem young. On average, Chinese doctors are

four years younger than similarly qualified American doctors. They don't go through a four-year undergraduate program prior to medical training, but rather start medical school immediately after finishing senior middle school (high school). Most Chinese doctors have studied medicine for at least five years, including a year of internship.

Finding a Hospital

Look on your trusty city map; most have red crosses indicating hospitals. Show your map to someone, maybe the *fuwutai* (desk clerk) at your hotel, and point at the various red crosses. If the *fuwutai* is local, she (usually these jobs are held by women) will have an opinion as to which hospital is best. If you are seriously ill, a taxi will get you to a hospital promptly. If it is an emergency, call "120" for an ambulance (a taxi may be hard to find late at night).

If you want, you can choose a Chinese medicine (*Zhongyao*) hospital where there are more specialists in traditional medicine. (It will have the character 中 *zhong* in the name on your map.) However, all hospitals offer both Western and Chinese medicine. The doctors will choose what they think is best (usually Western medicine for a foreigner) unless you express a preference.

Major cities have clinics and hospitals that specialize in treating foreign patients. They are much more expensive. There are also many private clinics everywhere, but my Chinese friends tend not to trust them — or the certificates displayed on their walls. At a hospital, the doctors will all be properly trained and certified.

I've had good luck, and gotten good treatment for a very low price. If you are sick and at a hospital where no one speaks English, don't despair. I think of myself as an animal and the doctor as a veterinarian. My role is to trust him (or her) and not scratch or bite. I've always been treated well. If you have a Chinese friend who will go with you, it can save a lot of confusion and often speed up everything, but it's a big favor to ask because it wastes your friend's time.

Always take paper with you. Many people in China have better written than spoken English. Often, you can facilitate communication with a note, carefully written in advance, which explains your problem as simply as possible. (Be careful to choose words that are in your dictionary.) Keep any notes you've written, as you may need them several times. If you have a choice, go early in the morning, around 8:00 a.m. Take your note, phrase books, and dictionary.

The doctors may be more wary of you than you are of them, as it is commonly believed HIV is more common among foreigners than in the general Chinese population. Your doctor or dentist will almost certainly wear sterile gloves while examining or treating you. Expect disposable syringes and IV rigs to be used. If such equipment isn't single-use disposable, *ask for it*. They will have it, but you may be charged a little extra if you are in a small place. Take responsibility for your own health: pay attention to these details.

I'm personally about as comfortable with treatment in China as at home. I consider both doctors and staff well trained, and sterile techniques reasonable. Would I accept a blood transfusion in China? Yes, if I was going to die without it. I'd use the same standard in the USA. Opportunistic infections lurk in hospitals, of course, which is a concern in China as well as everywhere else.

In larger hospitals, there may be some signs in English. Go to the outpatient department, if you can spot it. **The process** starts inside the main doors, where you will usually see a lot of people milling around. In one area, people are paying money, in another picking up medicine, and so forth. Somewhere in the lobby is a counter or desk with several nurses receiving new patients. Find your way there, and ask for help. Point at what hurts. Howl, if you need to. You may be afraid, but don't get angry. They will try their best to help you.

They will help you **register**, you will be asked to pay a few *yuan*, and you will receive a patient booklet for your records. They will write your name, age, and gender on it, or ask you to do so. After you have the booklet, they'll direct you to what they think is the appropriate floor and department. If you are really hurting or confused, a nurse will accompany you.

Once you get to the right floor and department, there may be another nurses' station. Hand them your booklet, explain your problem again, and you will be directed to the waiting area for the doctor they think you should see. If there are a lot of people waiting, you may be given a number. If you still have your book, hand it in, or put it on the pile on the doctor's desk. The books are stacked up in the order the patients arrived, and your turn will come. Smaller hospitals are simpler, because they have fewer departments, floors, and doctors.

Among other things, Americans will immediately notice that Chinese hospitals lack privacy. People are walking in and out and watching other patients being interviewed, examined, or receiving treatment. While it may be disconcerting, this is not necessarily a bad thing; children are less afraid (especially of dentists) as they have some understanding of what will happen. As a patient, you, too, can look around and evaluate the facility and treatments. It may make you squirm, but don't panic; make the most of it. I find the differences I can see educational and interesting.

After the doctor sees you, he or she will give you a slip (usually several copies) you will need to take somewhere to **pay** for the visit and any tests or supplies that were used. The cashier's window may be on a different floor. If you are carrying the slip around, the staff and most others will understand where you need to go and direct you. Hand in your slip; they will add up the charges and tell you how much you owe. Pay, get your receipt in duplicate, and go back to the doctor. He will have written up his diagnosis and treatment in your booklet, which he will give back to you when you give him his copy of the receipt. Be sure you get your doctor's name so you can see him/her again, if you want.

You'll need to **pick up medicine** if you were given a prescription. You can do that in the hospital, or at a medicine shop on the street. You may or may not have paid for it already. If you have not already paid, it may be cheaper to buy the medicine outside the hospital. Be sure you understand how to take it (if it's Chinese medicine, you may need to know how to prepare it), and when to come back.

If you are given Western medicine, the information sheet in the package will have the name of the medicine in English or Latin, and the strength in milligrams. Go to an Internet cafe and search for it with Google to find out what you have been given, and to get more information. While you are at it, check out the price back home. I find the difference interesting, and it always makes me feel better.

If you go back a second time, go directly to the floor and the doctor you want to see. If you take your patient book, you won't need to register again. Be sure to keep the booklet, as you can use it again and again. If you have a chronic problem, it will help the next doctor understand the problem, see what treatment other doctors have recommended, and evaluate the results. You'll need to register again if you go to a different hospital, but having your old booklet will make the process simple.

Chinese Medicine

You may be interested in exploring *Zhongyao* (TCM, traditional Chinese medicine) for a problem, perhaps something that is hard to treat with Western medicine. I have spent time experimenting with *zhenjiu* (acupuncture) treatments for a couple of things. It's inexpensive, with real doctors who have years of training, internship under specialists, and practical experience. Where could be a better place to try *Zhongyao* than in China?

In traditional medicine, treatment is especially varied between doctors. A *Zhongyao* doctor, commenting on the differences in the treatment he offered me, summed up his philosophy with the phrase, "One goal, many paths". Different procedures and medicine can lead to equally good results.

I find some Chinese medicine quite effective. For example, if I develop intestinal problems or diarrhea (I'm pretty nonchalant about sanitation, the cleanliness of dishes I eat out of, and other matters), I take a little yellow pill, Berberine Hydrochloride. The common Chinese name is *Huangliansu*, and the full name is *Yansuan Xiaobojian(pian)*. It's commonly available in bottles of 100, at a cost equivalent to about US 25 cents. Some pharmacies don't stock it, as the profit is too low. A well-known American herbalist, Ryan Drum, thinks this is an excellent treatment. He calls it a mild intestinal "calmer". I take one to three pills, three times a day as needed, depending on how bad I feel. Usually the problem is completely cleared up in two days or less. Two tiny pills once, and most mild problems are gone.

Popular over-the-counter remedies vary with cultures, and I like to try different ones. My current favorite cold medicine or immune booster is *Banlangen (keli)*. It's made from the leaves and root of the Indigo plant, and comes in small bags which one dissolves in hot water. It's popular, and I think it really helps. I take it at the first signs, when I start to think maybe I'm going to catch a cold, or when a lot of people around me have colds. I take a bag 3x/day, sometimes two bags, if I'm really worried. After I have actually caught a cold, it seems useless. Any pharmacy has bags containing ten or twenty little bags.

I carry a supply of each while traveling. They are both OTC, over-the-counter medicines requiring no prescription, which you can buy in most pharmacies. And I use both of them at home, too. You can also buy them in many pharmacies in Chinatowns around the USA. Not as medicines, of course, but as "nutritional supplements" with no claims made.

Saving Money

As long as you are in China, you may find it possible to pay for the cost of your trip by taking care of something you've been putting off because it's too expensive, such as dental work, glasses, or elective surgery.

With a little help or some careful research, you can buy generics of most medicines. Americans will find the price to be a fraction of what they pay at home, even for generic drugs. English/Chinese dictionaries of medicines can be found in many bookstores, so a little research will find the Chinese name of a medicine. Copy out the characters, or buy the dictionary. It's perfectly acceptable to read in bookshops in China, or copy information out of books without any purchase.

Glasses are easily acquired if you've brought a prescription from a recent eye exam. If you need a prescription, it can be more difficult because of language problems during the exam. If you buy new glasses, you'll be pleasantly surprised at the cost of the frames, and they probably come from the same factory as those you'd buy at home. Talk about a markup! Perhaps it's because frames are so heavy, bulky, and hard to ship.

Over three recent trips in China, I spent a lot of time getting **dental work** I had put off. Each trip, I spent a week or two with frequent appointments at a hospital in a medical university. Each of those times, the total cost of my whole trip (several months), including airfare and the cost of the dental work, was less than I would have paid back home for comparable treatment. The cost of this dental care has been about 5% of USA prices. I've received first-class treatment, and my teeth are now in better shape than at any time in the past forty years. As a side-benefit, I now have some good friends in the dental profession.

Beijing Fear

This bit is added for fun and to play down media reports which can blow many things all out-of-proportion.

It is a free translation of a popular joking poem which was posted around Beijing and common on the Internet during the SARS [Severe Acute Respiratory Syndrome] "epidemic" in April 2003, the new disease of that year. More in the stories. I was traveling in China throughout the SARS panic.

The latest news at the moment in Beijing,
Phobia of SARS has infected 2,500,000.
The symptoms are:
    Wearing masks and taking medicine improperly
    Frowning all the time without a smile
    Rushing to buy oil, rice, and Chinese medicine
    Sterilizing day and night without going to bed

A billboard in the Zhongguancun area of Beijing, April 2003. Note the empty streets of a city under quarantine during the SARS (Severe Acute Respiratory Syndrome) scare.

Dentist friends at a medical university. My teeth are in great shape now!

13

Money

TRAVELERS need to carry and use *RMB* (Chinese yuan), as few places in China accept foreign currency. The Bank of China charges a small fee, three-fourths of one percent, for cashing **traveler's checks** and a higher fee for changing US dollars. I seldom change **currency** at banks. All banks in China now have the right to cash traveler's checks, but only a few are set up to do it. The main branch of the Bank of China always can do it, wherever you may be. The fees may vary a little. Be extra wary if you need to change money at airports or in hotels; the rates may be very bad. Banks, at least, are pretty uniform, and operate under strict regulations.

In the bank, the process is slow. Stand in line, wait, present your passport, wait, sign forms, wait. It can easily take ten to twenty minutes or more for either traveler's checks or currency. For a long time, I've thought that all the government needs to do to completely stamp out the use of the black market by foreign visitor is to speed up bank transactions. A few banks do move quickly and efficiently, but they are exceptions.

Although illeagal, there are many **black market** moneychangers looking for foreign currency, especially US dollars. In contrast with the bank, a black market transaction can be finished in a minute or two. The moneychangers usually offer about one half of one percent more than the bank gives for traveler's checks, which is a lot more than the bank gives for currency. I use the black market for its efficiency, when I know where it is and feel comfortable with it, even though it's technically illegal. Others may be more comfortable with the bank, as there is always a small chance of being cheated or getting counterfeit currency in the black market. I've been cheated only one time, back in 1988 when I was new to it, and if I have ever received counterfeit bills, they were so good no one else spotted them either. Still, my Chinese friends warn me to be careful and keep my eyes open. Do your research and learn the current exchange rate before you change much money. Google can give you the current rate quickly.

The black market will often be **located** in front of a big Bank of China, maybe the central branch in the city you are in. It finds you; just wander up to the bank in no special hurry, maybe stand around outside for a few minutes. It doesn't seem particularly illegal and is done quite openly. Sometimes, the changers are in small shops (someone who knows will show you). These are the safest, as you can find them again if there's any problem. One such shop I've used in Beijing has been in the same place (near the back gate of a university that has many foreign students), with the same people, for more than four years.

The difference between buying or selling US dollars is typically less than 1% on the black market, for hundred dollar bills (the difference may be higher for other less-popular currencies, although you can change nearly anything. The rate will also be worse for smaller bills). Ask **both rates**, and if the difference is more than 1%, bargain for a better rate. A **typical black market transaction** goes something like this: having identified a trader, I ask how much *RMB* for US$100? The trader pulls out a small calculator and punches up 775. I take the calculator and punch up 785, or whatever the current exchange rate is. The trader laughs and punches up 780. I ask how much *RMB* to buy US$100? He (or she) enters 790; hmm, a pretty small margin. I agree and get out my hundred dollar bill while the trader counts out 780元. We each inspect and count the other's money carefully, and say thanks and goodbye. It's fast; this explanation takes much longer than a transaction.

Banks are even easier to find than Internet cafes; they are everywhere and almost always have signs in English, but the black market can be hard to find outside of big cities, so plan ahead.

I keep all my money with me in a money belt (see the chapter on safety), about half in currency and the rest in traveler's checks. I also carry plastic for insurance. In case of an emergency I could always buy a ticket home or get more money with it.

Many travelers use **plastic** such as **credit**, **debit**, or **ATM** cards, which work well in China. If you plan to do that, I suggest you check with your bank before you leave home. The only time I've used plastic in China was in '92, and it cost me 4% on the China end (split, I believe, with the USA credit card company), so I have little experience. I hate giving money to banks. Find out exactly what fees will be added, and exactly how the exchange rate will be calculated. Ask if your bank belongs to an ATM alliance that waives the fees, and which foreign banks belong to the alliance. The average foreign transaction fee in the US in 2006 is 3%, but there is one bank that charges no fee. There may be a fee as high as US$5 per transaction for cash advances using ATM or debit cards (some ATMs do not charge a transaction fee), and a cash advance with a credit card outside your home country may also have a higher interest rate. Many banks and credit card companies have hidden fees, and there can be multiple fees from your own bank, from the card company, and from the merchant. For example, there can be added fees for currency exchanging, and other special fees for transactions outside your home country. Some of these fees won't show up on your statement, but instead are added into the transaction amount by the merchant. Banks and other financial institutions can be quite creative, and fees can vary widely between different banks and card providers. Altogether, these fees potentially add an extra 5% to 10% to the purchase or cash advance.[1]

Do your research; if you didn't have time to consult with your bank, use the Internet. A good source for information are the forums on <http://www.lowcards.com>.

Whether you plan to use a credit card or debit card, contact the issuer and let them know you are going overseas. This will help avoid the possibility of fraud detection procedures.

---

[1] The Wall Street Journal, June 29, 2005, Personal Finance, page D2.

14

Standing in Line

QUEUES can be frustrating, especially so if there is no order. Most queues in China are more orderly now than they used to be, but there are still a lot of me-firsters, the pushers and crowders. In many places such as banks, the lines can be orderly and polite. These days, security guards are often watching and controlling important queues.

I've learned the following techniques by watching self-assured and polite Chinese who don't crowd, but seldom allow someone else to usurp their space. While standing in line, watch for these people and learn from them.

In train and bus station ticket offices, there usually are pipe barriers forming chutes to each window, with an exit chute to the side. Once I am in the chute, I **make myself big** by standing with my elbows out and my feet spread. This doesn't help before I'm in the chute, and doesn't stop somebody from using the exit chute to crowd in. I also **keep the space small** between me and the person in front of me, moving forward quickly with the line.

When I am almost at the window, I **politely hold my place** by stretching out my arm and putting my hand with papers or money on the counter. Any crowder then has to move my arm to get in front of me. If someone tries this, I stiffen my arm and smile (or glare) into the offender's eyes. I point at myself (but not with the blocking hand) and say "*Diyi*" (first). I can decide to give way after I assess the situation and the other person's need or craziness.

Most of the time everyone else in a line will ignore any confrontation. No one wants to get involved, they don't know whose son the crowder might be, and don't want any trouble; maybe it's the son of a Big Potato. (Shortly before he retired, Jiang Zemin said that the biggest problem facing the Communist Party was official corruption. Sometimes the children of officials, corrupt or not, seem to have peculiar ideas about their place in the universe.)

When getting on a city **bus at rush hour**: hold your place and don't leave any space in front of you. If you hesitate or leave a gap, you are lost. As soon as I am close enough, I extend my arm and put my hand on the bus, near the door, so a crowder has to duck under it. It's possible to hold my place that way and still be polite, not pushing, and even to let someone else go ahead of me. Pulling a crowder back doesn't seem to work, but blocking a crowder works fine. They usually back down.

Keep in mind that a crowder may be jostling you to distract your attention, teaming with someone who is trying to pick your pocket. Be aware of others around you. That also helps me notice the old ladies I may want to let get on ahead of me.

At a **toilet on the train**, you often can't stand close to the door without blocking the passage, so someone else will push past and stand closer to the door. When the door opens, don't waste a second. I immediately push past or reach in front of the crowder to retain my place while looking directly at him. The crowder usually won't meet my eyes and gives way. If they don't, I let them go first. Maybe he really needs to.

15

Telephones

THE phone system is excellent in China. Calls are low-cost, easy to make, and work to anywhere, any time. It wasn't that way in 1988, but China's telecommunications system is now excellent, perhaps the best in the world. China is by far the world's largest user of mobile phones, with a penetration of at least 30% countrywide, and over 100% in Beijing (4/2006). The service is excellent and the price low.

Public Phones

There are pay phones on the streets nearly everywhere. A few of these phones don't work, but rarely because of vandalism. They use IC cards instead of coins; there isn't any money inside, so why break them? Many of the phones look shabby because they have been used so much. Nonetheless, they are actually quite new. However, they are becoming a little less common again, because so many people are carrying *shouji* (mobile phones).

There is another kind of public telephone, in addition to the pay phones. Many small shops, including most newspaper vendors, have a phone or a row of phones on the counter. Often, there is a conspicuous orange, blue, and white sign with a drawing of a telephone on it, maybe the letters, "IP", and sometimes in English, "public telephone". Just pick up a phone and make your call. The phone has a meter and you'll be told the price after you hang up. It's a lot easier than dealing with a card, especially if you're passing through, and sometimes it's cheaper. I regularly use these phones for both local and domestic long-distance calls.

Some phones are for local calls only, but many do any domestic call. A few, usually signed "IDD" (International Direct Dial), can do international calls. Usually these "street phones" match the lowest rates for domestic calls. 0.2-0.3 元 per minute is the common charge to call anywhere in China. If you dial a local number and repeatedly get a busy signal, you may have picked up an "IP" (Internet Phone, or Internet Protocol) phone that is only for long distance calls. Show your number to whomever is watching the phones and they'll point at the telephone you should use.

For international calls as well as calls inside China, the best rates are often in small, private "IP" places. These are special little street-front shops with many phones, sometimes in small booths, and often nothing else. Most have "IP" on the sign, which may be blue and white. They are around, if you watch, but are becoming less common in the richer city centers. So many people carry mobile phones now. Look in the outskirts, back streets, and worker housing areas to find the IP phone shops, if you can't find one on the main streets.

Phone Cards

Sometimes international calls are cheaper with an IP card. A 50-100 元 IP card may have the same rate per minute as the IP places, but you can bargain for a discount when you buy a card, sometimes paying as little as 30% or 40% of the calling value, making the actual rate a lot lower. Offsetting this, you'll need to pay for a local call to use your IP card, unless you have a phone in your hotel room that allows free local calls.

IC (integrated circuit, with a chip, a "smart card") cards and many other kinds of phone cards are available in shops on the street nearly everywhere, or at the telephone offices. On the street, at newsstands, and in small shops, you can get a discount. If you buy the card in a telephone office or at your hotel, it will usually be full face price.

Many cards work in one province only, but cards that work in several provinces are becoming more common, as people travel more. The cards may have a code (often 17909) that you can enter to make IP calls. They are commonly available in 30, 50, 100元, and larger sizes. You can also buy a *quanguo* (all-country) card, but you usually have to buy it from a telephone company office, with no discount. If you are traveling out of the province soon, consider getting one, or give your partly used single-province card to a friend when you leave the area. Check the expiration date; maybe you can save it for your next trip.

With some cards, such as the 200 and 201, you must enter a code and a PIN before dialing a number. And there are IP cards that are good for international long-distance calls. Check the per-minute rate for the kind of calls you want to make. Different cards have different rates.

If the phone in your hotel room doesn't allow free local calls, ask the *fuwuyuan* what kind of card you need. A 10 or 30 元 card will let you make a lot of local calls, but it can be much cheaper to make long-distance calls on the street. If you can't figure out the rates and you care, make a couple of timed test calls on different phones and compare the rates. If the difference is significant, it will be easy to spot.

Shouji, Mobile Phones

In mid-2001 China became the biggest mobile phone user in the world. Earlier in the year, industry "experts" had been predicting that China might pass the USA, then the largest user, by 2005. In fact, by early 2005, if you included *Xiaolingtong*, China already had nearly three times as many mobile phones as the USA. In September 2006, the official numbers were 442 million mobile phones in China, plus about ninety million *Xiaolingtong* phones. Fixed-line phone subscriptions stood at around 360 million.

The 2006 <u>World Almanac and Book of Facts</u> doesn't show China on its list "Worldwide Use of Cellular Telephones, Year-End 2004". (They show the USA as the largest user with 159 million.) The previous five years also haven't included China (or India) on the list. Maybe it's because the Chinese don't call them "cell phones". Actually, they list countries by the percentage of population that subscribe. In the current list of 59 countries, China doesn't quite make the list. Choosing this measure for inclusion and providing no other statistics makes the list quite misleading.

If you want a mobile phone (*shouji*, hand phone, lit. "hand machine"), it's easy. Go buy one, many travelers do. If you plan to take the phone home with you, you'll need to buy a compatible "unlocked" one (Search Google for information). It is also easy to buy used ones much more cheaply than new ones, as many users want the latest popular model. Calling rates in China are much lower than in the USA, but still expensive against Chinese wages. Rates are difficult to compare directly, as there are so many different "calling plans" in the US with "free" minutes and the like.

Xiaolingtong

Xiaolingtong looks like a mobile phone, walks and quacks like one, but it isn't and isn't counted in the mobile phone tally. It's called a wireless phone, not a mobile phone, a regulatory difference. The *Xiaolingtong* ("Little Smart", named after a science fiction comic book hero) phone system has received scant attention abroad. The handset looks the same as a regular mobile phone, with all the slick variations such as cameras and color screens available, but isn't ideal for a traveler. They are sometimes called "city phones", and don't fully roam. (They aren't supposed to roam at all, but as of the end of 2004, they worked anywhere within the home province. Don't tell anyone: it's unofficial and wasn't advertised. In mid-2005, the government ordered them to quit roaming and the companies responded "quit what?". Compliance is slow, but so far as I can learn, in 2006, they don't roam.) The coverage areas are much more limited than mobile phones, but the charges are substantially lower, with one-way billing. The monthly fee and per-minute rates are about the same as for a home phone. Some toll calls actually cost less than the same call from a standard landline phone. And the handset costs substantially less than a *shouji* handset with similar features. Mobile phone companies have fought back by substantially lowering their rates to try to keep their customers.

Many ordinary Chinese have gotten XLT (*Xiaolingtong*) as their first telephone ever. XLT is an exciting, seriously competitive parallel system that has forced all wireless phone rates down. Some mobile phone users also carry a XLT phone, for the lower rates. There are even dual-mode handsets that are both mobile phone and XLT, but they are expensive. (One I looked at in 2004 cost more than US$300.) Some handsets available then could serve as a wireless modem for a notebook computer, with up to a 128 kbps data rate (about US 90¢/hour to connect to the Internet, as of 2005).

Per-minute charges can be less than half typical mobile phone rates (mobile rates have been falling fast in some areas, so the difference is decreasing). There's more: text messages (SMS) are completely free between XLT phones, billing is one-way, there are no connection charges, handsets are lower-priced, and monthly rates are much lower. (*Shouji* in some areas now also offer one-way billing in addition to lower rates and are experimenting with other incentives.)

While XLT voice calls worked seamlessly with mobile and landline phones, the mobiles did not initially accept SMS (Short Message Service, text messages) from XLT, a major factor slowing growth. In March 2004, the Chinese regulators required the mobile companies to accept XLT messages. The mobiles responded that it wasn't technically feasible. Then, through an "accident" (the work of an innovative employee?), the two systems cross-connected seamlessly for a day in the spring of 2004 in the city of Xiamen. This was widely reported in the Chinese press, but the mobile telecoms still dragged their feet. By January 2005, it was reported on TV that they cross-connected everywhere in China. XLT users now must pay a small fee per message (about US 1¢) to send to mobiles, and the *shouji* user may need to add a special code before the XLT number.

XLT phones are similar to a cordless phone with public base stations. The technology is also called PAS (Personal Access System), PHS (Personal Handyphone System), or WLL (Wireless Local Loop). They are low power, and need 200-400 base stations within a standard mobile phone "cell" bounded by four towers. If the phone is physically moving, it must switch from base station to base station more frequently than a *shouji*. Consequently, it's more likely to drop the connection, especially when the phone is moving much above walking speed. It is also positionally sensitive because of the low power: you'll see someone answer their phone on the street "*Wei?*" (Hello), and suddenly come to a stop, turn 90°, maybe take a few steps this way then that, all the time crying, "*Wei? Wei? Wei?*". That's *Xiaolingtong*.

At the same time, the lower power of these phones has a major advantage: battery life is phenomenal. At a usage level that requires recharging most mobile phones daily, a simple XLT handset may need to be charged only once a week. They are sometimes called "Green Phones" as, with the low power, there is little worry about any possibility of neurological damage from the radiated energy.

Of course, the lower power means signal quality is poorer. Yes, connections may be dropped more frequently. And people enjoy making jokes, calling it "*Wei? Wei? Tong*" (Hello? Hello? Tong), or, less politely, "*Wei? Wei?* Damn!", but most users hold up their XLT handsets and say "Good enough!". I think the USA needs *Xiaolingtong*.

Capitalism with Chinese Characteristics

What is the most interesting to me about *Xiaolingtong* is the competitive pressure it has placed on the mobile phone companies: the rates in China have fallen fast, and the mobiles have been forced to experiment with one-way billing and other incentives. Chinese central policy holds that good communication is an important component of continued economic growth. This policy recognizes that communication, to be useful, has to be priced low enough that everyone can afford it.

This "Capitalism with Chinese Characteristics" intrigues me, and

Xiaolingtong seems a good example: the government owns all the telecoms, but forces them to compete in a brutal fashion. In the early '90s, there was only one telecommunications company in China — China Telecom. Then the government began a policy of fostering or forcing price and service competition by carefully breaking up the telecommunications monopoly, and it was divided into China Telecom and China Mobile. Next, China Mobile was divided, with China Unicom split off. A few years ago, China Telecom was divided again, splitting off China Netcom. (There have been other smaller splits — China Railcom, using railway right-of-ways, has laid huge fiber-optics networks and offers fixed-phone service in some areas.) Currently, only China Mobile and China Unicom are allowed to offer mobile phone service, with landline services (and *Xiaolingtong*) operated by the others. This rule is set to change as 3-G (Third Generation) is ramped up.

In the late '90s, the landline companies were doing badly, as they were getting few new subscribers. New subscriber numbers are critical for drawing investment, and most new subscribers were getting *shouji*.

Along came an upstart company, UTStarcom, running *Xiaolingtong* in a few areas in the late '90s as an experiment. As soon as it proved itself workable, it was awarded by the government to China Telecom, putting them into wireless communications (but it wasn't called a mobile phone, as China Telecom wasn't allowed to offer that service). The mobile companies hated it, and their new subscriber number began to fall drastically. They have been forced to lower rates and experiment with various incentives to entice new subscribers, and to keep their old customers.

A co-founder of UTStarcom, Wu Ying, a young engineer? In the fall of 2004, he was said to be the eighth richest man in China. (2004 China IT Rich List by Rupert Hoogewerf) It was only an idea in 1996.

What is harsh for the companies (and their investors) is a windfall for consumers who benefit from ever-lower prices, new services, and rising quality. Will XLT be around next year? Is it a good and desirable telephone option? I don't know, but it has already dramatically lowered the price of telecommunication for Chinese people and given wireless phones to many who previously couldn't afford them. It most certainly will be appearing in other developing countries around the world.

Added to this complex picture is a new and different wireless service: *Dalingtong* (Big Smart). A few of my friends are trying this service, but its subscriber numbers are still low. Some commentators predict it will grow fast. *Tianzhidao*; this is an intensely competitive market.

16

License Plates

V EHICLE license plates: every traveler needs to know about license plates. Why? Because it's fun and interesting and you can amaze (amuse?) your friends with your insider knowledge.

There are four main types: yellow ones with black letters are mostly commercial, on buses and trucks; motorcycles (*motuo*) also have yellow plates, but they are physically smaller; blue plates with white numbers and letters are the common ones; and the central (national) government plates, especially those for the police and army, are white with black letters.

Motuo with engines of 50-100 cc may have a small blue-and-white plate. With engines even smaller than fifty cc, they need only a bicycle plate. (These small *motuo* are forbidden in many cities.) Electric bikes also need only a bicycle plate. There are arguments about what routes electric bikes should be allowed to use. Car drivers want them to stay in the bike lanes and many bike riders want them to use the vehicle lanes.

Driver training car plates have the word 学 *xue* (study, learn) at the end. Give them a little space. Temporary plates are on paper, stuck in the window. Joint-venture cars have special plates, and there are also special plates for embassy and consulate cars. The colors can be reversed on some of these special plates. For example, cars registered to foreign-owned companies have a black background with white letters.

On the common blue-and-white plates and most white-and-black government plates, the first thing is a Chinese character. It's the abbreviation for the province, autonomous region, or municipality: 桂 *Gui,* for Guangxi, 粤 *Yue,* for Guangdong, 京 *Jing,* for Beijing, 青 *Qing,* for Qinghai, and so on. Most dictionaries have a list of the abbreviations in the back.

Following this Chinese character is a letter designating the city: "A" is the provincial capital, or the central district of it; "B" is the second most important city, and so on, down the alphabet. (These letters were assigned to cities many years ago and don't necessarily reflect current importance or size.) A double letter on the blue and white plate, such as "A-A", probably designates an imported car.

The letter "O" is an exception, and never represents a city; it stands for "Official" and is on an important government official's car.

On most taxis, the letter "T" follows the city letter. Some provinces instead use "Y", and it can be yet different in other areas. That one is easy to figure out, as taxis are easy to identify.

The five-digit number following the letter has little meaning on the common plates, unless it is a number such as 88888, 88668, 00000, or other specials that Chinese might consider lucky. *Guanxi* (relationship, connections) lets someone get these. If your *guanxi* is good enough, nearly anything is available, including special letters on a common plate.

Sometimes a red Chinese character follows the numbers on blue-and-white plates, and has various special meanings.

On a white-and-black "O" plate, if the number is 00000, or 00001, it belongs to high officials. And if the "O" is red, the highest.

If there is a red Chinese character at the start or end of the plate, be careful. Don't kick the car or curse it when it forces you off the road, or is parked in the middle of the bike lane. They have more power than you.

On PLA (People's Liberation Army) plates, the first word is red. There are twelve different words (the Chinese zodiac), designating different regions. The next letter designates the group, such as border patrol, security, or air force. The red letters, "WJ" (*Wu Jing*), designate the Armed Police. Next are black letters and numbers. A special number such as "0001" may have some meaning on these army plates.

There are web sites devoted to Chinese license plates, with photographs of common examples and of special and interesting ones. Search around. Surprise your friends with your esoteric knowledge.

Most new drivers have learned about all this; they must know which cars they cannot afford to hit, even if it means their life.

Regulations are continuously changing; new plates appear, and old plates are canceled.

17

Getting Out, Coming Home Crazy

REVERSE culture shock: Coming Home Crazy is the title of a revealing 1990 book by Bill Holm, written on his return home to the USA after a year spent teaching in China. Nearly the first thing that strikes me when I arrive in an airport in America are all the obese people with jiggling flesh. Soon after, I'm struck by how shabby the cars seem (they are all so new and clean in China). The food isn't fresh, the vegetables in the supermarket have been in cold storage for days or weeks. I can't speak to kids, or kid around with them, unless they are the children of my friends. The kids will be scared, and someone might call the cops. The police all carry guns and I know that many other people also have guns. It doesn't make me feel safe or free.

I get to vote for my country's leaders, but I don't seem to have much to choose among. Most of America's elected leaders seem caught up in short-term electoral cycle thinking. Are China's leaders different? They certainly aren't popularly elected. Is that better or worse? They seem to be doing an impressively good job of staying on track and keeping things from flying apart. Are our elected leaders doing as well? How important is stability? Most of my Chinese friends think it's crucial.

Freedom and oppression: they can both be found in China in plentiful supply, depending on where you look and what you look at. There are countless degrees of freedom and oppression, wealth and poverty, and at least two sides to every issue with many different factions in every group, impossible for the outsider to truly assess. I tend to avoid the richest (they don't seek me out, either), and never see the poorest, who are inaccessible to me. I rarely see the extremes. What is "most", anyway? I like to think I see the middle 90%.

I think again and again of a conversation I had five years ago with a brilliant young friend when he was a postgraduate student. Late one

105

night in his apartment, looking down and not meeting my eyes, he asked "What do you think of human rights in China?" I answered carefully that they could be better, but that human rights could be better anywhere in the world. He looked up then, directly into my eyes and said strongly, "I feel free." Months later and far away across China in his home town, I saw another friend, an old woman in her eighties who speaks beautiful English. Telling her of my conversation with this young man from her town, a local boy who had gone on to attend a top university and do postgraduate work, she responded somewhat angrily, "The next time you see him, I want you to ask him for me: What does he feel free about? Just free to make money?" Perhaps half a year later, I saw the young man again in Beijing and relayed her question. He looked somewhat puzzled, shook his head sadly and said gently, "Is she still angry about the bad things that happened during the Cultural Revolution?" Generations and times change, but I feel good and my friend feels free.

I also think of a Tibetan friend, likewise a postgraduate student in a big city, asking me "Why do Americans think Tibetans are holy?"

My middle of the night questions: what is it about China that I want to know and understand? What is it that makes this country so interesting and exciting for me? What keeps a people, a culture, strong? What is assimilation, and is it necessarily bad? I'm confused: what is it that seems bad to me about the common Western policy of assimilation of minorities by deliberate culture and language extinction, that has seemed so much better in China, with the *shaoshu minzu* (minority nationality) schools and policies? Is it really better, as I think? Do I know enough to make any pronouncements? What's the relative value of a dialect, as compared to a language? What about the position of women in China, as compared to the West? Is it as good as it seems?

The modern world is encroaching. Most people want it, and the faster it comes the better they like it. Many "poor" farmers in the countryside have modern things: TVs, VCDs, mobile phones, washing machines, motorcycles, the latest gadgets. Are they richer or poorer? Certainly the gap between them and the rich is growing wider, but their lives are easier and they have a lot more money than just a few years ago. Does the arrival of the modern world extinguish culture? If it does, does it matter? If it matters, to whom does it matter? What (and who) determines whether a culture stays vibrant, or fades away? What is a living language, and if a language is dying, is it possible to support it? And who am I, to think I can be some kind of observer of all this, with an opinion that matters?

I'm lucky, that's what I am, to be able to occupy myself this way. (I once had a red MGA sports car which was nearly useless for anything but fun. I tried to pretend it was practical, and made ways to use it as a truck.)

So... This book doesn't answer any of these questions, or even attempt to answer them. Rather, it's about the process of traveling around China and does not necessarily relate to the country as a whole, to reality, or to the future. It's easy to generalize about China but always a mistake, as it's a huge country, dynamic and diverse and changing fast. Every possible variation exists somewhere, so take my notes as just that: notes, crumbs collected in many places over the past nineteen years while following my big nose (*da bizi*, a slightly pejorative Chinese name for foreigners).

I do know I'll return to China many more times. As my understanding deepens, I can learn and see more. Everything is changing so fast it's almost going to a new country each time. Maybe playing catch-up is my life. It is certainly wonderful.

Tales about Travel in China

18

Tales about Travel in China

THESE stories are a litany of boats, trains, buses, frustrations, and being sick (with a few other bits thrown in), but that's not what traveling in China is about for me. However, it's what this book is about, and I hope to provide an authentic "feel" of the process of getting around. Although that process dominates these stories, they represent only a tiny part of my experiences and pleasures. All these accounts stand out in my mind, and I selected them because each seems useful. I hope they provide support, comfort, and shared delight.

Be sure to note the dates: every aspect is changing unbelievably swiftly. Keep in mind that China is a huge country, generalizations are always a mistake, and everything will be different. Much will be more modern than anything I mention, and the oldest things described here still exist somewhere. The "newness" and my inexperience color the earlier stories.

1988

March 31

Guangzhou, the city buses: A few Chinese seem to try to not pay. Seems to be a bit of an art for some, riding the bus for free.

The boat dock: I messed up somewhere, didn't ask enough questions, got in the wrong line and missed my boat. I got my ticket changed to the next boat. It sure would be nice to be able to read the signs and understand the directions I'm given. People try to help me but I'm too dumb, I can't understand.

Walking the streets, people stare at me. My beard and long hair are very strange. I stare back, nod and smile, sometimes say "*Ni hao ma?*" (how are you?) if there is any response to my smile. Sometimes the response is a huge grin and "*Ni hao!*" or "Hello, hello, hello" or "OK, OK". With old people, sometimes the response is incredible. An

111

absolutely blank staring face becomes instantly a huge grin, smile, all wrinkles, twinkling eyes, nodding, "*Ni hao*". Then, click, a blank face again. Great fun, it makes me feel good. Some small children seem frightened, other children greet me with "Hello," or "OK," or "Hi," and less commonly, "ABC" said fast and clear.

People seem friendlier than in, say, Seattle, a fairly friendly American city. People are openly curious, stare blatantly, but usually respond warmly if I act in a friendly manner.

April 2

Wuzhou, Guangxi: It's strange walking down a street hearing calls of "Hello," "OK," "Very good", all directed at or caused by me, and often unable to identify who has spoken. Kids run up, yell "Hello," and are often shy when I respond "*Ni hao ma?*", collapsing in giggles and running away, only to come back or follow me for a way. Most people seem very friendly and I attract a crowd in an instant by stopping to buy an apple or look at something. I pull out a phrase book and people collect. I guess I'm much more interesting than TV. People laugh at me a lot, but it seems friendly, not condescending, or anything negative.

April 3

Met a student, Chen Qing, in a bookstore. He said only 20% of the students were women in his Guangxi College of Finance and Economics (total enrollment 120, a three-year program, and a very small college) because most women don't have the intellectual powers to pass the entrance exam. I wonder if such a belief is widespread among the men? And I wonder if he voices that belief in front of women?

He took me to his college dorm this evening. He walked into the twelve-bed men's dormitory room and said something like, "Wake up, I've got a foreigner", in English. Curtains were flung open, heads popped out of everywhere, someone leapt out of a top bunk to grab a chair, slide it front and center, and bid me to sit. Within minutes, there were fifteen or twenty students in the room, and others looking in the door and windows. I am hoarse from all the talking and an incipient cold.

These students were all about twenty years old, some with good English skills. Most of them were open and willing to talk about many things. I praised the progress their government was making, some of them contradicted me, and I countered with examples of bad US policy. They told me of a man and woman student they had played an April

112

fool trick on, setting up a secret assignation for them. The woman was furious and reported the misdeed to the college authorities. Everyone was most pleased, as no one got caught.

Altogether, it was like being in a semiserious freewheeling discussion with a group of college kids in the US, except these students were doing it in a foreign language.

April 4

Li Dezheng, the upper-class monitor (the eldest student, I believe, or maybe the best student) who acted as translator whenever there were problems last night, came to my hotel to offer to be my guide today. I thanked him, refusing the offer. He seemed downcast and I realized he wanted to spend the day with me. The college president had given him the day off for that purpose. Perhaps he is advanced enough in his studies to merit a day off. So I finally accepted his company.

We climbed Baishan (White Mountain). Mr. Li told me locals say you haven't seen Wuzhou if you haven't climbed Baishan. It was a beautiful view of the whole of Wuzhou City, the confluence of the two rivers, the Xijiang and Guijiang (maybe three rivers, as the Xijiang changes its name to the Xunjiang here), around which the city is built. Above the city are lush green forested hills. We took a bus out of town, down river, and took a trail up a small stream with some waterfalls. Mr. Li knew the way. He said he loved the walk, but he had no time, maybe only once a year for a busy student. He was very happy and as it wasn't a holiday there were almost no other people.

While we were sitting on the top of Baishan, I explained a problem I'm having with this notebook, trying to explain to people what I'm writing and why, and how my inability makes me feel uncomfortable. I asked him to write something for me on the cover to convey my purpose, my reason for writing. He seemed puzzled, and asked me what I wanted him to write. I asked him again to write something that conveyed what I had explained to him. He looked at me peculiarly and asked, did I want him to use his own words? I said yes, exactly. He laughed, got excited, and sat deep in thought, pen poised over the page. Several times he started to write, and each time stopped before he had begun. Finally, Li wrote three vertical lines of Chinese characters, from right to left, in the old way. He wrote very fast, and then handed my book back.

Having a guide is a bit strange, much different from wandering around by myself. I see less and ignore many people, but learn in more depth about a few. I don't want a guide all the time, but it seems difficult to stop once it's started. It's hard to explain my appreciation, but that now I want to be alone. I think it's more than a language problem.

Li did something wonderful: as we walked in town, he held my arm, pulling my head down near his mouth. As my presence generated comments and conversation on the street, he gave me a running translation. Comments such as "Is it a man or a woman?", "His hair is longer than hers.", "His hair is longer than mine!", and so forth. I had been uncomfortable with all the attention I had been receiving, and the comments I generated up and down the street. He made me feel easy and comfortable, a large gift. **N.B.** — In the rest of this first trip, and during my subsequent trips to China, I have not met another person who was willing to provide such a running translation without embarrassment. Li did it with great enjoyment, and it was his own idea.

April 5

On the boat to <u>Guiping</u>: I passed this notebook to a man who was watching me blankly, and pointed to the cover. He read the cover, studied the book for awhile, and passed it back with a smile. Now when he catches my eye, he smiles warmly. I'm glad I had Mr. Li inscribe the cover for me. It says, freely, "These are my memories of my travel in China. I look, and write what I see. 1988." At least, that's what Li told me it said. **N.B.** — A later translation: "This is a notebook about my impressions and reminiscences of China. It records my unusual traveling experiences there. 1988."

Accepting help, hospitality, and meals I'm not allowed to pay for makes me intensely uncomfortable, but there seems to be nothing I can do about it without being offensive. Compounding this, once I accept something in public, others around often seem to feel the need to offer me even more. These generous people who will never see me again freely and happily offer more than I can in any way imagine they can afford. And I haven't yet figured out any way to give back.

April 12

<u>Guiping</u>: I went for a hike yesterday with Huang, a young doctor from the town hospital, to what he said was a remote village. I could not imagine that a village only two hours' walk from this small city was as cut off as Huang said. I was right and he was surprised. He's not from here, and not a country boy. There was electricity, with TV sets, tape recorders, and the like in perhaps a third of the houses in the village.

The houses were quite nice, but since there was only a rough trail, no road, it was hard to carry in building materials. So the walls were made of cast or rammed earth, or mud brick. The villagers considered their dwellings poor, as they were not made of more permanent fired brick, but they were large, nicely spaced from each other, airy, light, and clean. The villagers said they liked the fresh air and quiet, but wanted a road which would much improve their lives, and they hoped the state would build one. I said a road was a mixed blessing, because then everything became faster, dirtier, and noisier. The villagers laughed and said it did not matter, they wanted a road!

As Huang had warned me, many did not speak with us, or respond to us in any way. It was a response he called "not moving." I would make a polite greeting, and be met by nothing, only a blank stare. Many of the children responded this way, even when older people were speaking with us. Some adults also watched or passed a conversation with a "not moving" response to any greeting. Huang said this was a non-response to our presence, neither disapproving or approving, not like or dislike, but a completely neutral non-response. It was easy for me (and I think for him) to feel this as resentment, a strong negative reaction to us. It was intimidating, but Huang assured me it was nothing and to ignore it, but it seemed to get him down, especially when a group began to collect at a slight distance, all "not moving" in response to greetings or attempts to start a conversation. He seemed to be right, though, for if someone was willing to talk to us, the others seemed not to exist, and not to bother the person talking with us, at least not in any overt way. So perhaps it is truly a neutral thing. We returned to Guiping at dusk, having walked, run, sat, caught crickets, laughed, and talked for more than ten hours. A very nice day, all in all.

Eating lunch today, an old woman leaned on my table and watched me with a happy smile. I asked her, with help, how old was she? She said 77, so I asked her to guess my age. She guessed I was over 80. I expressed amazement, and said I must look very wise. She said it was my long beard. My interpreter, a young student who is the daughter of the cook, told me she thought my light hair had something to do with it, since Chinese have black hair, only white in old age. Yesterday with Huang, another old lady in the village said the same thing. She was 78, and said all she knew of the outside world was what she remembered from before liberation. Both women seemed to have no reference, nothing on which to base a guess at my age, so they may have been sincere about the "over 80" bit.

April 17

Guangxi road manners: Trucks and buses want the right of way (bad brakes, always overloaded). They roar through towns, air horns blasting. People ignore them and amble diagonally across the street. Many near misses. Clearance between trucks is often only a few inches, but I haven't seen any collisions yet.

At night, nobody uses lights (Remember – this is 1988, not today.) Not cars, not trucks (well, occasionally...), and certainly not bikes. I have not seen a bicycle with a light on it since I came to China. This can be frightening in the countryside, with trucks and buses roaring along in the complete dark. My first ride on a bus at night was hair-raising. Maybe the driver could see where we were going, but I sure couldn't.

April 29

Guizhou, near Huangguoshu: I picked a likely spot and started hitching, the first time I've tried in China. It was easy. The first truck to go by was full, but the second, a big new Isuzu, picked me up. I pointed at a phrase in my phrase book, "Where are you going?", presented a map to the driver, and he pointed. I pointed at a phrase "I am going to___", and he said "*Meiyou*", the universal negative (don't have, can't do, won't work.) I pointed at a phrase "Can you take me part of the way to___", and he said "*You*" (have, can) and pointed to a town on the map, the village at the turnoff to Longgong. And we were off. I rode for an hour and a half, and approaching the end of the ride, offered him one of my Chinese-English business cards, which he liked, and offered him money, which he absolutely refused, three times. I added a few books of American matches to the card, which he also liked, and the ride was over. It was nice, sitting up high in the truck, with big clean windows and a soft seat. All that visibility and comfort, and we went a lot faster than a bus, too. I expect my card and the matches will give him a good story to tell at the next truck stop, about a crazy foreigner.

May 30

Beijing: The amount of construction happening in China is completely beyond my experience. I don't know what the situation will be tomorrow or next year, and I don't think anyone else does either. Everywhere, buildings, roads, dams, and bridges are being built. In the cities, even more so. Here in Beijing, everywhere there are forests of tower cranes. Imagine the biggest construction site you've ever seen in an American city, then picture a site larger than that every half mile and you've got a pretty good picture of Beijing. Tower cranes are the dominant feature of the skyline. It's truly impressive and yet most Chinese I talk with assume that since China is a poor country and the USA is rich, there must be more construction in America.

June 19

<u>Luoyang, Henan</u>: My hotel room is on the fifth floor. I look down on a busy street and a big free market (an area or street where farmers and others sell things) thronged with bicycles and pedestrians. There is a lot of noise, mostly horns. If a bus, truck, or car comes, there is much horn blowing in an attempt to clear a path, but more likely just making more noise. Nobody seems to move or hurry because a huge bus with air horns is preparing to run over them, or to move more quickly to let a truck through a market. Pedestrians seem confident in their possession of the right of way, and as a pedestrian, I like it. As a truck driver, well....

1991

December 14

<u>Dapeng, Guangdong</u>: I climbed a mountain yesterday. The humidity was a bit high for climbing, about 80%, and 70° F. The slopes were covered with an even-age stand of pines planted about five feet apart, the largest about eight inches. One stump I examined was seven years old, probably left from a thinning a couple of years ago. An extensive planting, it ran over hill and dale into the distance. This kind of planting is common in many places I've been, and represents a huge effort and commitment. I've read that vast areas of China were denuded during the "Great Leap Forward" in the late 50s and early 60s, for fuel for back yard smelters and the like. Large areas of China's forests had already been stripped by the late-1800s. The scale of these new plantings is almost beyond my conception, and cutting appears to be strictly controlled. There is evidence of pruning, lower branches being cut off close to the trunk, and thinning, but there are almost no bits of wood lying around. I guess it's all been carefully gathered for fuel. Due to these massive planting programs, there will be forests here again in the future.

I saw only four other people on the mountain, workers headed down together, but a lot of people must come up here. I followed a pretty well stomped trail, and there was trash everywhere along it. In places, the trail was damn near straight up and down. Down, then up and down again. I got lots of scratches. A small rhododendron or something with white flowers with a yellow center was in bloom everywhere, very fragrant. There was bamboo, a pampas grass, oaks, many plants I didn't know at all, and, of course, the planted pines.

The topographical map I had didn't help much, as the contours were 100 m. It showed this mountain as the highest, but not exactly which peak was highest, elevation as 867 m, about 2700 ft. There was very coarse grass at the top; otherwise it was barren. There would have been a spectacular view of Hong Kong, and north across Daya Wan, if it hadn't been hazy.

I started down at 4:00 PM and got to the bottom at 6:00. I hurried, got to my bike at dusk, and rode back to Dapeng in the dark. It was hard riding in the dark as I started on rough gravel roads full of holes (but without much traffic) and no light. I'd guess only somewhat more than half of the motor vehicles around here on the coast north of Hong Kong have working lights. Two-thirds of those with headlights leave them on high beam all the time. The remaining third use their dimmers, drive carefully and surely, and use their horns only when necessary, then only "beep beep". A good portion of the drivers play macho, careen along, lean on their horns, won't dim their lights or give right of way: I'm a driver, I'm a big guy!

1993

January 5

Zhejiang: At the airport near Huangyan, shivering. What a fight, getting into my seat on the plane. Everybody was trying to carry on too much, me included. The woman in the next seat had filled my seat and the luggage space with her stuff. I had to move it all out, with everybody waiting in the aisle, stuck behind me. I got even with her; while she was ignoring my problems, while the stewardess was trying to get her to move her stuff and she was also ignoring the stewardess, I accidentally dropped my pack in her lap. She quit trying to ignore me and moved a bit of her junk. Otherwise, she was going to be stuck with my pack in her lap for the duration. She understood that; good communication, cross language, cross cultural, cross inconsiderate idiot. Perhaps not so different from a bus, but sure a lot more expensive.

November 15

I had a long bus ride from Hangzhou to Jiaojiang yesterday, on a small bus which had fairly comfortable seats but not enough knee room for me. North of Linghai we were rear-ended by another small bus, which lost its windshield. An altercation ensued, with a man from the other bus trying to punch our driver, who I didn't consider to be at fault.

Money changed hands, our bus giving the other bus about 500元, although I wasn't sure who gave or received. That calmed things down, and we (our bus) went directly to the police station in <u>Linhai</u>. The police went out immediately and picked up the other driver, and we (all the passengers) wrote out statements, as directed. Mainly, we wrote that we had seen the other man try to hit our driver, who didn't fight back. All this took a few extra hours. I don't know if anybody will read my statement, written in English.

1998

February 22

<u>Wuzhou, Guangxi</u>: After breakfast, I wandered around for a couple of hours, onto smaller and smaller streets, going up all the time. Soon I was on a path with steps in places, twisting up the hill between houses. Quiet, peaceful, fresh air with sweet wood smoke and sometimes the smell of incense. At one point, a middle-aged woman with an angry face told me there was nothing for me to see. She was loud, her expression and scolding tone reminding me of a neighbor I once had in America. I went on past, and two houses up two old women greeted and welcomed me with smiles and invited me to walk on. My impression was that they didn't like the sour younger woman who had scolded me.

February 24

I was told at the bus station there was a bus at 11:00 AM, so I checked out hurriedly, got my ticket to <u>Guiping</u>, and found the departure time was 12:40, two hours to wait. I should have bought my ticket when I asked, then I would have really known. I was told to sit down and wait a little, but the place stunk of diesel exhaust, so I went across the street to a park to wait.

I went back to the bus station with thirty minutes to spare and was greeted by some disgusted and annoyed women who had been looking for me. They pointed at something stamped on my ticket, rushed me out and put me in a taxi, gave directions to the driver, and told me 10 元. My bus actually left from a different station, and there had been a shuttle earlier. When I was told to sit down and wait, they really did mean for a few minutes, not the two hours I thought I had to wait. They were annoyed I'd wandered off.

China has certainly been building a lot of roads. We flew along a two-lane highway that hadn't existed a few years back. It was comfortable, except the seat was a little short for my legs. The bus was empty when we started but picked up people along the way, the first few right outside the station. The bus would stop anywhere it was flagged down. Sometimes it was nearly full, although never so full I had to pull my pack off the adjoining seat.

In <u>Guiping</u>, Gao (a middle school English teacher I first met in 1988, now an old friend) told me the bus fare from <u>Wuzhou</u> was less than 10元 (I paid 33.7元). He says I should not have bought the ticket in the station, that I should have stood out on the road and flagged down a bus to Guiping. When I got on, I should have handed the conductor the amount I had determined was fair by asking around, and said "*goule*", enough. I understand now why I was the only passenger to get on the bus before it left the station. It's a private bus (maybe they all are private now) and the station takes a large cut for booking and printing the tickets, dispensing information, and providing toilets and a waiting room.

March 10

<u>Yulin</u>: There is a lot of new road construction here, the same as I see everywhere, with multilane underpasses being built under the rail tracks and new tracks being laid parallel to the existing ones. There's a diverse mixture of trucks, cars, tractors pulling wagons, motorbikes, bicycles (both often with sidecars), and small tractors with permanent small dump trailers. They aren't walking tractors anymore, as the operator rides on the trailer. Wang (an old friend who is an English teacher in the teachers' college) tells me pedal-powered trikes and sidecars are banned from the center of Yulin, except the special-use ones, such as the "street sweepers".

March 12

In the evening, I went to an English corner at the teachers' college as I had promised some students. It was a big night, a real mob scene. There were three other foreigners there, a new foreign teacher who is a woman in her fifties from Canada, and a young British couple teaching in a private middle school outside Yulin. We were each surrounded by ten to thirty students (they, ten each, and me with thirty, my animal magnetism) who wanted to talk with us. So, four different clusters. It broke up after 10:00 PM, nearly two and a half hours. I was told these evenings lasted only one hour. Some students will stay as long as you do.

I had the biggest crowd because the American accent is popular. I talked mostly with three students while the rest listened and occasionally threw in a question or comment. I had a boy to my left, a pretty girl in front, and another pretty one with short hair to my right. The young man was very angry with the Chinese government and wanted to talk about it. Other students tried to hush him, saying he was wrong. I suggested they allow each other to speak freely, if they wanted to talk with me. The shushers left and one girl asked about the CIA, a subject I was more comfortable with as it was about my own country. We talked about secret police, and how they are a law unto themselves. We moved on to Clinton's media-mania sex scandal, but I shied away from the angry man's comments about lack of human rights in China. I told him China was not my country, I would talk about my own country, he could tell me what he thinks about China and I would listen, but it's not my place to tell him about China. They wanted to know where I had been, both in China and the rest of the world, and where I planned to go, so I gave them the list, ending in Kunming. I told them I had old friends there whom I hadn't seen for ten years, a man about my own age and his mother. The girl with short hair asked how could they remember, how could I remember? I told her I remembered conversation with my friend as though it was yesterday. She was disbelieving and said I must have a good memory (of course, they are all about twenty, and ten years is half of their lives). I said how could I forget my friend telling me about his time in the Red Guards, the wonderful and terrible, at times with tears streaming down his face? How could I forget when someone honors me with a story like that? How could I possibly forget? (This is typical of the free-ranging conversation in English corners.)

March 20

In <u>Nanning</u>, nobody is honking their horns. An order was passed last fall (1997), making it illegal to blow horns unnecessarily, with a stiff fine for violators, enough to get people's attention. I was told that within a few days, taxi drivers had cut the wires to their horns because they were so much in the habit of honking they couldn't stop. With the wires cut, they pound out their impatience, frustration, and importance to their hearts' content, whacking on the disabled horn button.

The new law makes the city much quieter and even bicycle bells are seldom rung now, although the rule doesn't prohibit that. Many, enjoying the peace, have taken the bells off their bikes and thrown them away.

There are occasional discreet toots from the buses and large trucks, but even that is rare. In Beijing in 1991, there was such a rule but it wasn't enforced, making the no-horn-honking signs seem silly. I remember thinking it was the most disregarded law in China. This is nice!

The Xida (Guangxi University) campus is quiet and beautiful, with many trees and green areas. It's far enough out of town that the air is better than in the city. Much of the air pollution, which isn't very bad, comes from two-cycle motorcycles and trikes. They've proliferated in the past two years. People riding motorcycles on the campus are considerate and quiet; they whisper along. There must be an enforced noise and speed rule.

March 27

<u>Xingyi, Guizhou</u>: I miss the no-horns order of Nanning — this place has terrible horn honkers. The horn honking is getting to me, especially bus drivers who blow their loud horns nearly continuously, except when they must take their hand off the horn button to shift gears.

1999

December 14

<u>Hong Kong</u> — the new airport. At the old airport, I always saw special-forces type guards wearing berets and carrying Uzis, but they are gone. I'm told the airport has better security now, the cops are still there but discreetly out of sight. Designed-in surveillance is so good that if someone lights a cigarette, a hand is on their shoulder before they get a second puff.

December 30

<u>Xiamen, Fujian</u>: There are new propane or natural gas-fueled city buses on the streets with "Green Bus LPG" written on the side in English. Nothing in Chinese except fare and route information, which isn't presented in English. I assume that "green bus" is an English language slogan used to mean environmentally friendly.

Deng Xiaoping said "To get rich is glorious" and "Some must get rich first." There are many new expensive fancy cars and SUVs here, but few Chinese even dream of owning one. These cars are washed daily (by someone else).

2000

January 1

<u>Xiamen</u>: A couple of notes about this street market, the Xiaxi, and most similar markets around China. Permanent shops are in buildings

on both sides of the street. The market itself is in the street in small stalls or on tables, leaving enough room for a small truck to pass down the middle between the stalls.

The shops are all open-front, with many of their wares and displays moved out onto the sidewalks in the morning. There are workers cleaning the street at all times, sweeping up the fruit rinds, fish guts, paper and plastic bags, and so forth, working in and around the throng of customers. The trash is hauled away constantly on *sanlunche* (freight tricycles or trike trucks).

Early each morning (4:00-5:00 AM), the street is washed and fresh (although it's hard to believe this by midmorning). All the street stalls are gone, put away to allow for this complete cleaning. Most are dismantled by around 9:00 PM, when the street is already getting fairly clean. At one end of the market, there is a small office for the officials in charge of the market. A customer can go to this office to lodge a complaint, ask to have a vendor's scale checked, register to sell there, or whatever. Most of the vendors are regulars. I see the same faces day after day.

January 17

At the airport, I missed my flight. I learned something about my new Chinese bike: it can fly without me! I was a bit late getting to the airport, took the bike apart, packed it in a hurry, and checked in. They charged me nearly a third of my ticket price for the bike, excess baggage. I had understood my bike was included, but maybe they only meant it was allowed to take the bike. I complained bitterly, but paid. Then off to the security check. Oops, must go back to pay the airport tax, then back to security, what's this pocket knife, what's in the camera, what about this wrench. Finally off to the gate to find my plane was gone with my bike and pack, but not me. When I rebooked for the next flight, they refunded the excess baggage charge, I'm not sure why, maybe as an apology. I didn't argue or insist on an explanation. I was willing to be an hour and a half late for that. With the extra charge for my bike, taking the plane was expensive.

In Guangzhou, I found everything waiting for me. I assembled my bike in a quiet corner near the luggage carousels. A few people wandered over to watch and two security officers kept coming over to joke with me and help. When the bike was assembled, I asked the two officers, with a bit of Chinese and sign language, if they rode. Receiving an affirmative, I pushed the bike hard toward one of them and let go of it. He caught it as it went by, looking a bit worried. He jumped on it and rode it around the area and around the luggage carousels, to the amazement of everyone there. Then the other guard did the same, with a huge grin. They gave the bike back and I tied on my bags and bid them farewell. I hope they didn't get in trouble.

January 26

Wuzhou, Guangxi: Took a bike ride, 25-30 km, trying to find a new railroad from Yulin to here. It showed as a completed line on some of my maps, as planned on others, and not at all on the rest, which made me curious. I rode out of the town, off the edge of my detailed map, and took a side road I thought would cross the rail line. The road became a trail which became a path which got smaller, through duck ponds, past small farms, and brush and hills. I started to get worried, as it was close to dusk. I spotted a group of kids, young adults, and a couple of middle-aged women all watching me and laughing, so I parked my bike and walked over to them, to many exclamations of "*Wa*!" and "Oh!". We exchanged pleasantries, where I was from, how old I was, all of the other questions, and I got out my best map which lacked detail for the area, showed them where I was trying to go, and they pointed across a field. I thanked them, said goodbye, and headed along the dikes between the fields. I had to carry my bike across several single-plank bridges, and finally got to a "road" leading up a small valley. The group of folks watching, now tiny, way back across the fields, waved and pointed that I was on the right route. I waved, yelled thanks and goodbye, and started up the unpromising track. After fifteen minutes on the path, I started to catch sight of tips of buildings in the extreme west of Wuzhou. I would have been happy being lost, except it was getting late and I was getting worried, with less than half an hour until dark. I got back to my hotel well after dark. I never did find the rail line, maybe it wasn't built yet. **N.B.** — 2006, the line shows as "under construction" on my new maps.

February 15

Yulin is quiet. Now this city, too, has an enforced "no horn honking" law similar to Nanning's, two years ago. Yulin is different, compared to my first two visits when, in addition to the horn honking, public loudspeakers started blaring music at around 6:00 A.M. every day, often common Western stuff such as "Jingle Bells", or "Happy Birthday", that sounds silly and inappropriate to my Western ears. Now, without the racket, the mornings are relatively peaceful with only construction, traffic, and people noises.

Of course, what sounds inappropriate is culturally determined. I think of a Chinese piece by A Bing, played on the *erhu*, "*Er Quan Yin Yue*". I love it, and the beautiful melody makes me happy. My ex-wife got a bit angry whenever I played it, saying it was something to listen to when very sad, that it made her want to cry, the story of a blind man trying to imagine what he cannot see, the reflection of the moon in a quiet pool.

2001

March 14

To <u>Nanning, Guangxi</u>: The new *Nan Bei* (Nanning-Beihai) expressway is a high quality multiple-lane, divided limited-access freeway, with no pedestrians or bicycles to be seen. It has nice on and off ramps, with tollbooths controlling access. Nearly all the new expressways are toll roads; if you drive, you pay. The signing on the expressway is first class international standard (of course in Chinese).

March 31

Another bus: these Daewoo coaches are made in Guilin, not Korea — maybe a joint venture. The video fare is something, we've had two: the first, about a Chinese warrior or diplomat or... from the far past who is sent into the present to do something. He is sex-starved and most of the plot revolves around that. Next, *Qigong* (mystical powers), past and present, wizards, monsters, and lots of *gongfu*. Later we got MTV, some kind of fashion show with the singer romantically singing through and around everything.

The bus trip was efficient and boring. I prefer the train; it's nice to get up, walk around, and meet different people. The train takes longer than the bus now, although it was much the fastest, only five years ago.

June 5

<u>Nei Menggu</u> (Inner Mongolia): I caught a bus from <u>Wuyuan</u> to <u>Hongqi Gongshe</u> (Red Flag Commune). Even this small but new local bus had VCD, playing another Jackie Chan *gongfu* movie. I came out to Wuyuan hoping to find a Mongolian man I had met last year in Guangxi. He had given me an address written in Mongolian script, but most of the people around here are *Han* (ethnic Chinese) and can't read it. I like to have small "quests", something I'm trying to do to give me a reason for poking around, going places I otherwise wouldn't see, a reason for talking to people. In this case, it's interesting tracking down the address of someone who is probably in a different part of China.

The road to <u>Linhe</u> is a wide and smooth two-lane asphalt highwa with no shoulders (hard edge with a concrete block curb). It's an od mix of traffic: bicycles, pony carts, small tractors with trailers, big farn tractors pulling four-wheel wagons, *motuo* (motorcycles), three-wheelee *motuo* and trikes, buses, trucks, and high-speed cars. There ar windbreaks of trees on both sides. Although there are no shoulders, th lanes are nearly two standard lanes in width, wide enough to allow fo slower vehicles and breakdowns. There are km and 1/10 km marker down one side. About 1 1/2 hours before Linhe, the road changed to four-lane, with emergency pull-offs every .8-.9 km on both sides.

Huhehaote, Hohhot, <u>Huhhot</u>, Hoshi, or Hushi: The first is th *Putonghua* name, the second the old name familiar in the West, the thire a Romanized spelling preferred by many Mongolians, and the last two *Ho*, or *Hu*, *shi* (city), is the common name used by everyone here. *Hot* i Mongolian means city, it's common for Chinese to shorten names, an Huhehaote is too long. Everyone, both the *Mengguzu* (Mongolians) an the *Hanzu* (Han Chinese) seem happy with the name Hushi, it doesn' rankle many feathers. Spellings of place names can be a problem ir *Shaoshu Minzu* (minority ethnic group) areas, as it's government policy to respect the minority names and there may be no fully standare Romanization of the language. Three different Chinese maps with Romanizations can show three different spellings for places in this area. Probably the only completely correct spelling is the *pinyin* of the officia name.

A *Mengguzu* friend talked about environmental degradation in Ne Menggu: there is agriculture with bad practices, over cutting of trees fo fuel (due to increased population density), mining, gravel and ston extraction, and the digging up of the grasslands to harvest a valuabl hair-like fungus. Ten or so years ago, many people from other parts o China came here to dig for this fungus. This digging damaged larg areas of the grasslands, which will take ten or more years to recover This harvest is now banned, or at least closely regulated.

And drought: this is the third year of a severe drought. Man animals have died, and milk production is way down. He says the tre planting programs aren't the best. The species selected are right, but th newly planted trees aren't cared for, so many die. The land reclamation he envisions includes taking care of the planted trees so they will grow and prosper. And a lot of education.

June 14

Huhhot, the weather today was something: In the morning, it was cool and sprinkled a little. The air was clear, visibility good, mountains clear. Then a great dust storm blew up. It started with a little rain (not enough to get damp) and very clear air. Suddenly there were strong winds, and in less than an hour visibility was down to 100 m. Three hours later, the wind had died, the dust had settled, and things were back to normal. I was out on a bike in the worst of it and got my ears and hair full of sand and dust. The gusts were nearly strong enough to knock me off my bike, and small pebbles bouncing off me hurt. People were hiding any way possible, ducking down and behind things or running into buildings. A friend told me a storm such as that happens about once a week in the summer here, and that a really bad one can last a day and a night. The evenings have been cool and fairly clear.

June 21

This afternoon, we had a heck of a thunderstorm. It poured. Thunder crashed loudly enough to set off car alarms all over the place (car alarms in China? You bet).

In China, many people will answer what they think you want to hear. So if you ask if someone has something they don't have that they think you want, they may answer "yes". Or if you are asking directions, people might give directions to make you happy, although they haven't a clue. Others are more direct, and yet others will answer '*Meiyou*" (don't have) even when they have something you want, because it is too much trouble for them to sell it. I guess I mean each person is different.

Chinese seem to have a much better understanding and knowledge of the USA and the rest of the world than average Americans seem to have of any place outside of America, even of our close neighbor, Canada.

Just about any person you meet abroad who is from the PRC is special, the cream of the crop by several measures. (There are also a few rich kids with no qualifications whatsoever.) It is sad for China that many of the people who leave are the best. They find little to do in China that truly uses their abilities, so they leave, but this is changing very fast right now.

July

Here in <u>Erlian</u>, the "North Gate" of China, pedicabs, *sanlunche*, are the common transport. They cost about 2元 per person to anywhere in town. I find most drivers friendly. They offer their services and move on quickly when I thank them and say no.

July 2

<u>Erlian</u>: With a mob of students, Narsu (A *Mengguzu* [Mongolian minority] English teacher in a *Mengguzu* school; about thirty, beautiful long hair) and I collected a taxi, actually a small van, for an impromptu school field trip, US$10 (I paid) and we went out in the desert to the east of Erlian to hunt for rocks and dinosaur bones with half a dozen of her students. These kids picked up just as many rocks as American kids would. No luck finding fossil bones.

August 1

Overall impressions of <u>Huhhot</u>: Streets are being widened, new pipelines buried, a big conversion to natural gas underway. The widening seems to be for beautification and parking. The newer big buildings are mostly set back from the streets, with small buildings along the street. Most of the small buildings are marked for demolition, 拆 *chai*, the character painted on the walls, big and red.

Huge crews are at work, hand labor and big modern machines too. As work is finished, different crews arrive and plant blooming flowers and then others arrive to water them. Seems to work.

On one street, as old buildings are knocked down, new walls are being built at the rear. Almost before the plaster is dry, artists arrive to paint huge murals of the grasslands running for a hundred meters. In one place, the foreground of the mural has red and yellow flowers perfectly matching the color of the real red and yellow flowers planted in a three- to four-meter strip in front. In the painted grassland are people and *gers* (*Menggu bao*, yurts). The impression of depth, the endlessness of the grassland, especially at night with the flood lamps, is impressive and beautiful. I wonder how long it will last? Maybe for years, if they used good quality paint.

Street lighting is changing from the old standard of an incandescent lamp every hundred meters or so, to twin sodium vapor lamps every twenty to thirty meters. A month ago, holes were being dug along *Xilin Lu* (a main north-south street) and then concrete poured. Last week the lamps on galvanized poles were installed. They are all operating now.

128

Light filters nicely down through the young trees, many less than two years old.

August 15

Gansu: Horn honking in Lanzhou is restrained. There is still a lot of honking noise, but most of it is made by a few jerks. I watched a big dump truck edging its way down a small street. Its horn was adjusted to a barely functional croaking buzz. The driver could honk at will, giving a signal without destroying the peace. Later, a mini-van taxi with a shrill horn passed, also honking at will and driving too fast, but the idea, the concept, is spreading, and many drivers don't use their horns at all. A few years ago, it seemed as if everything with a horn or a bell had to blast away all the time. It's not as quiet here as in the places that have outright banned horn honking, accompanied with stiff fines, but it is still a big improvement I had thought impossible ten years ago.

August 22

Ge'ermu has some of the characteristics of the town at Huangguoshu Falls in Guizhou that I visited in 1988. This place sees a lot of foreign visitors, but usually only sees them once. Lonely Planet gives Ge'ermu a bad rap, so most foreigners arrive expecting to hate it. Nearly all are on their way to Lhasa, and many of them have a preconceived idea of China to start with. It's a good example of one of the worst aspects of tourism.

So I get overcharged a lot. Most sellers and restaurants try to skin me, while pretending to be friendly. Not nice, not fun. The seller smiles and smiles, says what good Chinese I speak, and asks two or three time the normal price. I'm unused to having to bargain so much and I don't like it. There are many people on the street who smile and say "Bye-bye." When I planned to come here, I forgot about those aspects of places such as this. Ugh. Glad I'm leaving today. I think Lonely Planet guidebook negativity goes a very long way toward creating these kinds of places.

There are little kids here who yell "Fuck you!" as did the kids at Huangguoshu in '88 who yelled "*Yanggou!*" (foreign dog, lit. "ocean dog") and spat on the ground; there's just more English now. These kids are colored by the kind of tourism the place sees, tourists with no interest at all in the place, only a transit point that they have been well prepared to dislike. Huangguoshu had its attraction, but had day-trippers arriving by the bus load. Almost no one stayed overnight, much less longer. The result is very similar.

The place itself is okay, but the people have come to dislike foreign visitors and travelers because of the kind of tourism they see. I came here because I had a little extra time, and the side trip seemed reasonable.

Erlian, on the Mongolian border, was different, although as a border town it also was a transit point. It had a lot of business travelers, and people entering China for China's sake. Here on a major land road to Tibet, many of the foreign visitors have preconceptions about China because of what they "know" of Chinese treatment of Tibetans from Hollywood movies. Everyone knows Hollywood is a lousy source of factual information, but it still manages to form people's ideas. No one seems to remember or have any knowledge of the CIA's role in the Tibetan uprisings of the '50s, or of the understandable Chinese fear of this outside influence.

The place where I've been eating breakfast (a tent in an alley) is fine. I get a good and cheap breakfast, and it has been good and cheap since the first time I ate here. I'm comfortable, sitting at a table and writing. They make beautiful *youtiao* (a fried bread) and don't care whom they sell it to. They treat me the same as they treat everyone else, from the first time I came in. I'm likely the only foreign customer they've ever had, but I imagine they have many Chinese customers who aren't from this area. *Waidiren*, not *waiguoren* (outside person [not a local] vs. outside country person), but that may be a fine distinction here.

I met a Spaniard, a painter, who has been living in Bali for 21 years. He complained about the lack of English in China, why don't "they" speak English at the bank, at the hotel, in the restaurants? I would have thought a guy like him would know better. Takes all kinds.

August 24

As everywhere in China, Xining, Qinghai too is in a furor of construction. Xining is a somewhat remote and arid city in the western "underdeveloped" provinces, elevation 7,500 feet. Streets are being widened, old buildings knocked down, new water and sewer mains being laid. And there is a big flood control and park project along the *Huang Shui* (a branch of the *Huang He*, the Yellow River). A park or promenade is being built on both sides of the river, five to fifteen meters wide and one to two meters lower than street level. When the river rises above its walls, it can spread out half again wider into these areas while rising another meter or two. The project looks good and creates a nice public space. There are many other public space projects: trees are being planted along the streets, rows of thousands of three-inch saplings being transplanted. All have their trunks carefully wrapped with heavy straw rope, to protect them from injury during the transplant.

Road and street construction goes on with all the traffic mixed in. There are no detours. It rained heavily last night, so some of the areas of city street construction are a real mess. Dust and mud everywhere, spilled from trucks hauling debris. There is also a major limited-access expressway under construction toward Ge'ermu, and east toward Lanzhou.

Modernization comes at a price: the cities, even moderately remote cities such as this one, are getting more modern and convenient, but places lose their individual character. The old neighborhoods are being demolished, but people lived there. The old houses (not very old, most less than fifty years) may have been pretty miserable places without running water and sewers, but they were locally different. These older places often added greatly to air pollution, with small inefficient coal heating and cooking, while the newer places have modern central heating plants which use fuel as much as 20-30% more efficiently, but.... The people who lived in old places certainly won't be able to afford the new housing. Where will they go?

August 26

Everywhere, construction: roads and streets are being widened, all the small buildings fronting the streets are being knocked down, back to the front of the high-rises. It has all obviously been planned. The front walls of the high-rises all line up, and they appear to be two to four years old. Apparently the one and sometimes two story stuff that fronted the streets was temporary. The character, 拆 *chai*, is painted on the walls of buildings to be knocked down.

Biked around for a few hours. Up above the city to the south, there is a new six-lane bypass with a beautiful and impressive cable stayed bridge, sort of a centerpiece for the city. Totally by chance, I saw the explosive demolition of a four story concrete frame building. I had paused to blow my nose, looking down a nearly cleared strip for a new road. I was looking directly at a huge concrete frame building right in the middle of the strip about two blocks away, when Ba-Boom! The whole thing fell apart and straight down, disappearing into a huge cloud of dust.

On the bus to <u>Lanzhou</u>: It looks as though it'll take about two more years to finish the expressway. Major tunneling looks complete, but there are a lot of bridges to build. It could be finished in a year, I suppose, although that strains even my faith in the Chinese ability to get major projects done in a hurry.

The <u>Lanzhou, Gansu</u> airport is 75 minutes by bus outside the city. It is new and modern, with many areas still unfinished. There are modern boarding gangways, not yet in use, and coffee bars and rest areas, not open.

Two Chinese teachers from Kunming were waiting at the airport. They looked as if they had been in a fight with a tiger and lost. Both had cuts and scratches all over their faces, hands, and arms. The man had a big gauze patch taped under an eye, and the woman was barely able to walk. She had blood spots all over her shoes. They had been in a bus head-on wreck near <u>Dunhuang</u>, and in the hospital for a couple of days. It looked as if they were lucky to be alive.

Big terrorist attack, or supposed terrorist attack. The World Trade Center in NY was destroyed, and the Pentagon damaged. It'll be interesting to hear the Chinese reaction, and see the Chinese news. All airports in the US are reported closed. It will be interesting to watch the news on Chinese TV tonight. I was in China when the Gulf War started, and for the duration. The coverage I saw on Chinese TV, and listened to on short-wave radio (these days, I look at news on the Internet) was much more broad than what people saw in the US. My sister is well-informed and skeptical of news reporting, but I found I knew much more about that war than she did when I returned home. Chinese coverage of events outside of China seems more complete and balanced than what most US viewers see.

The USA: TV footage of the World Trade Towers and the Pentagon is most impressive. 110 story towers brought down very neatly. The Pentagon was hit hard. The good Internet news sites are swamped, and the networks overloaded. It's very hard to get anything. It's unclear what was attempted or by whom, but what was done is an impressive technical demonstration of the possibilities and the vulnerability of modern society. It is certainly interesting to look at the US from the outside, with the help of other peoples' eyes.

2002

The bus ride to <u>Yueyang, Hunan</u>, was rough. I wanted to catch a riverboat to <u>Nanjing</u>, and needed to get from <u>Changsha</u> to the port at <u>Chenglingji</u>. We met a traffic jam, trucks stalled solid for a couple of km.

The driver took our small bus down the shoulder, or when he met with an impasse, down the oncoming lane. To manage, he negotiated his way between the trucks which were too big to do as he did. Finally with further progress blocked, we all got out and stood around. A man from Shanghai told me a woman was trapped under a truck up ahead. There were many police and a couple of ambulances. Finally we edged through, to squeeze by a big truck slewed across the oncoming lane, wheels blocked, with a lot of people working underneath.

Once we were past the accident, we started negotiating the stalled oncoming traffic, where all the smaller vehicles were doing what our driver had done, trying to drive down the wrong lane.

Past the jam, our driver began to drive as fast as possible to make up lost time. Crazy, in the back seat on a rough road. My knees were crammed sideways against the seat ahead and I had a splitting headache, but I survived.

July 4

<u>Beijing</u>: Fat — There seem to be more fat people than last year, both old and young, and many more fat students. It's a building epidemic of major proportions, according to Chinese government reports. But it is all relative; the fat people here wouldn't be noticed on the streets of the United States. They'd look normal.

July 5

The China Cartographic Publishing House seems to have fallen on hard times. Their shop was dusty and all the maps seemed old. Pirate map printers, with large-format scanners and large-format color printers turn out perfect copies with no warehousing and no development costs, print on demand. It could kill the publishing house, but hopefully this problem will be solved. Their work seems critical for the continuing rapid development of China.

July 9

I left my hotel a little late for the long bike ride to the main train station. I allowed one hour, but should have allowed an hour and a half. Beijing is a big city. At the station I started dismantling and packing my bike in a great rush. A man came over and wanted to help me. He was drunk on *baijiu* (white spirit, distilled alcohol), I could tell from the pungent smell. I didn't want his help, but he wouldn't go away. He truly wanted to help, but he only got in my way. It was like having my old neighbor Jimmy's help on a bad day: some help.

133

I finally got the bike packed, and he went into the station with me even though I was telling him goodbye. He insisted I go upstairs, which turned out to be wrong, so I had to go back down, carrying the bike, and I was very late. Then he wanted money, dragged me to the wrong platform, kept pulling me around. Finally I got rude and told him to get lost, "*Zou, zou, zou!*" (leave). I had tried to be polite to him, but when I lost it, I yelled at him loudly. He seemed surprised, and left after a quick look around showed him I had attracted the attention of some guards. I found the right platform and got on my train with a bare few minutes to spare. I was running hard.

Ugh, just what I needed, help from a drunk. Oh well, it was the first time I'd had this problem in China. Having to deal with drunks in public places is a more common experience for me in the USA; I'm far too familiar with it.

July 20

<u>Huhhot</u>: Today I met Lan, a rather fat student I had met on the train. He had asked me to call him, said his mother and father were civil servants and if I needed any help.... I met him at the east gate of *Neida* (Inner Mongolia University). With him were his mother and girlfriend, and his father's driver and car.

Turns out his "civil servant" father is a local Party Secretary. Lan is one of the new little emperors. Whew, not quite what I had in mind. We spent the whole day in an expensive SUV, a Mitsubishi Pajero Super Sport GX something, complete with electronic siren and a louder "CLEAR THE ROAD" warning klaxon. Cars such as this drive down the wrong side of the road sounding their klaxon horn and even the police cars pull off to let them by. I wanted to hide my face, being in such a vehicle. It had an "O" and a red character on the license plate.

July 22

I watched the *Wujing* ("Armed Police", the civil arm of the PLA — but few guns, only a small sidearm on the belts of higher officers) engaged in a "Strike Hard" campaign for traffic safety, pulling over trucks and buses for safety checks. Passengers were dumped off anything that didn't pass, the vehicles towed away, and the drivers arrested. The *Wujing* were checking brakes, tires, steering, lights, other legally required equipment, and registration, very efficiently, with well-trained teams of six or so soldiers to each vehicle. These soldiers come from a different area, to reduce the chance for corruption — no local contacts. The *Wujing* also watch the local police, who don't look happy during these campaigns.

August 4

Xinjiang: Yesterday in Pichan (east of Turpan, and around sea level), I found Abdul, a Uyghur middle school Chinese teacher I met last month in Beijing, where he was attending a short English course. I communicate fairly well with him in English, which he says is his worst language. He speaks, reads, and writes Uyghur, *Putonghua* (the subject he teaches), Japanese, French, and now a little English. He tells me he likes language. He does this on his own, but his school leader allows him time for study. He's about thirty, and had invited me to visit him.

We got on what he called a bus, a Beijing Jeep with seating for a maximum of ten. A Beijing Jeep is a vehicle something similar to a USA WW2 jeep, often all-wheel drive, simple, couple of front seats, couple behind them, and a couple of short benches long-wise in the back. If it was carrying a crew around in a logging operation in the western USA, it would be called a "crummy". There are also new Beijing Jeeps that are spiffy SUVs: just much lower priced than the US and Japanese brands.

In the "bus" was the driver, an old man, Abdul and me, and two teenaged boys. We were going to his home village Kukyar, in the foothills nearly two hours and 45 km away, to stay in his family's home for a few days. The first part of the trip was on rough and potholed pavement, and the last third on ungraded gravel. The road wandered through rocky semi-desert, came to an old fort, and then suddenly dropped down as steeply as possible for a vehicle on wheels, into a deep and narrow canyon. In the bottom, amidst signs of rushing water, was the village.

In the morning I got up about 7:30. Abdul was still sleeping so I joined his father and brother for breakfast: bread (*nan*) broken into a bowl with tea poured over it, and a dish of green beans, eggs, and meat. Abdul is up now, and I'm drinking tea. Abdul told me not to help with cleanup; it would be bad for me to do that, he said.

August 5

Woman in the village: Abdul's brother's wife stands in the cooking area while the men eat, then eats while standing after the men are finished. She wears a skirt that ends ten cm. above her knees, and no stockings. Her hair is tinted and she wears no head-covering. Most of the women in the village (which is Muslim) wear headscarves, long dresses or robes, and have their legs and ankles covered with pantaloons and stockings.

Nang: the oven is round, about a meter in diameter and not quite so tall, made of stones and clay. It has a hole at the bottom for draft, and is hollow, tapering smaller toward the top opening. A hot fire of small wood and brush is built inside to heat it, taking a couple of hours. The *nang* dough is shaped into 1.5 x 20 cm. round cakes which are stuck to the vertical curved walls inside the oven, maybe ten or so at once. The cake is patted with a little water, then mother reaches deep inside with a big flat glove and sticks it to the wall. Then the top hole is covered. Abdul says he thinks the *nang* cook about twenty minutes, says he would have to ask her, he's vague. He doesn't know anything about this "women's work". The oven is built by the women, fired and used only by them.

Abdul completed his college education by self-study while teaching in the primary school, studying and reading until he passed the examinations. He would go up onto the plateau and walk for hours reading and studying, in all weather. He knows very little about the natural area or farming life. He grew up here and taught school, but it was only a place for him to study. He says his father and mother didn't allow him to do farm work, instead telling him it was his job to study.

August 8

Yesterday, Abdul and I went walking up on the plateau, which is one- or two-hundred feet above sea level. We hiked about fifteen miles in 40° C. sun. At the foot of the mountains we found a bit of shade made by a gully wall, almost wide enough to hide in. We hung out there for an hour, drank a couple of bottles of water apiece, and started back. Crazy barren rocky country, very beautiful. I was nearly sick from heat exhaustion when we got back around 5:00 P.M. I had a blinding headache and broke into a cold sweat as soon as we were back in the cooler, more humid canyon (humid is relative here, this area may be as dry as any place I've ever been). I drank a lot of water, took a couple of APC tablets (asprin, phenacetin, and caffeine), nearly vomited from the heat exhaustion, and then slept for a couple of hours. I felt okay later in the evening, and feel fine this morning.

Back to Pichan: The Beijing Jeep had sixteen passengers this morning, very crowded. Two were small kids, but two fat women balanced them out. A tight fit. The man next to me said they had once had 21 in the Jeep.

Abdul has been very generous, taking me into his home and village, but to many of my questions he answers, "I don't know, I don't care about this." He is afraid of, and perhaps hates, most wild things. He says all the snakes here are poisonous, and he hates and is afraid of lizards. Toward the end of our time, we were mostly at cross-purposes. I am tired and glad he is rushing off to other things. Maybe he is relieved, too. I am grateful for his time, and the opportunity he gave me to see life in his village.

August 10

Got to Bugur (west of Turpan) at 4:00 A.M. I've come here to meet another Uyghur I met in Beijing, a high-powered researcher in nanotechnology. It was dark and the bus driver, going on to Kuqar, dropped me on the highway after waking me. I was still half asleep and groggy. There were several taxis around and one driver got out. I asked him about a *zhaodaisuo* (budget hotel). He said he would take me to one for 10元, I said too much, 4元, and we quickly agreed on 5元. We loaded my stuff and he took me to the Luntai *Binguan* (hotel), a two star place. I said "*taiguile*" (too much), a "*zhaodaisuo*." The driver laughed, and took me back to where we had started, the bus station hotel which I hadn't seen in the dark as all their lights were off. The driver helped me wake someone and I got a room. It was pretty funny to give the driver 5元 for a circle ride, but he was helpful once he truly understood what kind of hotel I wanted.

August 12

Uyghur manners: blowing or wiping my drippy nose is bad, especially when eating. I must completely leave the room if possible. And when washing my hands, it is bad to shake the water off. I should leave my hands to dry in the air, or use a towel if one is available. And farting: unacceptable.

August 14

At breakfast in a small place on the street, an old Uyghur man traditionally dressed in a cream-colored robe and trousers, probably from the mosque behind this place, came over to my table and asked me something in Uyghur language. I told him in Chinese I didn't understand, and then told him I was an American, the obvious question. He was satisfied and said with a nod "*Ah, Amerik man*".

My friend and his father asked me a couple of days ago why the Chinese call the US "*Meiguo*" (Beautiful Country), when Uyghur call it the "real" name. I answered that names were funny things, that America was not entirely correct, that "United States of America" was better. We talked about the historical reasons for the short Chinese name, "Beautiful Country", and the name "*Jiu Jin Shan*" (Old Gold Hills), for San Francisco. And the strangeness of the name, "*Meiguo*", for me, given our history of imperialist relations. The name developed at a time when the US, while perhaps better than some, was pursuing the opium trade and gunboat diplomacy, raping and pillaging. And yet this short name has stayed in the language and maybe the hearts of Chinese people, through many other evil times.

In the afternoon, I went on a bike ride through a village eleven km to the north of Bugur. I kept going, but found the road dead ended a few km farther on. I turned back, and found everyone in the village was waiting for me. They knew... It was hot, so I bought and ate a watermelon in the middle of the village.

I let an older guy, maybe a bike repairman, take my bike for a spin as he was very curious about it. When he got back, having run it through all its gears, he held it up above his head with one hand amid much laughter, to demonstrate how light it was, or perhaps how strong he was. Good watermelon, good company.

Uyghur sense of humor: after buying the melon I got out my pocketknife, which was much too small for the job. Someone yelled "Ha!" from over where some young men were playing cards. I looked up in time to see a large Uyghur knife sailing through the air toward me. I quickly considered my options: try to catch it, and cut my hand if I missed, or let it go by to land in the pile of rocks where it was headed, ruining the knife. I caught it by the handle (the man had tossed it nicely), whew, and everyone looked elsewhere, as though no one had been paying attention. After I cut up and ate the melon, I cleaned the knife and took it back to the man. He didn't even look up when I handed him the knife and thanked him. Test passed, I guess.

August 22

Shang You, a village near Turpan: Aanisa, a 22-year-old Uyghur girl who has studied English only one year, invited me to go to her home town with her. I've been allowed to pay for nothing but my hotel bed, and two ice cream cones. She has said, after an argument, that I can pay for our return bus tickets to Urumqi (50元), but I don't know if she will actually allow that. I hunted for and bought a couple of Uyghur/English dictionaries, a small one and a big one. They'll help her with her study, and I think she'd never spend her money on them. I've been using them to help with our communication, and will give them to her at the end.

At her home village I went with her father on his motorcycle to look at his grapes. We sat under them and ate four different varieties. Very nice, interesting, we ate a lot and picked more to bring back to the house. Aanisa says her father has an angry heart, and her mother a happy one. Yesterday when we arrived, her father was working on and writing pages and pages of papers. He and I are the same age. Easy for me to see him as an illiterate peasant much older than me, but incorrect on both counts. Right now, he is reading a newspaper and pointed out a story about the US, Bush, and Iraq.

For the first time, I find myself in places where I sit on the floor, no chairs or stools. My knees are pretty creaky, not to mention my back. Pretty hard for me to adopt the posture.

When we arrived in Turpan, Aanisa wanted to take me to the famous places. I could see her money flying away, so told her it was her home town, what did she like to do? Round and round, then finally "Do you want to go to my family home, cook lunch?" This was what she wanted, to spend a little time with her mother. So, off to her village, to her living room, and into her bedroom where I am sitting on rugs on her *kang*. Pretty plush, very private. What is acceptable is so different both ways from *Han* culture. I would never be in a bedroom with a *Han* girl in her home. I am completely at sea. She went out, brought in tea and melon, went out again, brought in her younger brother to keep me company. She told me he is *nongmin* (a peasant), and speaks very little *Hanwen*. I took a nap on her bed, in her bedroom. She went somewhere else for her nap.

I talked with her a little about money, being a guide, taking friends around. I'm unsure how much she understood, and I hope I didn't make her feel bad, that her bringing me here was unwelcome or bad. I told her that she could sometimes make a little money as a guide, while giving the tourist a good deal, and that she could bring friends such as me to her home, but that it made me feel a little bad when she paid because I knew how hard she worked to buy books and to go to school. She agreed that was all true, but I think I made her feel bad. *Meibanfa*, needed to be said. It's hard to guess what she understood or understands, or misunderstands. Her English is very limited, most of our communication is in English, and I'm the first foreigner she has ever met.

Outside, watching Aanisa wash dishes while her mother is cooking: her mother is talking a blue streak, and Aanisa says "mm", every two or three seconds. At one point, her mother quit talking and Aanisa said "mm" once more anyway, right on schedule. Her mother gave her a sharp quick look. When her mother gets on to more interesting subjects, sometimes Aanisa says "ah", or "oh". Occasionally she tosses in a question, comment, or answer, and seems happy and relaxed to be with her mother.

Aanisa's hair is sleek on her head, but bushy and kinky in the tied back tail. The color seems black, but is actually brown in the sun.

The animals have names here. In Aanisa's family's place, the donkey is named "Mang", the goose has a name, the chicken....

I think there has never been a foreign visitor in her home before, and she didn't tell her parents we were coming. When we arrived and pushed open the gate, her mother and father looked at me with a seeming total lack of surprise and offered me food. Uyghur/Arabic culture, I think.

Back in <u>Urumqi</u>, I gave her the two dictionaries and she was delighted. Aanisa lived up to our agreement and let me pay for our return bus tickets. I was allowed to buy our bottled water on the return, and pay for the city bus to the small restaurant where she works. I gave her the big E-U dictionary before we said good night. I had written a dedication to her in it. I estimate she spent around 130元 on the trip and our first night. I gave her dictionaries worth 90元. Our time together has cost her at least three days' pay, minus the dictionaries, which she will use but never would have bought, they were too expensive. I feel OK about it.

2003

January 11

On the <u>Hong Kong</u> to <u>Guangzhou</u> bus, there was something new in security: the conductor video-recorded all the passengers before departure. Looking for known smugglers, maybe. Some passengers kept their heads down "accidentally", or turned, looking out the windows. No one was forced to face the camera.

April 7

Northwestern <u>Guangxi</u>, on a short trip into the mountains near <u>Leye</u>: there was major reconstruction on the main road, so the bus took a long detour. It was sort of similar to roads in the mountains from my childhood, in the northeastern Sierras of California. The highest pass was about 2000 m, over 6000 ft. My maps didn't show elevations, other than occasional peaks. The bus was a nineteen passenger modern Iveco fast coach, no smoking.

The trip back was in a larger Daewoo 23-passenger coach, somewhat

140

too big for the road. The guy in the next seat was car sick, barfing into plastic bags. He was careful, but miserable. The alternate driver tried to get me to move to another seat, but it was next to a fat man, not much room. Besides, I'd have had to climb across the poor sick guy, while he was vomiting. Not great, but *meibanfala*, tough luck. When we arrived at Baise, the sick guy apologized by politely saying goodbye.

The driver of the small bus on the way out honked his horn too much. The driver on the way back honked much less, mostly only when necessary. The mountain road detour was nearly all dusty gravel. People living along the road seemed (!) to dislike the traffic. Not much of the dislike was overt, but small things showed, such as expressions of disgust and dislike on the faces of young children. And some young men casually threw their melon seed husks at the bus when it was stopped, as though they didn't see it. Mostly, people stood or looked with blank faces, as the bus passed them in a cloud of dust. Certainly, the traffic doesn't improve the quality of life. The locals are monetarily poor, but live in a land of great natural beauty which is normally (without the detour traffic) peaceful, with clean air.

2004

January 15

Hong Kong, waiting for a bus to Guangzhou, I watched once again what would be eccentric behavior in the USA: old men (my age or older) doing strange exercises in public places, on playgrounds or the sidewalk. A well-dressed man unbuttoned his dress shirt, leaving it tucked in, and jogged/ran/danced forward and backwards in circles on the sidewalk, while briskly rubbing and patting his arms and chest and sides inside his unbuttoned shirt. After five minutes or so of this, he buttoned back up and walked off, looking the same as everybody else on the street. No one paid him the slightest bit of attention.

February 17

Over nearly twenty years, I have perceived a continued general improvement in street-level air quality in Chinese cities, largely due to conversion from coal to bottled gas as home and restaurant cooking fuel, and more recently, a move away from two-cycle, to four-cycle *motuo* (motorcycles).

This year, using Nanning, Guangxi as the example, I feel a striking decrease in air quality. Commuting is increasing; people are living farther from their work. The city is growing, its population is expanding rapidly with workers arriving from the countryside. Buses are more numerous, *motuo* are ubiquitous, and the number of cars is increasing rapidly. In previous years, Song, a young lawyer I've known since he was a student, used a bicycle and lived close to his work. Now, he has two houses, one for his mother on the far north side of the city, and the other on the southern fringe in a new suburb. And he works in the city center. He has a *motuo*, drives his company's car whenever possible, and seldom rides a bike. From one house to the other takes an hour by bike, and to his workplace, more than half an hour from either house. He doesn't want to waste so much time. The change in his behavior reflects many.

City and suburban infrastructure has been and is being built on an enormous scale, making this commuting possible and even necessary. Bicycle parking on the street is becoming limited, displaced by *motuo* parking which earns the keeper more and uses more space, three or four times more than for the same number of bikes. Car parking has been developing rapidly. Electronic card-reading parking meters, which I first saw in <u>Urumqi</u> in 2002, are now common in urban centers everywhere I go. Underground parking garages are being built everywhere, and are standard in new buildings.

Song also feels air quality has become considerably worse since last year. He notices it in the city center around his office and says the air is much better out where his house is. He feels a lot of the air pollution is caused by all the construction. Construction certainly adds its part: large numbers of trucks and heavy equipment running around the clock, and I'm seeing ready-mix trucks, transit-mixers, for the first time in large numbers. (They are nearly all brand-new Nissans, the nicest I've ever seen anywhere.) Solvent fumes from paint and adhesives, and dust from construction, excavation, and demolition all add their contributions. Huge volumes of concrete are being poured. I don't know anything about emissions from curing concrete, but I can smell it.

He hopes air quality will improve again as construction is finished (will it ever be finished?), but I fear the increased number of cars will continue to worsen the pollution. He plans to own a car next year.

February 22

Buses in SW <u>Hunan Province</u> still have roof racks, with luggage on top. It's forbidden here, same as elsewhere, but VV, a Hunan girl, says Hunan people are different: rules aren't made for them; they do it anyway, who is going to stop them? I've come here with her and her new husband to meet her grandparents.

Suining, SW Hunan: We had an elaborate lunch in the home of some *Miaozu* (Miao ethnic group) foresters up in the mountains. Their house was all wood, the common structure around here. It was built on a fairly steep hillside, with two main floors, plus a 1/3 basement used for chickens and storage of animal feed. There were three large houses, about fifty feet apart, owned by the different brothers and their families, all built twenty to thirty years ago. There were older, dilapidated buildings of the same style around the area, plus many new ones, including several under construction. These small clusters of houses were isolated, not grouped in villages.

The construction was post and beam, the cross ties all through-mortised and wedged with no metal fastenings used in the frames of the buildings. The foundations I looked at were a bit casual, 8-10" posts up to twenty or more feet tall, resting on a rock on the leveled or terraced ground. The first crosstie was often only a few inches above the dirt or rock. The floors were live and springy, moving nicely when someone walked across the room. The paneling was nearly all vertical with a match joint edge, fitted into slots in the cross pieces, and wedged tightly between the posts, providing a lot of sheer strength for the frame. Nails were used in the small stuff, such as door and window frames. These buildings all had heavy tile roofs.

The cooking hearth was set flat in the floor, so the fuel included long branches, small logs, and a few small blocks. The fuel was advanced into the fire as needed. Above the fire was a heavy metal tripod with a ring at the top, to hold a *guo* (wok) or other large pot. The smoke exited through a grill in the ceiling above. All the walls were blackened by the smoke, and I assume the women's lungs were as well. (Luckily for the women, they had wood for fuel and weren't burning coal.) Hanging on the walls and around the ceiling grill were various kinds of foods, mostly meat, drying in the smoke. I sat near the hearth and watched the cooking for awhile. The dogs allowed it, but didn't allow me to touch them. One, named "Hero", had three legs. He was an old dog, and got his name after he had been caught in a trap for wild boars, and found after he had been in the trap for a week. The eating table had *huotong* (fire bucket) under it, with a nice charcoal fire to warm our feet and legs. These *huotong* are common here, as opposed to building heat. *Huotong* are also often used in a low wooden box you put your feet into, with a blanket to wrap around your knees and the top of the box. Inside is a wooden grill with space under it for the fire, held in a pot shaped like an upside down coolie hat, full of glowing charcoal.

Nice and comfy! In town, the fire in the box is electric, but people still call them *huotong*.

The host told us the rice we ate was grown by them, fully natural, no fertilizer. He was proud of that. Even though they could have grown little in their tiny fields on the steep hillside, they had all the necessary cleaners and polishing equipment. The rice was excellent.

The industry in this mountainous region is mainly forestry, a forest preserve said to have a few southern tigers and many wild boars, with bamboo, fir, pine, and many different deciduous species. There are many small hydroelectric plants, micro-hydro. This county is a designated experimental area for such plants. The elevation is about 800 m, rough and beautiful country. It's a strictly closed area, because of some military bases. Don't ask how I'm here, it's too complicated.

VV's grandparents have their coffins stored in a small shed behind their house, carefully covered where they have waited for years. On one side of the back courtyard, under another small roof, there is a stack of fairly large short logs carefully piled off the ground. They have been there for more than ten years and are to be used to make coffins for one or more of the uncles.

April 26

Xining, Qinghai: At the bus stop, I said good night to her with some longing in my voice. As the bus moved away, a Tibetan guy standing nearby threw his arms around another guy, pretended to give him a big kiss, and said "Good night" in English. He was pretty pleased with himself. I walked back to my hotel alone.

October 15

Time isn't with me: I lost my watch down the toilet on the train. It was my good fake Omega, two years old and working well. I need to buy a new one. I'll get a copy-Rolex, this time.

Beijing: Got my new watch, a Rolex Oyster, 25元. The price was marked 58元, the seller asked 50元, I offered 20元. I got it for 25元 when I started to walk away. First time I've owned a Rolex, I'm moving up.

No way Beijing pollution is as bad as is reported again and again, one of the ten worst cities in the world. The weather is nice, blue sky, but a little cold tonight, I need a light jacket. Dinner at *dapaidang*, I'm sitting on small street with bumper to bumper traffic behind me and what I smell are good cooking odors and sweet charcoal smoke. I rode my bike a lot in the heavy traffic today. Street-level air quality seems pretty good, but I've got a bad headache. I don't really know but the air doesn't seem bad to me, a picky country boy used to clean air and intolerant of American cities.

November 5

<u>Urumqi</u>, <u>Xinjiang</u>: I waited for a Kazakh friend for half an hour, then called him. He said he had waited for me two hours earlier. I was two hours late as I had assumed local time, and he assumed since I was a foreign visitor I would use Beijing time. Next time, I'll be sure to ask: local or Beijing time? He said he usually used Beijing time, and always when dealing with foreign visitors. He uses local time when dealing with locals, or foreigners from the 'stans and Russia. The first time we met, I had used local time, but no confusion as I had also said "In 25 minutes." China is a big country for one time zone.

December 12

<u>Xining</u>: At my hotel, the *fuwutai's* name is Shu Yu, "comfortable happy". Today, I gave her 100元, and told her for two days. She wrote out a receipt, and gave me back 60元. I said again "Two days", and she smiled nicely, told me to pay again tomorrow, that she wanted to talk to me more.

It's cold at night, 10°F. but very dry, 8% humidity, so it warms up nicely. Today was a beautiful warm afternoon, so I went for a walk to the foot of the mountains. I noticed a girl, ten or eleven, following me at a distance. When I started down, she sidestepped off the trail without looking at me, then turned and followed again, walking among the boulders off to the side. So I greeted her and stopped. She came down, shyly joined me, told me her name, and we walked back together. She was quiet after she told me her name. Whenever I'd stop to greet and speak with others (often old women sitting in the sun), she'd wait a few feet away, smiling and looking somewhere else. When I'd move on, we'd share a secret smile. Fun and nice. When we came to her small street, she said goodbye and ran off, fast.

December 18

I stopped on the sidewalk to watch some young guys break dancing. They put each other down, pushed each other to do more, more, more! Tough kids, in really good physical shape. They ignored the girls watching them, and focused only on each other. A couple of them were studiously cool and nonchalant.

It's fun wandering around, I never know what I'll see. Some shops here hire musicians, or something like the break-dancing kids to perform in front, attracts quite a crowd. I saw a new thing in street food: chocolate popcorn. Throw in a handful of cubes of chocolate while it's popping....

December 21

<u>Xining</u> is near the geographical center of China, elevation 2295 m. On a map, find the big blue dot in the middle of China (Qinghai Lake) and Xining's to the east of it. I've been here nearly two weeks, and ice that was here and there on the streets when I arrived hasn't melted yet. My hotel is near the bus and train stations, so this is a mobile neighborhood. There are a lot of Tibetans from nomadic areas wandering around, doing shopping and looking at me in wonder. I look in a mirror and don't see anything so special. These folks are wearing huge robes, and a few have gigantic fur hats. And the pretty young girls are all eating ice cream! In this temperature. Some of these Tibetans in their robes look like pretty tough characters. You'd cross to the other side of the street if you met one near a bar in the USA.

Warmed up enough to snow this morning, the first day of winter. The streets were actually wet(!) for a brief time. It's all gone now, evaporated, except in the shady spots where I expect it will last until next summer.

December 22

I come to <u>Xining</u> to visit an exceptional English training program in the teacher's university. But this city is a good example of the urban infrastructure development I see all over China, even in fairly remote and underdeveloped cities.

I was first here in 2001, and I've been back three more times. The wide city streets seem as if they've always been here, fronted by big buildings. If I hadn't actually seen the narrow streets and construction three and a half years ago, it would be difficult to convince me that it had been different so recently. Maybe ten or twenty years ago, I could believe that.

And these new wide streets: they are plugged with traffic. Rush hour is as bad as anywhere. There are many city buses, packed solid during rush hours. These big new buses wouldn't have fitted on the old narrow streets. The first time I was here, there weren't enough cars to create much of a traffic jam, even on the narrow streets.

There is still some road and street construction, but it's limited now. All the dust, noise, and nearly impassible roads I remember are finished.

But major building construction goes on at a great pace. The streets are edged with planting strips and young trees. Now, in the middle of the winter, the trees are bare. It's hard to guess how it looks when they are leafed out.

I remember <u>Beijing</u> in 1988 as a birdless and treeless place. Now, Beijing is a moderately green city, and there are wild birds everywhere in the trees, including big birds such as ravens and magpies and a few raptors. A year ago, I remarked on this to a Beijing friend, how the planting of trees on an enormous scale had brought back the birds. He was skeptical, and said that the banning and collection of guns in the early '90s, and the added banning and collection of air guns a couple of years later had more to do with the return of the birds. This year, a different Chinese friend joked that the countryside was so contaminated by pesticides that the only place birds could live was in the city. The birds migrated to the city to find refuge, he said.

<u>Beijing</u>, as the centerpiece city of China, got its trees earlier than other cities, before the Asian Games in the early '90s. The trees there are of respectable size now. Tree planting in other places came later, so the trees are smaller. Here in <u>Xining</u>, six to nine inch trunks are common. The scale of this greening project in cities all around China, the tree planting along highways especially in areas of desertification, and the reforestation over mountains, over whole ranges of mountains, is staggering.

2005

January 13

<u>Nanning, Guangxi</u>: I traveled by deluxe express bus to <u>Hong Kong</u> and back to get a new visa. The bus from here directly into Kowloon took 12.5 hours, including the border crossing. We changed buses at the border, left-hand to right-hand drive. Both trips were overnight, leaving at 7:30 P.M., arriving at 8:00 A.M. This luxury coach was 2 1/2 months old, and the reclining seats were comfortable, about the same as airline business class. The bus stopped once for a meal, and made three additional toilet stops.

A third of the bus route was on expressways I've seen before, nearly half was on expressways that didn't exist two years ago, and weren't open six months ago, and the rest was on older ($\approx$5-8 years) but still good highways, which I'm sure will be replaced by expressways next year. By express train, it takes about thirteen hours to reach Guangzhou, then another train and a couple more hours on to the border.

The whole round-trip 25-hour bus ride cost less than US$75. There are cheaper ways to do it, but this was easy. And I avoided the *Chunyun* travel rush, as I boarded the return bus in Hong Kong. It would have been difficult to get a bus out of Guangzhou.

These new expressways bypass nearly all cities and towns, so I had little sense of the route. My maps didn't help much, as they showed a number of expressways as "under construction". I was sure of about half the route. My best map was dated 2004/11, the newest I found, but already out of date.

January 17

Baise: Tried to find a new map of the city, but only found the old one (2000/6) that I used the last few times I've been here. I wished for a newer map last year, too. It seems really outdated then. The main bookstore didn't have any city maps at all and said they were waiting for a new one that was supposed to be ready soon.

February 12

Guiping: Gao, an old friend, is one of my benchmarks in China. His job is the same, English teacher in a middle school, and he has the same position as when I first met him in '88. His wife is a nurse, also in the same position. Their son will graduate from a college in Wuhan this year. Three years ago, he told me they wouldn't be able to buy anything or save any money until their son was out of college. A year ago, he had a new electric bike, and his wife, a new motor scooter. I expressed surprise, and he happily told me that in addition, they were saving more than ever before in their lives.

They got their first telephone ever in 1998. Now his wife wants to disconnect it, as they both have *Xiaolingtong* phones, and their son has a mobile. He says "Let it be", although they don't use it much.

He tells me the cost of food has gone up about 5% in the past six months, something he considers insignificant as the cost of everything else continues to fall, and their salaries continue to rise.

I watch their lives steadily spiral upward, in possessions and ease. And they have little *guanxi*. In other places, friends in small cities and towns seem on the same path although I know less of their lives. In the countryside, I often see farmers plowing their fields behind an ox, the plow unchanged for more than 100 years, with a mobile phone (maybe a *Xiaolingtong*) dangling off their belt, and *motuo* parked alongside the field. If they stop me to chat, they ask me what I think of their area, their place. I'll comment on the fresh air and other nice things, and

148

they'll reply, "Yes, but *qiong, qiong, qiong*" (poor, poor, poor). I point at the phone, and they say "This? It's ordinary, had it half a year". I point at the *motuo* "Yours?" "Yes, had it a year and a half". I ask "Then are you so poor as you were?" And get as a common response "*Qiong, qiong, qiong*" as they walk laughing back into the field to work. I don't know if they are richer, but they certainly have more possessions and modern conveniences in their lives.

Ten days ago, Song took me to visit his grandfather in a little village to the southeast of <u>Nanning</u>. His grandfather hadn't been to Nanning for more than forty years. Song told me before we went that the village hadn't changed since he was a small boy (twenty years). When we got there, I saw that most of the houses had electricity, and the equipment looked new. He said yes, installed two years ago to most of the houses. Many houses I looked in had TVs and some had DVD players. I pointed out the new things I saw, one by one. Song laughed, and said "Yes, but not so much as Nanning". To me, these changes seem huge, unimaginably fast. To Song, it seems like no change. It's a matter of perspective.

On traffic fatalities, the statistics I've seen for China total 110,000/year, horrific. For comparison, the US, with a fifth the population, has more than 40,000 fatalities each year, but we don't worry much about that. And yes, I expect the death rate is higher in China. However, many of the survivors in the US, ignored in the fatalities count, are permanently and seriously disabled. From what I read, China's railway safety records are some of the best in the world, in injuries per person/mile.

September 23

In <u>Shenzhen</u>, I found the right bus station (*Qiaoshi Xizhan*) and a bus to <u>Xiamen</u>. The bus I got is an unregulated sleeper, not a nonstop coach, so it stops again and again to pick up passengers. It slowly filled up with workers, some sitting in the aisles between the beds. They are loaded with tools and bags, so the bus is packed.

October 27

<u>Huhhot</u>, transit mixers, concrete trucks: a couple of years ago, I saw the first ones in any number, and they were all shiny new Isuzu. Now transit mixers are everywhere, and there are several shiny new Chinese brands in addition to the Isuzu and Nissans. I see few of the Isuzu here, or in Xiamen or Beijing. The Isuzu stood out because it was a new thing, but the Chinese ones look ordinary now and blend in

with the rest of the new vehicles of all sorts. Here in Huhhot, most of the mixers have an insulated jacket. It's cold.

All these streets: I'd never know they were new. Daxue Lu, running east and west in front of *Neida* (Inner Mongolia University) was terrible four years ago. Now it's a nice street lined with trees, and very busy. Lots of good street lighting in the busier parts of the city.

Ulan, the next major street to the north, is a six-lane street, divided bike lanes on each side, with trees and modern street lighting. The major east-west artery, Xinhua Lu, a long block farther north, is eight lanes plus bike lanes, and has overpasses and interchanges at major intersections. Five years ago, most of these streets were under construction, a mess, no trees, and little street lighting. The construction caused little traffic constriction as there were fewer vehicles. These are busy streets now, all with trees and lighting.

November 13

Another reason for the policy of knocking down old neighborhoods and houses: most of the old places are not connected to district heating, so burn coal inefficiently for heating and sometimes cooking, although it's easy and not too expensive to convert to bottled gas for cooking. With the new housing developments, the population density is much higher (necessary because of the large numbers of people moving from the countryside to the cities and towns), but the air pollution contribution per person is much less.

The low temperature burning of coal is a bad source at low level, the smoke hangs right on the street. The big heating plants burn coal more efficiently at higher temperature, and their stacks put the smoke and fumes up high. Maybe it only moves the pollution away, but I think it also reduces the problems significantly.

It's the tobacco smoking that regularly gets to me. It's still the worst source of air pollution for me and makes me feel worse than anything except possibly strong solvent fumes. Chinese government policy is addressing this more and more, although a substantial part of government revenue comes from tobacco. This year, it has been announced that no new tobacco factories will be built, and within a couple of years, all tobacco advertising of any sort will be banned, and health warnings will be required to cover 30% of all packaging (very carefully spelled out as 30% of the area of each surface of the package including prime areas). Smoking bans in public areas are becoming more common, but smoker education (awareness, consciousness, acceptance) has a long way to go. Smokers know it is their right to fume away and few notice their effect on others, or at least pretend not to notice, but more and more young educated men are not smoking. Though women were heavily targeted by advertising (good old Virginia Slims, and other American companies spotting an untapped market) ten to fifteen years ago, not many young women smoke. The smokers must be feeling the pressure; many seem belligerent.

November 26

When I am on the streets here in <u>Huhhot</u>, there is a lot of traffic noise, people talking and calling, and some horn-honking. The honking is pretty restrained except for the usual few jerks. Many taxis have special very soft horns so they can freely warn bicyclists and pedestrians, nice. And most taxi drivers here are polite, not pushy. The trees that were being planted along the streets five years ago are nice and of respectable size, some a foot in diameter.

When I leave the street and go into *Neida* (Inner Mongolia University), it's a different world, quiet and peaceful. It's almost as though my ears are relieved of a pressure I didn't know was there. And *Neida* is full of trees and grass.

December 22

<u>Xining</u>: I met Tserang, my lovely Tibetan friend, yesterday for a last lunch. On a crowded city bus, she called it "squeezy". I liked the term, and told her I'd like to squeezy her.

We stopped at a shop to recharge her bus card. To get a magnetic transit card requires a 30元 deposit, and the card is refillable. She did hers and her sister's, added 50元 to each. It costs 0.7元 to ride with a card and the cash price is 1元. Most women and students carry the card in the side of a purse or bag and slap the bag against the reader in the bus and listen for the beep. Take the bag or card away and the reader resets, put it close again for a second rider, wait for a second beep. Using the card saves money and there is no need to be sure you have the correct change, as no change is given on buses without conductors.

There are many city buses here and they are frequent, I haven't waited more than ten minutes except one time late in the evening, after 9:30 PM when the bus had stopped for the night, I didn't know as there were no start and stop times on the bus-stop sign. A different bus was running later, so it wasn't a problem. A taxi would have cost 10-12元.

The biggest problem I see with the clean, modern city buses is the brakes. Here and most other places, the bus brakes work well but squeal loudly. Standing at a bus stop can be painful, and the squeals can be heard blocks away when the buses brake suddenly. They need different lining material, or some sort of vibration dampeners on the drums. Or honking could be allowed again; then I wouldn't be able to hear the squeal.

The new roads and expressways: what portion are being built with private investment for the right to collect tolls for twenty or so years? I understand this is common. What part are being built by the government? How good are the inspections, controls, and engineering on the privately built stuff? The highways with no toll gates are certainly government-built, but I don't know how to tell about the ones with gates.

Trains

1988

April 30

Instead of finding a hotel in <u>Anshun, Guizhou,</u> I bought a ticket to <u>Kunming</u> on the Kunming-Shanghai train. It's said to be the most crowded in China. I was only able to get a hard seat ticket with no seat assignment. It was a real fight to get in the car, to push in far enough so the door could shut behind me. It was a rough thirteen-hour all-night sardine-packed standing room only no sleep endurance test. I was aboard for almost half an hour before I was able to get my pack off my back and get it reasonably situated on the mucky floor. Hot water for drinking ran out about two hours after I got on, so for the rest of the trip all throats were dry.

There was only enough room for about a third of the standers to hunker down, so we rotated, the most exhausted getting more squatting time. Good thing there wasn't any water, as there was simply no way to get to the toilets, and in any case they were full of standing people too. Some near me had boarded the train eighteen hours earlier. Their standing trip was 31 hours and they were hurting. I couldn't really complain or feel too sorry for myself. I stood nearly the whole time with my pack on my feet, clutched against my knees. I did manage to squeeze up to a wall so I was able to rest my back. I never got farther into the car than about six feet from the door.

1998

March 26

<u>Guangxi</u>: I'm trying the not-quite-finished *Nankun Tielu* (Nanning-Kunming Railway). The station in <u>Baise</u> is clean, open and bright, high ceilings with lots of windows. I'd call the architectural style

"Station Modern". There's nice Chinese music playing on a good quality PA system on the station platform.

One of my seat mates, an engineer, said there are 288 tunnels between <u>Baise</u> and <u>Xingyi, Guizhou</u>. The train is moving slowly as this is a test train, the line really isn't open yet. And it doesn't go all the way through, only to <u>Xingyi</u>. I may have to take a bus from there to <u>Kunming</u>; information wasn't clear.

We are in mountains full of limestone formations, a poor *shaoshu minzu* (minority nationality) area. Some young country women got on at one stop, to get off at the next. One of the women sat down on the end of the seat across from me without noticing me. She looked up, saw me, and I said hello. She hopped up and moved to another seat fast, with all her stuff. She glanced at me once or twice as though I had bitten her, before they all got off. There are many wooden houses along here, and lots of horses. The houses tend to be scattered rather than clustered in tight little villages as is common in most of China, the parts I've been in, anyway.

March 29

<u>Yunnan</u>: I spent a couple of nights in <u>Xingyi</u>, and continued on to <u>Kunming</u> by bus. The road paralleled the new rail line much of the way. I observed the huge construction project from the bus window. There was still a lot of subsidiary work going on, retaining walls, drainage structures, and the smoothing and shaping of spoil piles from the tunnels. Many tunnels and bridges, rough country.

The standard bridge design uses a line of tapered concrete columns, with huge precast beams and deck, long spans. They are elegant, and a lot of work has gone into blending the whole rail line into the surrounding countryside. Many of the "bridges" are one-sided, leaning against the canyon walls, and running up the river from tunnel to tunnel, instead of crossing. The new line will bring big changes for the way of life along the route, an area which had been pretty inaccessible. I hope it's mostly a good change.

April 10

<u>Baise, Guangxi</u>: After a few days in <u>Kunming</u>, I'm going back the other way on the *Nankun* railroad. Being on a new railroad is interesting, as the train is full of engineers and I am learning a lot. This is the most advanced electric railway in China, one of the most advanced in the world partly because it is new and partly because the grades require high currents. The passenger run from Baise to Nanning started last

September, 1997, Baise to Weishe started November 30, and a direct train from Nanning to Xingyi started on April 1, a few days after I tested it. About November this year, direct Nanning to Kunming passenger service is planned to start.

At the railway yard, I visited a substation, electrical and mechanical repair buildings, testing facilities, a grand tour. It was all new and much of it unfinished. Lots of equipment wasn't set up, and jury-rigged, wires dangled all over the place, good enough for temporary use. The equipment in the shops and on the line was nice, most of it made in China. At the substation, there were also automatic switches from France, and in the control room, computers from Taiwan and printers from Japan.

There are two independent power lines to each railroad substation, for reliability and serviceability. Between substations, a built-in safety interlock allows only one engine to get power at a time.

There was a bad derailment a few weeks ago, a freight test train where ten or twelve cars went down an embankment. On the way from Kunming, crews were working all along the line, ballasting and truing up the tracks. A lot of it is bumpy now, limiting speed. Meanwhile, the trains go slowly, especially the ones carrying passengers.

2001

August 16

The <u>Lanzhou, Gansu</u> train station is under major reconstruction. They are adding another level of tracks and a new building. It's pretty confused, trying to keep the station going full blast while completely rebuilding it, but this is common in China now. I see major expansions of infrastructure facilities like roads, railroads, and stations, but the existing ones are still running on full schedule. It's almost more than I can conceive, keeping the existing services and facilities running at full-speed while expanding on this scale.

August 31

This *Nankun* (<u>Nanning-Kunming</u>) train is not air-conditioned. That explains the difference in ticket price. When I bought the ticket at a booking office in Lanzhou (a long way to the north) I paid 117元. The schedule book said the price was 170元, and that the train was air-conditioned. I had half expected to be charged the difference by the conductor. Mystery solved.

My ticket, marked <u>Lanzhou</u> as point of sale, did give some amusement to the conductor and other passengers. That's a long way away to have bought a ticket. The new computer ticket system connects all offices, so a ticket for anywhere in China ought to be able to be purchased at any ticket office. Two years ago, the tickets were computer printed, but the networking hadn't been completed. Now it seems to work well if I can get the ticket seller to try. The conductor had never seen a ticket like mine before.

I have a young friend on the train, a little girl from Baise. She's about eight, and will get off with her family around 3:00 AM. She's been sitting with me, looking at all my maps and books and bringing me snacks such as sunflower seeds and oranges. A guy I met by chance in the station is my compartment mate. His English is good, and he has a job with a small Nigerian company that buys shoes and jeans for sale in Nigeria. He works with two Nigerians, has been working for them four months. His main interest is English, American English.

I told him what I tell all students: practice English with all kinds of English speakers including Nigerians. English is the national language of Nigeria, and Nigerian English is correct, just different. It is important to train the ear to understand all kinds of English; make the most of this opportunity to expand his international English.

2002

June 22

Jiangsu: My compartment mates are two women and an unconnected guy in their late twenties. They've been looking at a Chinese art magazine called *Images*. It's all underwear shots featuring male and female Western models, mostly hunks with stuffed shorts. They seem to consider it natural, and enjoy it while laughing and pointing out details to each other.

In past years, many people sought me out to practice English. Now, fewer do this. I've had a long conversation with a grad student from *Nanda* (Nanjing University): we started with my painful Chinese, and completely exhausted my ability. Then we slowly slipped into English, of which he had a good command. He had not hinted that he knew English.

There is trash including plastic bags along the tracks, but it is much cleaner than the early '90s, when Styrofoam one-use food boxes had come into use on the trains and made the sides of the tracks look like snow. I thought then that it could never be cleaned up.

July 27

Nei Menggu, a new thing I've seen on the trains this trip: some of the railroad employees, the ones who sell water, snacks, and beer, are also selling gimmicks and toys, with quite a show and pitch. A guy came by with toy gyroscopes. He was good and did everything but balance them on his ears. The guy was a good showman. Another has been selling socks he runs through a lighter flame or sticks with a knife without damage.

And there is a stunning woman in the next compartment. She is casually dressed, fashionable but inexpensively. She has flawless skin and beautiful long black hair. As she reads, she smiles at her book. I think many of the men on the train would trade a year of their lives for one of her smiles.

Some of the other people around me in the train that I've spoken with include a Uyghur man from Urumqi who is some kind of government worker in agriculture; a primary school teacher of Chinese, *Hanzu* (ethnic Chinese), also from Urumqi and on her way home after visiting her boyfriend in Huhhot; a girl from Harbin with good English, just graduated from middle school and traveling with her father to Xinjiang for the first time. She hopes to go to *Renda* (People's University in Beijing) to study chemistry and physics; a middle-aged mother with a ten-year old girl, *Mengguzu* (Mongolian) from Lanzhou; a grandfather, 60, who bought one of the gyroscopes, probably for a grandchild although he himself was excited by it and had the salesman show him many tricks. They are all in my compartment and the next one, except for the Harbin girl, who is a few compartments up. The stunning woman is in her late thirties or maybe forty, but I've had no contact with her. The primary teacher is pretty, and in the berth across from me.

Gah — The stunning woman won't even look at me. I'm heart broken. Her casual grace is wonderful. She is aware of all the men who notice her (most of us), but she is aloof. She knows she is glorious: just watching her put on a light over-shirt, and flip her hair back, while glancing at her reflection in a window.... She gets off the train at Wuhai. *Kelian*! (pity).

August 1

Hard sleeper to Urumqi, Xinjiang, a 22-hour trip from Lanzhou: When I got to the gate, the train was already loading. I got on and tried to get my bike under the berth. It didn't fit, so I pulled it back out, with people holding up their feet, and discovered there were several railcar umbilicals (big cables that connect the cars at the coupler) under the bed, in a nest of dirt and dust where they had been for some time. I dragged them out with piles of dust, got my bike shoved under, people put their feet down, and I got the big cables and connectors shoved under another berth, washed my hands and sat down. The train was moving five minutes later.

Immediately an army officer, 38, with fairly good English came to speak to me. He's a career army man, armor. In college, he studied the power systems for tanks and such. He is from the countryside in Henan and his father had only five years of school, his mother, none. They valued education, encouraging and supporting him. He told me he thinks the Uyghur people are very smart, only their educational opportunities are limited and poor so they have fewer chances. He has studied English on his own for twenty years. His vocabulary is good, although he has little chance to try to communicate. When he is at a loss for a word, he often comes up with the exactly appropriate word after a brief struggle.

There is an exceptionally tall and pretty young woman in the next compartment, an army cadet. She was shy, didn't talk to or look at me at first. Eventually with the officer's help, she loosened up. She is an actress with an army troupe whose job it is to entertain soldiers at remote bases. Her troupe is based in Beijing and she is a dancer.

2003

January 14

I rode up to the <u>Guangzhou</u> train station on my bike to look over the situation. It was tightly organized chaos, with unbelievable crowds. I estimated there were 30,000 people outside. The crowd was controlled, with lots of cops keeping order, and no beggars. What a mass of people, huge long lines snaking around the square in front. It's two weeks before *Chunjie* (Spring Festival), and *Chunyun,* the travel rush, is in full swing. Everybody in China comes to Guangzhou to seek their fortune, and now they all want to go home. All the students from the colleges and universities are also on their way home. I think it is fairly easy to travel toward Guangzhou right now, but nearly impossible to leave.

2004

February 12

<u>Nanning, Guangxi</u>: Wei's sister also got her a ticket to Nanjing, so we went to the station to get a refund for the one she had bought. Hers was full price, and the one her sister got is a reduced-price student ticket.

The refund, about thirty hours before the train departure, was 80%. We could have sold the ticket fairly easily at the station for full price as they are hard to get during *Chunyun*, but we thought of that too late. Wei is a third-year student at a university in Nanjing, an old friend I've known since she was in middle school.

One of her teachers said in a hydrology lecture about a river in Nanjing that in the '50s people could wash their vegetables in it; In the '60s they could wash their clothes in it; In the '70s people could still swim in it; In the '80s it could be used for watering plants; And in the '90s they could use the water to kill insects. Not a hopeful commentary. What did he say about this century? I asked. "He said nothing."

March 29

Kunming: On the train to Chengdu. I've been engaged in fairly standard train entertainment, talking to people, playing with kids, plus a new thing. A guy came by, pointed down the car, and said "*Zou, zou*" (Walk, walk). So I got up and walked with him as far as we could go, through four or five hard sleep cars, one soft sleep, and four or five crowded hard seat cars. There were a few passengers sitting on the floor, although most had seats and it was easy to pass through. The dining car was between the hard and soft sleep. I've never had someone take me for a walk before, a long stroll through about twelve cars, but a good way to get a little exercise. I guess he thought I ought to try it, or perhaps he wanted company.

People get off, new people get on. So far, I've met no one with more English than my limited Chinese.

April 4

Gansu: The train arrived nearly one hour late, most unusual, but I got on the connecting train I wanted. It was very crowded, standing room only. I wouldn't have gotten on by myself. I went to a crowded scene to try to buy the ticket and met a guy with good English who said "Let's just get on the train." We picked up a girl on the way whom I had bumped into hard with one of my bags at the ticket counter. We three crammed ourselves onto the train, my bike and all. He got off at a small stop, but the girl stayed with me, and we collected another girl, a student in Chengdu.

Qinghai: Made it to Xining. The two girls stuck with me and helped me off the train. One was met by someone and rushed off. The first one was worried about me, wanted to stay while I put my bike together, and offered me her mobile phone to make a call. She obviously had other things to do; I thanked her for her help and offers and let her go on her way.

April 23

Got my ticket to <u>Nanjing</u>. The schedule had changed; a new schedule book came out April 18th, and I hadn't noticed. The train leaves at a slightly different time, and is more than three hours faster, about thirty hours now, for 2050 km with about twenty stops. I arrive at 2:00 A.M., a bad time to look for a hotel.

April 29

Leaving <u>Nanjing</u>, onto the train, what a rush: the train was ten minutes late arriving and only scheduled to stop here for nine minutes. That was cut to six minutes, to try to catch up. Big train, long scramble, bells ringing as people ran to get on. I dumped my bike in the end of the car, and managed to get my bag on the rack after the train was moving. Then I went back for the bike. Everybody was helpful, and I got it under the berth with a minimum of hassle.

Trains in China mostly run right on schedule, it's rare one is even a few minutes late.

May 7

<u>Lanzhou, Gansu</u>: I'm on the train and stowed, ten minutes early. What a struggle. This lower-priced, slower train is packed with people carrying too much luggage. I thought my ticket said car #1, but it actually said +1, an added car and I didn't notice that; I walked the full length of the train, dragging my packed bike, no car #1. I was told to go back to car #3. There, I was told to go to car #1, which didn't exist. I was finally told to go to car #5, which is where I'm stowed. I had to move a lot of luggage around, but people were mostly amused and cooperative. I hope I'm in the right place, when the conductor collects the tickets.

May 8

<u>Zhengzhou, Henan</u>: I was unable to get a sleeper ticket to Guangzhou, so I got a *yingzuo* (hard seat) ticket for the seventeen-hour trip tonight. I'll be tired and smelly, sure glad I managed to get my longjohns and tee-shirt off last night, it's a different climate here. No sleeper tickets available for the next two days right at the end of a "golden week", the Labor Day holiday, but I must get to Hong Kong

for my flight home. Oh well; I put my bike and pack in "left luggage" and headed out to find *wangba*, check email, and eat lunch.

Met a young American woman while I was wandering outside the station who stopped me and asked if I spoke English. She wanted to know if I knew where she could use a bank card "In this shit hole of a city". I told her any bank, and told her how to find a bank. She said she spoke Chinese well and could read, that wasn't what she wanted. She hurried off in a huff, me staring at her back and shaking my head.

On the train: my bike won't fit entirely under the seat. I got on when the gates were opened, a good thirty minutes early. Now, ten minutes before departure, the train aisle is absolutely plugged. All the people who were in my set of seats when I got on are gone. I'm the only one of the original bunch who had a reserved seat. It's going to be rough. I haven't been on a trip such as this in many years, I don't remember when. This may be the longest trip I've done in a seat and not my idea of fun, but it will get me to Guangzhou on time.

One hour into the trip, things are settling down. I'm in an aisle seat, on the three-seat side of the car. A few people are able to sit in the aisle and the rest must stand. Often, someone is leaning on my shoulder. A window seat might be better. My knees are giving me twinges and my back is already aching.

May 9

The train is overcrowded, but it's been possible to get to the toilet and to the hot water. Once, I bought bottled water as it was easier. The aisle has been nearly full at times, and many seats have an extra person. I've talked with a guy from Henan who likes to sing, and plays guitar and sax. The past two months, he has been earning money singing in a coffee bar. In China he is considered fat, but would hardly be called stocky in the US. He's traveling with his sister who also speaks some English, neither of them have seats. And there is a pretty girl across the aisle by the window, we've been flirting mildly to pass the time, mostly with eye contact. Our flirting creates amusement for others, some of whom encourage us. She has a great smile and her eyes twinkle, hard to manage near the end of a seventeen-hour hard seat trip.

People are sure different: when I or others go down the aisle, there are some who get up and make space politely, and others who won't move an inch, just stare at you coldly as you climb across them.

October 14

Hong Kong to Beijing express train: a Hong Kong engineer on his way to Beijing told me I could have bought my ticket for this train much more cheaply in Shenzhen and boarded there, rather than in Hong Kong. Then I could have gotten off at <u>Zhengzhou</u>, which was what I wanted to do. A few cars on the train start in Hong Kong and are sealed until Beijing. I've bought tickets before at the Shenzhen station, but I was in a bit of a panic and thought only of the Guangzhou station and how I didn't want to go there. These days, there are many trains that start from Shenzhen, or such as this one, add cars there. Good reason to keep a train schedule book, as I wasn't able to find any information in Hong Kong about trains in China. I can't get off this express in Zhengzhou, or anywhere before Beijing. I can't even get out of the car at platforms to buy food. I actually clear customs and enter China in Beijing.

October 20

I got on the train to <u>Gansu</u> as early as possible, with only a few people in the car ahead of me. I stashed the bike at the end of the car, got my bags on my bunk which was right in the middle of the car, got my pack onto the overhead rack, and pushed my way back through the rapidly filling car to get my bike. I slowly got the bike back to the compartment, and found a man and a woman were there, stowing their stuff. They were wonderfully helpful. One of the bunks had a railroad box under it. The conductor was disapproving but I assured him the bike would fit, that I had done it many times before. He watched with a concerned expression, but didn't try to stop me. The guy in the compartment was great, helping me cheerfully. I must really like having a bike as it's an enormous amount of trouble, carting it around.

Then an elderly couple arrived, with lots of stuff and a huge middle-aged son who was helping them get settled and stowed. The box under the other bunk a real problem, but the helpful guy kicked off his shoes, climbed up on the bunks, and got everything stowed nicely in the overhead.

These cars are new, the same as the Hong Kong express, which was the first time I'd seen this design. The old style overhead luggage rack is gone. There is a ceiling over the corridor, and access to the overhead is from the bunks. It's better and worse, more difficult access but people don't block the aisle while stowing their stuff. It's much safer, as what little could fall off can't fall in the aisle. The old ladder in the aisle that provided access to the upper bunks is gone, replaced by fold-out steps between the bunks. Each bunk has an individually switched reading light. Gone is the rod over the window to hang towels. The walls and ceilings are covered with a melamime-like paneling. It looks good, is low maintenance, bright, and easy to clean. There is an LED sign at the end of the car showing whether the toilets are empty or full, controlled by a switch in the door lock. The wash area is totally redesigned, as well as the boiler for hot drinking water. There is a soap dispenser at the sinks, and in the toilets, a little net holder for your mobile phone. I wonder how many of them have gone down the drain (an open hole dumping directly onto the tracks) like my watch?

All this modern and thoughtful redesign shouldn't be surprising; after all, China has the biggest passenger railway system in the world and it is expanding rapidly.

On the train, I talked with Yi, 52, who had fair spoken English. He was pretty shy about it at first, but had just returned from three months in UK where he had worked full time on a tire factory that was being dismantled and shipped to Lanzhou. He called it a "qualified" factory, but a little old. He is a mechanical engineer, mostly rubber machinery. For a while we sat with a group of other men, talking about many things with Yi acting as interpreter. He was embarrassed by many of the questions the others wanted to ask me, questions I am used to and consider ordinary. For example "How much money do you make?" It was fun and entertaining until lights out at 9:30.

Yi told me a little about his time during the Cultural Revolution. He joined the Red Guards at fourteen, but his parents were judged bad as they had the name "landlord" so he was kicked out and sent to the countryside with his family. He worked days and studied at night. In 1977-8, he passed the college entrance examinations and went to Qingdao. He was nervous talking even so little, and that in a roundabout manner. Memories and habits of the Cultural Revolution last a long time. He didn't offer me his full name or contact information, although I told him I'd enjoy meeting him again. He said something about sending me email.

2005

October 8

Xiamen to Beijing, passing through a lightly populated area of low misty mountains in Fujian with a small river, green fields (maybe late rice), tired looking villages, many fallow fields, and a few small factories. On the train last night, I talked with a student, 24, in her senior year at China National Agricultural College. She's returning to Beijing from Xiamen where she applied for graduate work in politics. She knows nothing about this subject and is uninterested, but wants to study at *Xiada* (Xiamen University) because of the clean air which is more similar to her home. She's from Zhoushan Dao, a big island off Ningbo, south of Shanghai, maybe the fourth or fifth largest island in China (depending on whether you count Taiwan). Her parents are farmers and her father also makes salt in the old way. This used to be a common business there but now few do it, his salt is special and shipped around China. The island was famous for salt. I'll meet her in Beijing and go visit her school in the Haidian district.

I also talked with a group of PLA soldiers (one had good English), and another girl studying in Beijing, a senior in international logistics (some kind of business degree) who is doing an internship at Dell. I'd enjoy meeting her again, but she will only be in Beijing for a couple of days and won't finish her internship until late October. Another girl was doing graduate work in international business in Beijing, on her way back from visiting her family. And a businessman from Jiangxi, now living in Australia. I met him in the station, he is friendly, hyper, and a little overwhelming. He insisted that the pronunciation of Haidian was "Haiding". I'm told the phonetic part of the "*dian*" character is "*ding*", and that many outsiders make this mistake.

In the next compartment is an unpleasant fat man. He has a bad face and is repellant. An attractive woman in her late 30s from the same compartment started talking with me, no English, Chinese only. He pushed in, sat close, in my space instantly and deliberately. Turns out she seems to be with him, ugh. He stinks of cigarette smoke, but at least doesn't try to smoke in the compartment.

My compartment has gotten a little crazy. A woman and a child in a bottom berth got off at a small stop, and part of a family from the next compartment immediately took possession of the vacant berth. There's five of them, they have the four upper and middle berths in the next compartment, and the last one probably has a hard seat ticket. They have a fairly big and lively boy, not counted as he's under the height requiring a ticket. My berth has suddenly become undesirable as the boy yells a lot. 7:30 PM, lights out in a couple of hours.

December 22

<u>Xining</u>: Something new at the train station; smoking is not allowed in the waiting rooms. There are small modern prefab rooms for smokers in each waiting room, about 3x6 meters or a bit bigger. I wasn't able to explore how they are ventilated, and didn't want to enter, looked terrible inside. Sure makes the waiting room nicer, a big improvement.

The train was fifteen minutes late arriving from Ge'ermu so there was a mad rush. No room for my bike under the berth, I got it out of the aisle, waited and helped others with their luggage. I'm taller than most, can get stuff onto the rack without too much trouble. Patience worked well, everything got sorted out by the conductor, a train box got moved, and I got my bike under a berth. People were carrying a lot of stuff, the conductor had to shift a lot of luggage around, but fifteen minutes after the train was moving we were settled and stowed.

This non-air conditioned train has clear no-smoking signs, smoking seems well-controlled. The train is full, been talking with a guy doing postgraduate work at the CAS (Chinese Academy of Sciences) Salt Lake Institute who is traveling with his director to a meeting about library apparatus in Mianyang. He was a middle school chemistry teacher for three years, then to CAS for a master's, one year in Beijing, one year in Xi'an, now a year in Xining. If he goes back to teaching he wants to teach in a college, or find work in industry. He doesn't want to go back to a middle school. His director is a professor, a solution chemistry expert.

I had instant noodles for breakfast, and on the platform in Lanzhou, got a chicken leg and an ear of corn, 8元.

There is a *Zangzu* family a few compartments down, a pretty young woman, probably a working professional of some sort, with her mother and father. Her father is red-eyed, rough looking, wearing a traditional robe with a knife on his belt, *shouji* around his neck. He has a silver prayer wheel that he swings around and around, it tinkles gently. He checks his mobile phone regularly. Her mother is also traditionally dressed, wears a special hat with big wings, and keeps her eyes down most of the time. I greeted them "*dimo*" (probably not the right dialect, but understood) and they are friendly and pleased. The daughter has beautiful hair and is in her late twenties or early thirties. Tried to talk with her a bit, she works in Qinghai, but I couldn't understand what kind of work. Her mother's face is beautiful. The daughter's face is similar, bigger nose, a beautiful smile and beautiful eyes. Her mother keeps her eyes down, but when she glances up, she has the same smile and twinkling eyes. Both the mother and father are using prayer wheels.

In Lanzhou, a Hankou-Urumqi train disgorged a dozen young foreign women. I had fun calling the attention of my compartment mates to the *laowai*. We discussed whether they were French or Italian or American....

Been smelling *baijiu*, finally realized a red faced guy in my compartment is guzzling the stuff out of a paper cup. It has a pungent smell similar to gin. Whew, better not light a match. Unpleasant, but better than smoking. The guy is drunk by now, but quiet and well-behaved, whew, he can really put it away, and now has a cigarette out, maybe not so well behaved. Hope he heads for the end of the car before lighting up. I hope his drunkenness doesn't slide into many cigarettes, the car has been pretty good 'til now.

Went for a walk through ten cars to the dining car. On the way back, I was stopped several times for conversation, but didn't meet more than a few words of English, such as "Hello" and "Hi". Some men in their 40s and 50s invited me to sit with them for awhile, told me that my Chinese was pretty good for a *Meiguo guizi*. I told them *Xiao Bushi* was a real *Meiguo guizi*, no Chinese language at all.

The drunk is jittery and hyper. I hope he'll pass out soon. He lit another cigarette, I asked him please not to smoke, he smiled at me and took another long puff. I went on writing and he got up and went to the end of the car, it worked. I didn't argue, just said please and dropped it. Maybe that's the way. Anyway it worked this time, with this guy. *Wa*, the guy's poured himself another cup full.

I spent half an hour with the solution chemistry professor and her student, helping with editing the English in a scientific paper written by another student of hers. I'd like to meet her again in Xining at the Salt Lake Institute. She's hoping to retire in two years and go to her home in Xi'an. She's originally from Beijing, but her husband lives in Xi'an and she lived there for five or so years, considers it home.

2006

January 9

On the train (<u>Chengdu</u> to <u>Nanning</u>, hard sleeper, 35 hours), the conductor is a stocky fat-faced guy in his thirties with funny wrinkles on the back of his head, shown off by a very short haircut. He's vigilant, going up and down the car fixing curtains, cleaning, taking care of details. He got on the case of some students, made them sweep up the floor of their compartment, lectured them about garbage and watched to make sure they did a good job. Nobody is smoking. The students, all from Hainan Island, are traveling home together for Spring Festival. There are about 25 of them, traveling together makes it easy as they book whole buses for either end of the trip and help each other with their luggage. They all attend a fairly large college in Mianyang, none of them knew each other before meeting in the college, and travel together for convenience.

An army actress with a dancing company en route to entertain soldiers at a remote base.

A couple of young girls.

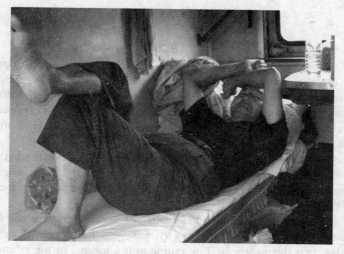

A fellow traveler from Japan carried only a small duffle sack with a shoulder strap. He had no camera and no computer. He said his traveling cost more because he had to buy clothes if it got cold, and abandon them when the weather got warmer.

The aisle in a nearly empty train.

167

Boats

1988

April 1

On the river boat to <u>Wuzhou</u>: Hard to write down anything, as there is so much to see I just want to look. The river passes through beautiful country: flats with cities on the side, a gorge, boats everywhere. All comes from the river, all goes into it, shit, garbage. Water from it is boiled to drink, clothes are washed in it.

Most boats of the larger sampan sort have the decks extended with a sort of permanent catwalk 14 - 18" wide all around. A small dinghy is often carried hung on the gunwale barely clearing the water, or carried off the stern.

My album about home has made the rounds of thirty or forty people, generating a lot of curiosity, talk, and fun. I've managed to explain that this notebook I'm writing in is a journal of my journey, a record of what I'm seeing, to help me remember. I've given out two of my business cards. Maybe I didn't have enough printed.

April 6

Above <u>Wuzhou, Guangxi</u>: My bunk on the riverboat is a bit more than two feet wide by six feet long with just enough headroom to sit up, although my head brushes the bunk above me. It's thinly padded, has a blanket and pillow, and a window at the head. The cabin is open, with ten to fifteen feet between my bunk and the bunks on the other side of the boat. The beds are separated by removable bin boards four or five inches high which fit into slots. They are easily lifted out, joining a couple of bunks. Often a family or group will remove a series of them. There is a lot going on under the blankets. A young couple across from me are snuggled tightly; I take them to be lovers or newlyweds, from friends joking with them.

I've spent a couple of hours in show and tell, the album, journal, dictionaries, phrase book. So far, no one has surfaced on this boat with more than a few words of English, yet most know more English than I know Chinese.

Our boat met a small motor-sampan in mid-channel, rafted with it, took on six or eight passengers and let off a few. I guess that's the way it's done where there aren't docks. I had my head out the window, I've got to get away from the cigarette smoke every so often. A phrase, "I don't smoke" is very handy. Without that, I think there is no way to refuse all the offers of cigarettes without being rude, or at least impolite.

Some of my new friends, young men, spotted the phrase "You are very beautiful" (*Ni hen piaoliang*) hand written in the back of my phrase book and started pointing at me and at each other, asking this one, that one? I rejected all of them, and pointed to an old lady nearby and used the phrase. My pronunciation is bad, and I had to repeat it for her five or six times. When she at last understood what I was trying to say, she was all smiles. My friends thumped their heads and rolled their eyes.

There is a big wood-fired water boiler; I watched it being fired. They've been having trouble, their firewood is wet. They keep spooning waste oil onto the fire, and it flares up and then dies down again. The crew filled the big hot water thermoses. River water, I think, heated to about 125°F. I'll pass, wait for water until I get off the boat.

The boat's been parked on a mud bank for several hours. I took another nap, perhaps this delay is a long one. About a dozen people have left the boat by sampan to a mud bank and across the mud on foot to a small town, perhaps to catch a bus. Two nicely dressed young couples picked their way across the mud with many shouts of encouragement, groans, sighs, and laughter from the audience on the boat. One dropped his jacket crossing a treacherous spot. What noise! Next, a woman lost her footing and stepped into mud over her ankle. Again much noise. The party responded with long suffering smiles and waves.

I am front and center most of the time, the main attention on this boat. Among my fellow passengers, the one with the most English I've met so far has a vocabulary of a couple hundred words, self-taught. Many seem to have a few words of English: "Hello!" "Bye-bye!" "Very good!", and, "America very good!". By now, I've learned about ten useful phrases in Chinese. It has been a long boring trip for everyone. It was supposed to take about twelve hours, and now looks as though it will be closer to thirty hours by the time we get to Guiping. I slept for a couple of hours, woke worried that we had passed Guiping. I got out my map and wandered around the boat until someone called me over. After some consultation, he pointed out where we are, Pingnan. Opening a map is often all I need to do to get help.

I'm unsure what has slowed us. We've stopped several times with the bow on a mud bank. The problem might be poor visibility due to fog. It's the dry season, the river level is low and the channel narrow. Some sections we've passed through after long stops have been rocky and constricted. I wouldn't want to try it blind in a small boat, much less a boat this size. I'm told the river is highest in July, the peak of the rainy season.

Maybe we arrive in <u>Guiping</u> at 10:00 PM. Hope I can find a room in the dark. I need a good wash, although the boat has been very comfortable. This twelve-hour boat ride of nearly 29 hours has cost me 15元 (US$3) including food and place to sleep. Crazy.

1991

December 14

<u>Dapeng, Guangdong</u>: In <u>Nan'ao</u>, a small village on a peninsula north of Hong Kong, I looked at boats. There are many fiberglass motor boats, four to six meters long with ten to forty horsepower outboard motors, and a few aluminum ones. Most of the fiberglass construction is very heavy and rough, designed to be knocked about. The designs would look familiar at home, owing nothing to traditional Chinese boats with one exception: there is a nice sort of sampan shape, more lightly and finely built than the others. I watched a man with one of these, unloading a half-dozen empty oil drums onto the concrete pier. He was very quiet and workmanlike, but most the boat operators are teenagers or a bit older, *wulai, liumang*. They are loud macho showoffs. Their favorite operating position is sitting on the outboard and steering the motor with their butt. The entire front third or half of the boat is out of the water when operated this way. Most of the motors are Suzuki, with a few Evinrudes and Mercurys, and some other Japanese makes. The boats seem to be mostly taking people out to larger boats anchored offshore.

When I asked about the *liumang* running the small motor boats, I was told these young men are fishermen, or at least they hold fisherman ID cards. This gives them the right to make a day trip into Hong Kong every week or so. They bring back all kinds of goods to sell and make lots of money. Hence, their attitude. I was also told that the closest they ever get to fishing is to take dynamite out and drop it in the water and then collect anything good out of what floats up dead, after the blast.

1992

January 30

On the boat to <u>Guiping</u> I'm into the routine of passing my album with maps and pictures of my home island. Two young girls, thirteen and fifteen, took great delight in watching me brush out my fourteen-inch ponytail. I asked them *"haobuhao"* (Is it good or not?). They answered me seriously but I didn't understand anything over the engine noise. We

170

were standing at the rail by the door of the engine room.

I've been squatting on the deck, writing this. A crew member came by and got me started flirting with a pretty *xiaojie* (miss), also a crew member. I told her she was pretty, and she invited me to sit by her side. This is fun, even better than my first boat trip in 1988. I've been up on the bridge, down in the engine room, and used up two rolls of film. It's been a beautiful day and I've found many new friends, but only one has more than a very little English. For the rest, I've got my pictures, card file (business cards of people I've met in China), and notebooks.

It's after 9:00 P.M., we'll be in Guiping in about an hour, the last stop for this boat. It's been fun standing at the ramp at each small stop, saying goodbye to my new friends. This time, I know where to find a hotel, as I've been here before. The first time, I had quite a time on the dark streets.

February 8

Gao, my old friend, arranged a boat ticket from Guiping to Guangzhou for me. It's the end of Spring Festival and the boat is full, as many people must return to their work in Guangdong. An old home mate of his has a position at the Northern Wharf. Without his help, the first ticket available was for the 19th, ten days later.

On the boat, I promptly met the director of a psychiatric hospital in Wuxi, his son who is studying architecture in Nanjing, and his wife. His English is limited. Next, an English teacher from Liuzhou with his wife and two daughters. Down the river we go. This boat is smaller than the one I came up on, but the twin diesels are turbocharged. I've had a good tour of the engine room. The engines run at 700 RPM and the room is neat, with a carefully laid out small shop. They have equipment to work on and test the injectors. It's noisy in the engine room, and neither the engineer nor oiler wore any ear protection.

The river is nasty in this area, with lots of rocks and turbulence. Needs a good pilot, although there are many navigation buoys. Midnight — The ventilation on the boat is good. I've been having a late night talk with the boat crew, showing pictures. One guy picked apart the pictures showing boats around Waldron Island (my home), noting details such as navigation lights, fenders, tillers, and rudders. Another crewman brought a bird in a nice bamboo cage out of his cabin for air. It's a nondescript black bird, but probably sings beautifully. Back to bed.

It's turned cold suddenly and two guys are sharing one bunk (small

171

for one person) right next to me. So they edged, feet and elbows over the low divider into me. Luckily, the couple with a double bunk on the other side appreciated the situation, and somehow managed to give me a few inches of their space. Two people aren't allowed in one bunk. I could have complained and had one kicked out, but neither of them have adequate clothes for the cold. They were both huddled under a blanket all afternoon. If I had complained, one of them would have been miserable, I didn't do it, but it sure would have been nice to have had a more comfortable sleep.

Too cold to stand out on deck now, and it's been raining off and on. I wish there was room to crawl back into my bunk. Scratch that – one of the pair is smoking. Remind me not to travel in the winter in this part of China without long underwear, even if it is the south. I'd have been a lot more comfortable with longjohns most of the time I was in <u>Guiping</u>. I should have bought a pair. And it was really cold in <u>Wenling</u>, a little south of Shanghai. Gao says you shouldn't travel in this southern area from September to April without carrying long underwear. You may never wear it, but if you need it, you'll have it.

1993

November 26

<u>Zhejiang Province</u>, near <u>Jiaojiang</u>: We took a boat to <u>Shang Dachen Dao</u> (Upper Dachen Island) in the East China Sea, Qiang's wife's old home. Qiang is a young lawyer who has been helping me with business. He speaks the local dialect, which is important.

Tomorrow, we go to <u>Xia Dachen Dao</u> (Lower Dachen Island) where he used to teach school. It's about the same size as my home island. Shang Dachen is a little bigger, but has a smaller population, about 2000 people. Xia has more than 3000 people. (My home island has a population of about 100.) These islands are roughly twenty miles off the coast east of <u>Songmen</u>, 200 miles south of <u>Shanghai</u>.

From the boat, I saw a few small fishing boats under sail. Most probably have engines and use a small junk rig for work and steadying, and to save fuel when the wind is right. I hope I can learn more about these boats and see some up close. Our ferry was a small ship, about 150 passengers and freight, and the three-hour trip cost US 95¢ each. We arrived before noon and spent the afternoon climbing to the top of the small mountain and wandering around the island, the fish docks, the ice plant, and a small temple, the *Ping Shui* (Flat Water) Temple. "Flat Sea", or "Calm Water" might be a better translation.

Everywhere we went, any available relatively flat ground was covered with fishing nets being repaired, and drying off the seaweed. We had to walk on them, as there was nowhere else to step. I'd never seen so many nets before in my life. The island is steep and rocky, and there is little flat ground.

1998

February 16

Hong Kong: On the night steamer to Guangzhou, with a ticket that cost only a little more than I was paying for a tiny room in Kowloon. I have a bed in a four-bed cabin, all to myself. The ticket lady assured me it was what I had asked for, but my Chinese is uncertain at best.

I talked with a pair of Hong Kong Chinese old ladies, 67 and 70, who are also on their way to Guangzhou. They have a house, or houses somewhere in the suburbs of Guangzhou, because it's cheaper than Hong Kong. The younger sister had traveled a bit, to Italy and France several times. They had great fun finding out about me, and telling me about themselves. Their English was fair. I carried their bags onto the boat for them, and at their invitation sat with them in their cabin until nearly 11:00 P.M.

Sophie Leung, the younger sister, said she would divorce her husband and marry me, as she's tired of him after 46 years and wants to travel. I could take her on a honeymoon to Niagara Falls, and all over, she said. I told her I had to think about it, to give me a few years, and that she must bring her cat, Nancy, who is three and has a short tail only six inches long. Nancy weighed six ounces when she adopted her from the SPCA, Sophie tells me. She fed her with an eyedropper for a week before she began to eat bits of fish from her fingers. Now, Nancy sleeps between Sophie and her husband, on their bed.

The boat is nearly empty, only about fifteen passengers on a ship with a capacity of 300-400. The old sisters told me this is the last trip for the ship, that it is being taken for mending, and maybe it's too old and can't be fixed. They wanted tickets for a few days later, but were told this was the last trip. There used to be two ships. One went to Guangzhou every night, and the other came back every day. Apparently, only one of them has been running for at least the past two months, so only every other day service. That, and this being the last trip, explains some of my confusion at the ticket office. I guess this boat is too slow for most people now that there are many other ways, and it has few passengers. In the past, it's been packed. There's now fast bus service on the new expressway, a fast rail link, and fast boats, catamarans and hydrofoils, but I liked this old ship, with a bed to sleep in.

1999

December 17

<u>Hong Kong</u>: Like San Francisco, the air is fairly clean because the sea breezes sweep away vehicle exhaust. The amount of newly filled ("reclaimed" is what it is called on the maps) land is staggering. One area of boat moorage I explored in '88 and '91, the <u>Yau Ma Tei Typhoon Shelter</u>, no longer exists. It has been filled to the extent of about 400 acres, with another 800 acres filled a bit north of that. It is now all a wasteland of "works in progress" (the designation on my map), freeway interchanges, the new airport railway, and new construction. It's filled to about fifteen feet above sea level.

In the government mapping office, I looked at historical maps of the Kowloon area. From 1924 until 1991, the shape of the waterfront was nearly static. The large-scale filling ("reclamation") seems to have started in '92. There is also a lot of newly filled land on Hong Kong Island around Central and Wanchai. Soon, if this keeps up, the Star Ferry won't be needed to cross from Kowloon to Hong Kong Island.

December 21

Waiting in the China Ferry building in <u>Kowloon</u> for the *Jimei*, a coastal steamer to <u>Xiamen</u>, Fujian, an eighteen-hour trip. It may be rough as force six to eight (22-40 knot) winds are predicted in the South China Sea, and gale warnings are hoisted.

We're off, got warped away from the dock by a tug. The hazy day is beautiful with warm sun, a good day for a sea trip, wind warnings or no. The *Jimei* is 9878 tons, 609 passengers, and 211 crew. Restrictions: twenty nautical miles offshore, force ten winds (48-55 knots) and five meter seas maximum. My cabin has two bunks, and I have it to myself. It's tiny, with a sink, small wardrobe, desk, and chair. No port. For HK$50 more, I could have had a larger cabin with a port. I didn't think about the port, it would have been worth the extra.

Outside the harbor, in about one meter seas, the ship rolled a mite. We made twenty knots as we crossed the entrance to <u>Dapeng Wan</u> (Dapeng Bay). It was too hazy to get much idea of the land, and the wind was blowing the carpets off the sun deck. By late afternoon the sea was running about two meters, with spray blowing off the crest of occasional waves. There were teeth on almost every swell and spray in the air, even on the upper deck. Everything was tied down and except for me, only crew member were out. The coast was dimly visible through a dirty looking haze. The roll of the ship and the thrum of its engines was comforting.

Wandering around, a pretty young woman and some guys tried to entice me into the slot machines (casino). I told them my money had wings and would fly away. One of the guys said the *Jimei* was the Vegas of Hong Kong. The girl was up front about it being her job, when she invited me in.

I watched a crewman fling a plastic sack of garbage overboard. I've read all the posted notices, at least the ones with English translations. I read several that warn against throwing garbage overboard within such and such distance of land. The notice continues that all garbage dumping must be recorded in the garbage disposal log, and warns of 100,000元 fines for violations. One of the disposal warnings in English and Chinese was posted right where the man picked up the sack.

2000

January 21

On the riverboat to <u>Wuzhou</u>: When I bought my ticket, I learned there is only one boat a week now. My bicycle should have cost me 10 元 more, and they wanted to charge me after I was in line. I started back to the office to pay, but they were already loading so they just put me on the boat. I had to carry the bike, still assembled, across two other boats. It's tied to the rail on the stern deck, with a bunch of motorcycles to keep it company.

The riverboat is familiar. There were many students who wanted to speak to me (right before Spring Festival). On earlier trips, there were few English speakers on these boats. I've spoken with three different groups of students, and a few others. Most have only basic English and the talk was only practice, but there was real contact and a lot of fun with old people and children. I ate dinner with a couple of students from two different universities in Guangzhou, one studying law. I asked why they took the boat, since it was so slow. They answered that it was easy on their bodies and restful. The bus is fast but tiring. Their family homes are in <u>Guangdong</u>, in a county across the line from Wuzhou. One lives near Fengkai, a boat landing about twenty km before Wuzhou. The other also gets off there but has a two-hour bus ride to his family's home up in the mountains. At one stop, a young man got off pushing a luggage cart loaded with a new computer, printer, and monitor, all boxed up. I wouldn't have seen that two years ago.

Surprise. I had thought I was the only foreigner on board, then found there were two other Americans on the boat. They've been hiding in a cabin the whole trip and only came out to go to the toilet. One, from NY, is teaching in Beijing. The other, from Philadelphia, arrived in Hong Kong four days ago, his first time in Asia. He's confused, and in a bit of shock. I guess the teacher is tired of talking to people. It seems a strange way to travel, shut in a cabin.

2002

June 15

Chenglingji, Hunan, a port on the Changjiang (Long River, also called the Yangtze River, *Yangzi* is correct *pinyin*). I have a fourth class ticket on a boat down the river to Nanjing, about 35 hours.

A big luxury tourist boat tied next to us disgorged a herd of Western tourists. Now I know why there was a luxury bus in front of the ticket office. As far as I know, I'm the only Westerner on this boat. I've talked with many other passengers, but no one yet who had much English, only a lot better than my Chinese.

Down the river at Wuhan, the boat filled up. A sour fat young Westerner got on with a Chinese girl. My cabin has six bunks on each side, with a one-meter-wide aisle between. I have an uninspiring saggy bottom berth. There is good ventilation — one advantage of summer, every door and window is open. The drinking water wasn't very hot, I wasn't sure it had been boiled, so I drank a beer instead of tea, long before I had my noodles.

The river is huge below Wuhan, with wide flat banks. There is an area of steep banks and rapids nearer to Nanjing, but the river is high this time of year so the rapids are covered and not a navigation hazard. We passed a huge rock sticking out of the water. I wish I remembered more of G.R.G.Worcester's book[1]. He wrote of this reach. There are low mountains on each side, and the river is much narrower. Hundreds of motor-barges as far as I could see were loaded with sand and headed down river. Some run with their rails under water, the water lapping against the washboards. One, a much bigger barge of about sixty feet, had three men busily digging and moving sand to the aft, adjusting the

---

[1] The Junks and Sampans of the Yangtze River, see Suggested Reading.

trim. Looked as if they had been at it for a long time. The narrowest stretch of the river, before it got dark, was about like the channel between Jones and Orcas Islands. Other parts were as wide as President Channel (in the San Juan Islands, Washington State, around my home). A major cable-stayed bridge showed a distinct water mark about two meters above the current level. No other marks were clear, although I thought I discerned one four to six meters above the water.

I talked with a 32-year-old man working on his Ph.D. in Chinese philosophy. He told me people have been living in this area on this part of the river for 7000 years, but *Han* Chinese people have been here for only 2000 years. He says that like the USA, China is a nation of immigrants, people from other places, but with a minor difference: they all came here 5000-7000 years ago. He hates the government, and thinks not one person on this ship loves it. But he, and all the rest of them love China. He described himself as Confucian and said any man's life is more important than any nation, and that no government has the right to scare any man. He was too polite to say, but I got the distinct impression he didn't like the USA's government any more than he liked his own.

2003

January 19

Guangzhou: A few days ago, I went to Dashatou to look at the old boat dock and see if there might be a boat to Wuzhou. The daily riverboat service was discontinued a couple of years ago. The old waiting room was discouragingly now a car repair shop. I looked around more and found a woman in an office reading a paper. She told me "*Meiyou, meiyou*!", but then suddenly "*You, you*!" There will be eight special boat runs up river to Wuzhou, put on for *Chunjie*, the first run on the 23rd, so I bought a ticket. I have no idea what kind of boat it will be, but likely the old river sleeper. There was some confusion about whether or not I could take my bike, but it will work out, I'm sure. I'm happy to be able to ride the boat again.

January 23

Including babies, there were only twelve people waiting for the boat an hour before departure, which was supposed to be 1:00 P.M., but it didn't leave until 5:00 P.M. The boat started farther down river in Dongguan, and arrived in Guangzhou about 3:00 P.M. Only twenty passengers were on the boat, and there are about 100 now. The boat capacity is at least 300.

The engine broke down at 6:30, barely out of urban <u>Guangzhou</u>. At first, I thought the problem was the timing gears. I watched the mechanics from a distance, trying to stay out of the way. Turned out to be the camshaft, broken right behind the first bearing, so the gears turned but no valves moved. It's 4:00 A.M. now, and the engine is nearly reassembled.

When the engine quit, the captain dropped anchor quickly. I thought the boat was stopping to pick up more passengers. Finally, a smaller freight barge tied alongside and eased the bigger boat skillfully up river. We tied to a convenient pier, and the mechanics got more help and tools. There were seven guys working on the engine, a big six-cylinder. The "convenient pier" was actually a fair sized shipyard with two covered dry docks, each about 200 feet long. I snuck ashore in the dark to look around but was spotted, called back, and told sternly (in Chinese) to stay on the frigging boat. I went back to bed.

January 24

We were under way by about 6:00 A.M., but had another breakdown around 11:00 A.M. which was repaired in twenty minutes. I have a bad headache, 3:00 P.M., but not as bad as the mechanics, who worked all night. And I'm sure the boat is losing money, with the small passenger load.

I've met four people with some English. One was a pretty Wuzhou girl, a third-year student studying law at a university in Chongqing. Then two boys studying navigation at the Huangpu Academy, and a young man working in Dongguan. He had a beautiful silver earring and a stud in one ear, unusual here.

The sixteen-hour trip actually took 37 hours.

January 28

<u>Guiping</u>: Market day is every third day, staggered between Guiping, Jintian, and Jiangkou. There is a boat that carries passengers and produce between the markets, two hours or a little more, 2元. It can carry about a hundred passengers.

April 25

<u>Guangzhou</u>, late evening on a ferry across the river, 0.5元. A man with only stubs of fingers was again playing the *dizi* (bamboo flute) beautifully. I gave him 1元, many others also gave him money and some clapped. How can he play so well without fingers? I wonder if he is on the ferry often, and what kind of arrangement he makes with the boat crew.

2004

January 16

Guangzhou: No problem getting a boat ticket, once I found the ticket office. All the old buildings around the dock at Dashatou had been demolished. It didn't look promising, but I asked some workers who were shoveling mud from the demolition. They said there was definitely a boat to Wuzhou, and pointed vaguely. I went around in circles for a while, then asked a woman in a bit of demolished building behind a scaffold, and she sold me a ticket. This year, as far as I understood, there are only two boats being put on for *Chunyun*, tomorrow and Monday.

In the afternoon on the phone, my old friend Wei told me she wanted to go on the boat with me. She was in Panyu, a little south of Guangzhou. She needs to get to Nanning, and can easily get a bus on from Wuzhou. Right now, the buses from around Guangzhou are triple normal price, and it's hard to get a seat. I've been to the dock and bought another ticket for her.

January 18

Wei made it to Guangzhou an hour before the boat departure. We met at the Nanfang bus station, and I got her on a city bus to Dashatou and headed there myself on my bike with all my stuff. We got on the boat fifteen minutes before sailing. Cut it close, but it worked. Took sixteen hours to Wuzhou this time, with no boat problems. The boat was full, no empty beds, but it was only a small boat with a capacity of 150 passengers. They had oversold, and several men had no beds.

Wei's father was a captain of *tuochuan*, river tugboats. He's retired now because of bad eyesight, and because there's little work anymore for river captains. We used her credentials to get permission to go up and sit on the bridge, telling them her father was a captain. She had often been on her father's boat as a child, but never before on a passenger boat.

I think this is the last year I'll find a passenger boat on this river.

2006

February 1

This year, the riverboats ran advertisements in Guangzhou newspapers, announcing boat service between Guangzhou and Wuzhou for *Chunyun*. I wonder how many passengers they found?

179

Bikes

1988

May 11

<u>Kunming</u>: A big day yesterday after all. I took off on my borrowed bicycle, stopped to get a cup of Yunnan coffee, fooled around a bit, and found the bike was gone. Stolen, I thought. I had locked it but left it in a foolish place, not a bicycle parking lot: I was being lazy and thrifty. I hunted for it and then went to find Zhuang, a pharmacist, to tell him his bike was stolen or at least lost. I was a bit embarrassed, to put it mildly. We went looking together, hoping some sort of block-watch person was angry because I had parked it in the wrong place and had grabbed and hidden it. However, those people aren't around in the evening. To complicate the problem, Zhuang's bike was unregistered, so he will have to get a letter from the leader of his *danwei* (work unit) to prove he owns it.

I was proud of myself; I started late and still created a lot of trouble in just part of an afternoon. It all turned out well this morning, just some small trouble for him. Confiscated bikes are usually turned over to the police after one day, but Zhuang found it chained with four or five other bikes, a heavy chain through the wheels. He paid a 2元 fine, got a lecture, and didn't have to register his bike. He explained creatively that he had loaned the bike to his "teacher from America" who didn't know any better. The block-watch people are the folks wearing red armbands. The block-watch watcher of public morality and decency had watched me park the bike, then carried it away and hid it as soon as I was out of sight. Because, bad boy, I shouldn't have parked it there.

1992

January 13

<u>Wenling, Zhejiang</u>: I rode east on my borrowed bike (the first time I've had a bike here) through a tunnel under a small, steep mountain and south toward <u>Yuhuan</u>. While coming back through the dark tunnel on my return, an end broke off the fork and the front wheel fell off. I'm glad I was in the tunnel: it was dark and I was going slowly, so I didn't go over the handlebars. I pushed and carried the bike for a mile or so, until I found a small welding shop.

The young man brazed it back together nicely. When he started to reassemble it, he found the axle was broken. He went down the road to get a new one from a bicycle shop, assembled it, and then saw a crack on the other side of the fork. So he took it all apart again, brazed the other side, and reassembled it once more, adding a missing washer. He was fast and competent, much more than a simple bicycle mechanic. He charged me 3元, I gave him 5元, refused change, and gave him one of my business cards. Altogether, a satisfactory repair in a hopeless situation.

1993

November 3

Guangzhou: Yesterday, part of the frame tube on the bicycle I've been using came apart. The only way to fix it was to get it welded. I pushed it over to a side street to look for a welding shop. I found a shop with an arc welder, but was told to come back later. I asked the young man for wire to tie the bike together. He looked around a bit, and then pulled out the welder.

He tried to weld it with me holding everything and helping. He was having a hard time, not a skilled welder, and gestured, could I do it? I said yes and we traded positions. I promptly burned a hole through the tube, then got the welder turned down to a more reasonable amperage. We attracted an amused audience, a small crowd. I managed to get it welded half way around, good enough. The sprocket and chain guard were getting in my way and I needed to take the crank apart to do a complete job, but no tools. Off I went with dirty hands; no charge.

1998

March 8

Guigang, Guangxi: A man went by riding in a bicycle sidecar. It was being peddled along by a small girl, working from one side of the bike with her leg stuck through under the crossbar. I said in Chinese "*Wa*, she is very strong," and he answered also in Chinese "We go slowly." The little girl ignored me, totally intent on powering the bike, working hard. Her father seemed as pleased with our exchange as I was.

April 6

Kunming: Yang brought a boy of about twelve with him when he brought me the bicycle to rent. He said the boy's parents were divorced, and the boy was living with an uncle who had been unemployed for two years and sometimes got drunk, no money for school. Yang has sort of adopted the boy and is giving him lessons and teaching him some small business, such as renting bicycles to foreign visitors. If the boy has one bicycle and rents it most days, he can earn enough money to live. Yang is a passionate do-gooder, or so he tells me. He says a man must first take care of his own health, then take care of his business and earn money before he can help others. He says that many Taiwan and Hong Kong Chinese use their money to help others in China. And that you can only do this if you are financially successful. I'm inclined to accept that he believes what he says. He encourages me to do business (maybe a partnership with him) so I can help others. His English is very good, largely self-taught, and he says he is not religious, believes only in himself. He has a college degree, computers or business, and has been sick the past couple of years. He wears a face mask most of the time, says he has to have special food cooked for him, that he had an operation about two years ago for cancer of the throat that he developed from second hand smoke. Now he must be very careful about what he eats and breaths because he is at great risk from infection.

April 8

Yang came back to the hotel last night with the boy, after I called him to retrieve the bicycle. Considering he only charged me 10元, it was a lot of trouble for him. Teaching is hard work.

1999

December 27

Xiamen, Fujian: I have a bike. In the market last night, I returned greetings to a studious and serious looking young man with glasses. He has a food stall making and selling fried cakes filled with peanut butter.

I thought he might speak some English and he looked friendly and trustworthy. I told him I spoke only a little Chinese, badly, and did he speak English. He said, no, only a little. I told him I wanted to rent a bike, or buy an old bicycle. Could he help me? He said, "*Keyi*" (can). By that time, a few people had gathered around, laughing, listening, and having a good time. The young man turned to the others, and one stepped forward, offering me a bike for 200元. "*Taiguile!*" (too much) said I. I offered 100元 and he backed away in disgust.

I said I wanted an old bike. The young man pointed at his beat up old bike and I said *hao*, good. I told him I wanted it for about a week and offered him a 200元 deposit, what the other man had wanted for a newer bike. How much per day? 10元, *hao* (good). So we messed around with the bike for a while. It was pretty funky, but all working. We tried to raise the seat, but too rusty, *meiyouwenti* (no problem). I gave him 200元 and my card. He wrote his phone number and name for me and I told him my hotel and room number, up the street from his stall. Xiao Ma and I shook hands and off I went, to much laughter from the onlookers.

2000

<u>Xiamen</u>: Bought a new bike with my Italian friend Adriano's help. He's living in Xiamen, has never had a driver's license, and has ridden bikes all his life all over the world. My new bike is a ten-speed with narrow tires that have a strip of hard tread down the middle for low rolling resistance on hard surfaces. It has a tall frame, tall seat post, tall handlebar riser, steer horn handlebars, basket, rack, two good locks, and a bell, altogether 750元 (US$90).

It was a project buying the bike. I was glad to have Adriano's knowledge of bikes and support in the negotiations. My bike had to be made up with parts from several others. I went around the shop and said, "This frame, those wheels, these handlebars".

The bike shop kept saying impossible, the parts wouldn't fit, whatever. I kept measuring, saying it will work. Finally, Adriano told them the price didn't matter, just do it. That made them happy and two mechanics went to work. Took them about an hour and a half and left them with a bunch of bikes to reassemble. Now I need to buy grease, find rags, borrow tools, take the bike apart, and lubricate everything. I also want to splatter it up with a can of spray paint to make it look dirty and old. Reduce its theft appeal.

Adriano will show me how to disassemble and pack it to carry on the bus and train. I'll need to get a bag made. This is old stuff for him he has it all worked out in fine detail and has done it many times over many years. He can't imagine why I haven't had a bicycle, and the main reason I've bought this one is to get him off my back, but I think I'll like it.

Today I returned Xiao Ma's old bike and paid him 80元 for eight days, and he returned my deposit. It was a good deal for me, put money in his pocket, and I returned the bike in better condition. I'd had the chain oiled and adjusted, and the brakes fixed, all for less than 5元.

My new bike is nice. On one long slight downgrade, I was relaxed and coasting along, passing people pedaling their bikes. I've greased and serviced everything except the rear hub (no freewheel wrench). I don't understand why new bikes are often unlubricated. Everything seems to be assembled dry, or with just a trace of oil.

I messed up the appearance of the bike with black spray paint. Splattered the chrome wheels and fenders, the white wall tires, and the beautiful silver frame. I tried to throw dust in the wet paint, but it dried too fast. To finish the making it ugly and old, I whacked a few dents in the fenders.

February 10

<u>Guangxi</u>: I went on a seventy km bike ride yesterday, a long day trip, with my old friend Gao and his wife and son to <u>Jiangkou</u>, their old hometown. Before we started, I noticed the chain on Gao's bike was worn out. I wanted him to get a new one, as it was ruining the sprockets. He refused, said it still worked, so we had to stop several times to tighten it. Soon, it was climbing off the sprocket regularly, and then it broke. He pushed and scootered his old bike for a few km until we found a bike shop and a new chain.

He said he was willing to replace it when it really needed to be replaced.

February 14

A few days ago, I started on a bike ride with all my stuff, 140 km south to Yulin by a scenic route (back road). I planned to spend an easy three days and climb one mountain on the way. Gao and family and friends decided to go with me on the first leg and climb the mountain, too, a place he'd never been but could see since he was a child.

The trip went more or less as planned except the middle 44 km of the road turned out to be loose sand, difficult(!) on a narrow-tired bike carrying a load. The first night after climbing the mountain, I stayed in a small hotel in <u>Madong</u>, a village (a small town, actually) at the foot of the mountain. The next night, I stayed in <u>Beishi</u>, a village (also a small town) in the middle of the stretch of sand road.

I arrived in <u>Beishi</u> about 3:30. Instantly, I started collecting children who were laughing, pointing, and following me with great joy. By the time I found my way to a small hotel, I had about thirty kids with me. They all crowded into my room to watch me. I was exhausted; it had been hard work trying to ride my bike in the loose sand. I managed to get them all to leave, and took a nap. When I woke up, I went out for dinner.

I immediately picked up the kids again, as they were watching for me. At the place I chose to eat, the woman was suspicious of me and made me pay before she started fixing my food. The kids all crowded around me. When she brought my noodles, she made the kids move just enough to give me room to eat. She told me I should forgive them, they had never seen a foreigner before. She didn't say she hadn't, either. The kids followed me back to my hotel after supper. I hiked up a hill behind the hotel with them to a cenotaph, a monument to war dead. The kids passed me on the way down, and ranged out in front of the hotel. I waved to them from the balcony of my second floor room and called, *"Wan'an"* (good night).

I left early the next morning in a misty rain. At the end of the sand road, I stopped in <u>Maijiu</u> for lunch and found myself in the middle of the largest fireworks factory I could imagine. As a professional blaster, I was impressed. Talk about firecrackers and rockets! I didn't light any matches and nobody was smoking. As I had approached the village, I noticed red paper drying on racks alongside the road. I hadn't seen that before and had been wondering what it was.

Along the way I was stopped several times by young people, always men, who wanted to know about me. Sometimes after we were talking, young women joined the group. Gao told me he rode a bike from <u>Guiping</u> to <u>Yulin</u> three times when he was in college, once the longer way by <u>Guigang</u> because the roads were better. He said it was sand road all the way then. Each time he made the trip in one day, 140 km on sand. *Wa*, after 44 km, I was ready to throw in the towel. He was a young farmer then, strong from ten years of hard work. Even now he is known as a strong man.

March 1

Arriving in <u>Guangzhou</u> by train from <u>Nanning</u>, I found that checking a bicycle into the luggage car is problematic. It was easy to do as I didn't have to take the bike apart and pack it, and the fee was reasonable. To retrieve it, first I had to make my way clear around the Guangzhou station through the crazy crush of people that is normal there, lugging my bags. (Although I use a standard backpack, it was packed inside a pannier that lets me carry it on my bike, and keeps it clean. I didn't want to unpack it and then have to repack it when I got my bike, so I was carrying it with my hand.) I finally found the freight pickup place and got in line to pay my 4元. Just before it was my turn the window slammed closed. Lunch time. Come back in an hour. However, I'm a foreign visitor so I prevailed. The worker stayed a few minutes longer and let me pay. The others waiting were out of luck. Papers in hand at another gate, I was told my bike wasn't there, maybe in an hour, why don't you go eat lunch? Ugh. I wanted my bike to ride to the hotel. So I sat and waited. If I had carried my bike onto the sleeper, I'd be at my hotel already.

I got my bicycle eventually, don't know where it was, or whether this was a usual delay. A man working at the pickup place took me in hand and led me somewhere else, and told me to wait. He reappeared after about twenty minutes with my bicycle. Altogether, it took more than three hours. I've heard I was lucky: sometimes checked luggage doesn't go on the same train as the traveler. At least my bike arrived on the same train.

2001

March 21

Packing my bike took less than half an hour, but I got hot and sweaty. If I took off my shirt when packing or unpacking it; I'd smell better and keep my shirt cleaner.

Carrying a bike, the total weight of my luggage doesn't matter as much. If the bike is packed in its bag and I'm humping it along with my pack, it's so awkward that ten pounds more or less makes little difference. And when the bike is carrying me and my stuff, rather than me carrying the bike, ten pounds is nothing.

April 25

<u>Xiamen</u>: At the *wangba* (Internet cafe) on Hubin Nanlu, I parked and locked my bike out front on the sidewalk, went in for 45 minutes to check email, and came out to find my bike gone, stolen. I looked around in a rush, up the small alleys where it could have been stashed, places where it could have been carried fairly easily. Some people were concerned at my poking around. I'd explain my bike had been stolen, and they'd say "Look, look", and wave me into the courtyard of their building. No luck, too many doorways, too many places to hide it. So I have no bike. Damn. It was a good bike, with all the special work I'd done on it. I can't replace that.

April 27

Xiao Liu, a systems engineer and programmer, explained something about bike theft methods: the professional thief wears a harness rig under his shirt that has an adjustable hook down near his belt, concealed by his shirttail. He hooks the seat or the luggage rack and pushes the locked bike along, carrying the locked rear wheel just off the ground. He appears to be pushing the bike, unless an observer looks closely enough to see the rear wheel isn't turning. The defense against this method is to lock both wheels. Then the thief has to pick the bike up bodily and carry it, which attracts a lot of attention. I had only locked the rear wheel.

I told my friend Zhou, a newspaper reporter on the daily here, about losing my bike. She laughed and said the bike was angry with me because I had said if it was stolen I wouldn't have to carry it to Beijing. I'd made the comment the other night when I met her for dinner. I had locked it to a convenient park fence and she had expressed worry about its safety.

May 4

<u>Beijing</u>: I bought a new bike, a 26" single speed. I think it will work for me, but I bought it with only a quick look at the options. I didn't find any ten-speed ones that were simple enough. The ones I saw, at a Giant shop, started at over 800元, and didn't have serviceable fenders or luggage racks. Fitted out, the lowest-priced one cost over 1000元, US$120. This one's only a single-speed, but cheap. Cost about US$30, including the two cable locks, one of good quality.

June 2

<u>Wuyuan, Nei Menggu</u> (Inner Mongolia): Watching bicyclists, I notice few have the seat high enough for efficiency, but the men operating the *sanlunche* (freight trikes) do. Most of them can completely straighten their legs and get in some ankle action at the bottom of the stroke.

August 15

<u>Lanzhou, Gansu</u>: The *wangba* I've been using locks all the customers' bikes left out front with a long cable threaded through the wheels. An Internet cafe is a good target for bike thieves. They know anyone inside is fully occupied and won't be watching. I sure wasn't watching when my first bike was stolen.

August 27

I'm right in the middle of the back to school travel crunch, and

187

found it difficult to impossible to get a train ticket to Kunming or Nanning. I need time in Nanning to get dental work done before I go home. So I bought an airplane ticket to <u>Kunming</u> for day after tomorrow, no direct flights to Nanning.

I'll dump my bike. It would cost 200元 or more to take it on the plane as excess baggage. I can buy a similar-quality new one for that, and this one already has problems and I never liked it. I'll try to sell it, but will dump it if I can't.

August 28

I made a deal to sell my bike for 45元 to a repairman down the street from the CAAC (China Airlines) office, where I catch the airport bus. I'd pumped up my tires at his stand two weeks ago and he remembered me. We bargained for fifteen minutes, both of us having fun, and reached a deal. He'll probably make about 25元. School is starting and it is an easy time to sell used bikes. He'll need to do a few small repairs and clean it up. I'm keeping the locks and the special tall seat post. It's convenient for me, I can drop off my bags, sell the bike, and walk back to my bags and the bus.

2002

June 28

<u>Beijing</u>: Bought a new bike, my third one in China. It's a twelve-speed Merida road bike, nicely made and fairly light. Not exactly what I wanted, but close. It's not as good as my first bike but a lot better than the second one. I paid about US$80 for it, with all my custom modifications. It's simple and utilitarian, except for the flashy paint job. It's nice to ride, but has a poor luggage rack. I need to oil and grease everything.

I made it as ugly as possible with black spray paint, like I did the first one. I hope the bike thieves will ignore it.

July 26

<u>Huhhot</u>: I need to get a move on to other places. I'm at the point where normal Chinese bicycle lane behavior is starting to annoy me, especially when people wheel fast into a busy lane from the side, right in front of everyone else, with no consideration at all. And nobody complains because it could bring trouble; just ignore it and forget it. Can't change it, better leave it alone. Paying attention only makes you angry, better not to be angry, better to laugh than cry.

Southern Guangxi — Farmers wanting to know all about me stopped me on the road.

North-west Guangxi, in the mountains. Like the Pied Piper, I quickly attracted an entourage of curious and friendly kids.

The frowning girl in the light blue sweater, center-right, was the organizer of this group for an outing to the home of a man they called a "witch doctor". The little kids were very afraid. The older kids said he had big dogs and many snakes. Later, we visited the schools and other special places.

Sometimes people walk four abreast down the bike line, blocking all the bikes. And taxis pull into the bike lanes and stop, blocking everything. If ordinary bicycle lane behavior is getting to me, maybe it's time to go home.

2003

January 22

Guangzhou: I visited a Dahon (a maker of folding bikes) shop, a little west of the Tianhe sports complex. They had only one 26" folding Dahon, a six-speed with no fenders and no rack, and no easy way to attach them, 750元. Unsuitable for my needs. Dahon makes only this one 26" model in China, but the price is okay and the quality looks good. The one I've looked at in the USA that might work for me is made in Taiwan.

February 5

Guiping, Guangxi: Gao and I went on a 6 1/2 hour bike ride to Jiangkou. Gao had a loose pedal arm on his bike. Together, we fixed it with a bit of tin can for a shim, an adequate repair. We did the work at a bike repair shop, but the man didn't charge us anything although we used his tools and his soap and water to wash up when we were done. The road was under construction part of the way, and dusty. When we got home, Su, Gao's wife, exclaimed loudly and made us go wash. We both had gray hair!

March 4

At the good small bike parts shop where I got my tubes, I got a new chain. I hadn't oiled the old one enough, and it was clicking and starting to climb the teeth. I also got a triple sprocket crank wheel installed, to give me six lower gears so my bike's now an eighteen-speed. They replaced both crank arms so it looks good. Total cost, 50元. The new chain was half the cost. It all seems to work well. They adjusted the shifters carefully, and fixed several other small problems.

April 10

Baise, Guangxi: At the train station, all packed, shirt changed, still hot and sweaty. Whew. A little trouble with my bike: I dismantled and packed it too close to the entrance door. So the guard at the door stopped me and told me "no bikes". I told him no problem and we went back and forth a few times, then he let me in. Impolite of me to have packed it where he had to see.

190

May 12

<u>Beijing</u> isn't as nice to bike across as it used to be. There are many new big roads, and most streets have been widened. This follows the standard pattern: knock down all the small stuff on both sides, back to the big buildings. This leaves parking and bike lanes, and a strip for trees, grass, and shrubs, but fronts on the high rises, uninteresting. All the small businesses and shops that used to line the streets and provide interest for me are gone. There are still some of the older streets left, lots actually, but they aren't direct through routes. Often, where the old streets meet the new big ones, there is no way across, and it can be a distance to a crossing. And then the crossing will often be an overhead or underground pedestrian crossing, requiring going up or down a lot of stairs, hard work with a bike.

2004

January 13

<u>Hong Kong</u>: In Seattle, I wrapped cardboard from a refrigerator box around my bagged bike. Looks like there is no damage this time. My bike has been somewhat damaged every time I have taken it on a plane. The extra protection was worth it. I left the cardboard behind a trash can at the airport in Hong Kong.

January 23

<u>Guangxi</u>: The express buses I've taken so far this year have been small, 25 passengers. The luggage compartments are too small for my bike. On the common medium-sized forty passenger express buses, my dismantled and packed bike fits nicely. On the smaller ones, my packed bike gets put in the aisle, and people must squeeze past it. I feel a little rude.

March 17

<u>Shuolong</u>: In Nanning, I had searched for an area map but didn't find one. Here on the wall of the hotel dining room is exactly the map I had wanted, dated 2003/11, Nanning *Shi Quan Tu* (Nanning City Whole Map). I had put a lot of effort into getting the most detailed and up-to-date maps before I started this bike trip. I bought the best small atlas and cut out the appropriate pages, but I didn't find this map.

At <u>Detian *Pubu*</u> (Detian Waterfall), I didn't go into the park. 30元 for a ticket was too much. There's little water for the waterfall this time of the year, and the gatekeeper refused to let me past the gate for a quick peek. I headed up the road toward <u>Xialei</u>. It was steep with many switch backs, but nicely paved. I had to push my bike the whole way. Halfway up, I found *houmen,* the back door (in China, it seems there is always a "back door" if you can find it, to parks, to offices, to everything). There was a tiny roadside viewing platform, with a trail down to the waterfall and no guards, no ticket office. I sat and ate oranges while enjoying the view. I couldn't walk down; there was no way to leave my bike and bags safely.

When I reached the top of the steep road, I discovered a problem. There was a beautiful newly constructed paved highway, not shown on my most detailed maps. The new road continued to climb up the mountains to the east and west, and a sign gave the distance west to Napo, a small town near the Yunnan border. My least detailed map, the province map on the back of my Nanning city map, did show this road but with no detail. The road on the other side of this new highway was signed to Xialei as I expected, but it was rough gravel, not what I anticipated. I was already exhausted from pushing my bike up the steep road for an hour and a half. I couldn't face more uphill, even paved, and I didn't know exactly where it went. So I started down the gravel road. Which, as it turned out, also went up. More pushing.

After an hour, I got a flat in a reasonable place, by a pile of bricks that served as a handy workbench. About the time I was remounting the tire, a couple of guys in a small truck stopped to see if I needed help. That broke the ice, and soon there were fifteen people around me. Some had passed on foot earlier as I worked, greeting me but not stopping. Others had been watching from behind bushes. I think they were all *Zhuangzu* (a minority), and a few sang in unison as they watched me. Nice.

I reloaded and started off again. Half an hour later, riding slowly down a hill, hiss, quick flat, darn. Eight or so *Zhuangzu* women I had passed earlier came walking by. To their "*Ni hao?*" (you good?), I replied "*Bu hao!*" (not good) to laughter. I mimed throwing the bike over the steep bank and told them feet were better, to their agreement. Later, tire fixed and riding again, I passed them, to cheers and thumbs up. I think they spoke only a little more *Putonghua* than me. I speak no *Zhuang* language and they no English.

Why do I do this, work so hard and put myself to so much trouble I often wonder? I guess it's the adventure, not knowing what is around the next corner. And the small contacts I make are fun for both me and the locals. They think I'm pretty funny and a little crazy. Maybe they are right. Anyway, the countryside is sure beautiful, rugged and steep with many waterfalls.

Tonight in <u>Huran</u> looking for a *zhaodaisuo*, I got pointed one way and then the other. <u>Huran</u> is smaller than <u>Shuolong</u> and totally without tourist traffic. A poor place with some kind of mining industry, possibly molybdenum, the word wasn't in my small dictionary. When I finally found this *zhaodaisuo*, it was the most miserable place I've ever stayed in China.

In the room, the first thing I saw was a spider behind the door, more than 2"x3" across the legs and a flat grayish-black. I didn't want to sleep with it, so I killed it. Boy, was it fast! I missed with the first blow but got it with a second, as it jogged when it should have jigged. It was the biggest spider I'd ever seen, and left me feeling a bit queasy. With a flashlight I hunted under the beds and behind things, any hiding places I spotted, for another one. Revenge a serious possibility... I think the worst part of the room will be mosquitoes. I don't think the spider would have helped with that; it needed bigger prey.

There's no electricity in town, shut off for some reason. I've got a candle on my table where I'm having a good supper. The hotel said the juice came on in the evening, but there are many candles in shops on the street. A few have electricity, probably from small generators or batteries. Looking down at the street (dark, when no truck or *motuo* is passing), I keep seeing people's faces lighted by the blue glow from the screens of their mobile phones.

March 19

My map pages showed a new highway as "under construction", north out of <u>Jingxi</u>. The page for the next county didn't show the planned road, only the old one. But highway was all finished, meeting the <u>Nanning-Baise</u> highway about fifteen km south of <u>Tianyang</u>. The last third of the road followed an entirely different route from the old road. This road that wasn't shown on my map was so new there wasn't a blade of grass anywhere on the cuts and fills, in a lush semitropical area where everything grows fast.

April 4

<u>Xining, Qinghai</u>, arriving at the train station: A group of men gathered to watch and help me put my bike together, and take it for test spins. Two of the men were skilled; either could have put it together easily. One kept getting out my tools to tighten something, and then carefully putting the tool back. It was the most real help I've ever had, really a bit too much.

April 11

Yesterday afternoon, I carried Tserang, a Tibetan university student, on the back of my bike down to the train station, about an hour's ride. We had a good simple dinner in a small traditional Tibetan restaurant. We ate yak meat and rice porridge (she says rice is new, fifty years, not traditional) and drank butter tea.

Riding around before dinner carrying her, I turned off on a nondescript side street as I like to do. We went under the rail tracks and up toward the mountains. It was industrial near the tracks, dusty and dirty. As we moved away, we entered a *Hui* (a Muslim minority) village. Soon, I was pushing the bike up the hill and we were being followed by a bunch of kids. I stopped to play with them. One boy, about ten, who had been following us kept saying in English "What are you doing?" Turned out Tserang loved it. She was excited to have gotten out of the city, even that little bit, and loved being in the *Hui* village. She said it made her feel like she was in her home town.

October 19

Beijing: I left a bit late for the long ride to where I was to meet Guirong, an old friend from Guangxi, in SW Beijing. I was hurrying, only a few minutes late but a little lost in a part of Beijing unfamiliar to me. I was looking at street signs in Chinese, peering really, as I need my glasses changed. It was rush hour and traffic was extremely heavy.

I glanced forward to find an idiot on a little electric three-wheeler cutting diagonally across the bike lane against the flow heading directly for me, only ten or fifteen feet away. I hit the brakes, swerved, and went over the handlebars. I landed on my hands and knees, running fast. I jumped up, snatched my bike up, and was slammed into by two girls on a bike. We got untangled, they weren't hurt, and I started to assess my own injuries. I never saw the three-wheeler again.

Meanwhile, several people who had seen me crash had stopped a short way on up the road. My hands were sore, but no blood, thanks to Chinese street sweepers: no loose gravel. My knees hurt but my pants weren't torn. The bike seemed okay. I got back on a little shakily. A man who had stopped rode alongside me for a few blocks, not entirely accepting my "No problem". I thanked him, waved goodbye, and made it to the restaurant, still shaking, about ten minutes later.

It was the worst bike crash I've ever had in China, possibly my worst ever. I'm really lucky. After dinner, I had an hours' ride back to my hotel in light traffic. My wreck was right in the worst of rush hour right after dark. By the time I went to bed, both my knees were already a beautiful purple.

And Guirong didn't even give me a hug.

October 22

<u>Gansu, Lanzhou</u>: I went for a good bike ride on the south side of the tracks. I had forgotten to tighten the rear fender brace screws; one fell out and the other was loose. So I started watching for a bike repairman.

I passed several that were busy, and then no more. Finally, I found an out-of-the-way guy who was packing up. I showed him my problem. He had a can full of old screws and nuts, carefully collected and saved. After looking at my bike, he dumped some out in his hand and selected two. I said no, too big. He went over to my bike while I sorted out smaller screws. His fit perfectly and he selected the best of the two, put it in, and then checked all the screws on the rear of the bike for tightness. I was worried about that, as his screwdriver tip was worn. But he was careful, held it straight, pushed hard, and didn't mess up any of the screws.

I asked him how much. He looked surprised, and finally said five *mao*. I had one *yuan*, and four *mao*, offered him the *yuan*, showing him the four *mao*. He refused the *yuan*, said four, and took the *ling qian* (small money). I thanked him and went on my way, no more rattle. Cheap for me, about 3¢, but I think a bit more than he usually charged.

December 6

On the train from <u>Urumqi</u> to <u>Lanzhou</u>, I got busted by the luggage police. A group of train cops were passing out tickets for excess baggage. My bike isn't really allowed, it's a little oversize, so they gave me a ticket to take to the head conductor. Cost me 42.3元 extra. It's the first time that has happened. Wonder how long before it happens again?

I was in car #5, and the conductor's office was in car #14, a long walk. Car #14 was hard seat, and full of young army guys in uniform. They and their officers were friendly but I played scared, holding my hands over my head. I said "*Da dao Meiguolao*" (Down with Americans, a cold war slogan). They all responded "*Pengyou, pengyou!*" (Friend, friend), and I shook a lot of hands. Some of the young soldiers knew a surprising amount of English.

2005

January 16

<u>Baise, Guangxi</u>: Tried something new, catching the express bus

195

from <u>Nanning</u>. I didn't disassemble and pack my bike. I asked the bus driver if I could put it in the luggage compartment assembled, with only the pedals and handlebars removed. Worked great, very easy, but it was a large bus and only half full. I went to the station, talked with the driver, went inside and bought my ticket, loaded my bike and stuff, and we were on our way twenty minutes after I arrived. Very easy and no extra charge.

September 26

<u>Xiamen</u>: Bought a new bicycle, a fairly nice 26" fifteen-speed Giant, 800元, US$100. I got 1.5" tires, wider than on my last one. I had the bike shop take off the popular knobby mountain bike tires and replace them with tires with smoother tread and a nice hard strip down the center. I think a basic bike like this costs around US$500 in America. Altogether, with a spare tube and two good steel U-locks, it cost me US$115. The next thing I did was to spray paint it ugly with a can of black paint I had already bought, and beat small dents in the fenders, I don't want thieves to want it. I painted the bike on the sidewalk in front of the shop, to their dismay and amusement. After they got into the swing of it, they started wheeling customers' bikes over, joking, asking me to paint them too.

Adriano's help was again very useful. He recommended the wider tires, although I was looking for narrow tires because that was what he had recommended before. He immediately chose this one for the wider tires and good rack, rejected immediately the two I'd selected, with good reasons. I was still following his advice from four years back, and hadn't considered the bike he chose this time. This one is much more modern, has excellent brakes, and incorporates some ideas from mountain bikes. It has aluminum wheels, the brakes are a new design with larger pads, frp (fiber reenforced plastic) arms (I still prefer metal). The handlebars are too low with the tall seat post I had installed, I need to do something about that. My new bike needs grease and adjustments and a trial fitting of the bag and panniers, also see if I need different tools.

September 27

Worked on my new bike most of today, hardly went out. Not much grease in the bearings, but on this bike, everything had been greased, if sparingly. The bearings in previous bikes were mostly dry. The front wheel was adjusted too tight, and way out of balance. I fixed the balance by judicious placement of two reflectors in the spokes. It took some time to get all the cables oiled and adjusted. It worked fine before I started, and now will work longer.

The bike doesn't fit in my old bag very well, as the rack is wider and longer and the frame slopes up a bit more in the front. I'll have a new bag made. Found a long U-lock, 65元, expensive but looks to be high quality, bought it. It can lock two bikes together, and locks my front wheel to the lower frame tube, my preferred way to lock but it takes a longer lock on this bike. Before I bought the lock, I test-fitted it and found two ways I can carry it fairly neatly. A friend pointed out that the brake levers and wheels still looked attractively shiny and new, so I bought a small file and scratched them up. It will take a little time for the bike to get dirty.

September 30

My new bag is finished. Cotton canvas again but untreated, a natural off-white. The guy showed me that the heavy nylon he had tore easily, and that the treated material also tears easily. This untreated stuff is much stronger (and more expensive). Working with him, we redesigned the bag so it will work better, completely enclose the bike with no gaps like the old one had, and he says the material won't shrink. He had the basic bag made when I returned in the evening, so I took the bike apart and packed it, tied it all up, and put the wheels on the bag. Together, we adjusted things, figured out where reinforcement patches needed to be added, how to sew on two sets of double handles in exactly the right places, and added the necessary loops for the luggage wheels. 160元 altogether with dinner thrown in, as his wife invited me to eat with them. I left the old bag on top of a trash can for someone to salvage.

October 7

At the Xiamen train station on my way to Beijing, it took me forty minutes for a leisurely packing job in the new bag, came out nicely. A small mistake where I chose to pack my bike: the place was near the freight pickup and consignment office, and several workers or managers came out and berated me, told me to put it back together and give it to them, that I wasn't allowed to take it on the train with me. I kept on packing and eventually they went away. Another location to avoid when packing, must keep my eyes open.

2006

January 25

The bus took 3.5 hours from Nanning to Guiping, very fast, nearly to <u>Guigang</u> on very good expressways. The bus, a big one, carried my bike easily. I removed the pedals and handlebars and lowered the seat. It went into the luggage compartment laid flat. The bus was a 52-passenger, full now during *Chunyun*, and everybody was carrying lots of stuff, gifts for their families. When I bought the ticket a few days ago, I asked for *da kuaiba*, emphasizing the "*da*" (big). I also told them I didn't want *xiao kuaiba*, again emphasizing the "*xiao*" (little). The luggage compartment was plenty big enough to accommodate my bike, much easier than disassembling it and packing it in the bag.

Safety

1988

April 6

Two weeks into my first visit to China, I feel no danger or threat to me or my belongings, even walking around in a strange city in the middle of the night.

June 17

<u>Luoyang, Henan</u>: Miss Betty, a college English teacher, and I spent yesterday on bicycles riding around the city and out into the countryside. The day before, I had looked at a wall along a street that puzzled me. The wall was massive with long shards of broken glass embedded in cement along the top. The gate was steel and locked with a padlock and chain. Some people used the gate, unlocking it and carefully relocking it. Others walked around the wall, as it simply ended thirty or forty feet either side of the gate. There was no fence, or attempt to prevent people from walking around it, rather than using the gate. I had seen similar things in other places in China. I stopped and asked Miss Betty about it. She smiled and said "Some people say the Chinese have a wall culture." I got no more explanation from her.

1991

December 10

<u>Dapeng, Guangdong</u>: Here and there around the construction site (a nuclear power plant) are guards in army uniforms with machine pistols. They are posted at gates that divide the site into sections. The gates all seem to have obvious and easy ways around them. Often, the

198

gate is only attached to ten or so feet of fence at either side. Clearly, from their expressions and body language, the guards want everyone to pass through the gates they control. We go any way we want, and ignore the guards. It seems people only pass through the gates if it is the most direct route to wherever they are going. No one seems to pay any attention at all to the guards. They look intimidating to me.

1992

January 20

Guangzhou: Had a pickpocket attempt on the Renmin Lu pedestrian bridge at Nanfang today. Three little girls, seven to ten years old, had their hands all over my pockets. I put my hands on my pockets, and one girl said "Sorry!" in English with a big smile. When I didn't smile back, they split. I assume there was an adult nearby, running them. It made me feel sad.

2000

January 22

Guangzhou: Thursday, Miyuki (a Japanese student majoring in Chinese language and culture in Japan and traveling in China as part of her course work) had her pocket picked in Qingping Market. She had 100 or 200元 in her jacket pocket, and then it was gone. She spent the rest of the day at the police station, filling out forms. She was angry and upset, mostly with herself. It was a foolish place to carry money. Next time she says she won't bother with the police.

February 29

Nanning, Guangxi: I have met *xiaotou* (thief). I went to *wangba* (Internet cafe) this morning after checking out of my hotel and leaving my bags at the desk. I was carrying my day pack, with dictionaries and phrase books, reading matter, maps, hairbrush, what I want on the train. At *wangba*, I put the bag down beside my chair. This net bar was classy and brightly lit, run by China Telecom, so I was careless. I did not put the bag in front of me, or between my feet, or hook the strap around my ankle, nothing. When I finished my email and got up to go, it was simply gone.

I gave the people there my card and the phone number of a friend. They will watch for it but I don't think it will be found. The thief will certainly be disappointed as there was no money in the bag, and little of value to anyone except me.

2001

August 3

Huhhot: A *Wujing* ("Armed Police", the civil army, a branch of the PLA [People's Liberation Army] concerned with things inside China) officer and I had supper and three beers together at a street restaurant with tables on the sidewalk. He said I was the same age as his father, so he called me "Baba". We were on our second beer when cops suddenly arrived with two dump trucks, and, amid loud protests, started throwing all the tables and chairs into the trucks. When the cops approached our table, he put on his uniform hat and the cops bypassed us. What a lot of muscle a hat has!

Soon, we were the only table left, an oasis of calm in the center of the sidewalk. When we finished, we carried our table to the side, one of the few tables the owners managed to keep. That'll teach them to set up a restaurant on the sidewalk without a permit. The street restaurants did make the sidewalk completely unusable, the way they were set up. People had to walk out into the street to get around them. I sympathize with both the cops and the food vendors, but I liked eating there.

August 11

In a new national "Strike Hard" campaign against crime, there are *Wujing* soldiers everywhere, three or more together and often on each corner of main intersections. They also patrol in small groups. They are armed with batons, some with electric "stun" capabilities. (Point the thing at someone and press the button: hot sparks race around the electrodes at the tip. The display is enough to calm most people right down; no need to actually shock them.) An occasional officer has a small pistol on his belt. "Armed Police" doesn't mean they carry and display guns, as it would in the USA.

These guys are young, extremely alert, well trained, and no-nonsense. They have no contact with the local police, to control corruption and prevent *guanxi* (connections). And they are all from outside the area, none are local, so they don't know anyone or have any local contacts. They often pull trucks off the road for impromptu safety inspections. Nobody is arguing or fighting near these guys. They mostly ignore me; I'm not what they are watching. If they pay any attention to me, it isn't obvious. But the *Wujing* are obvious, highly visible and meant to be.

The young *Wujing* officer I had dinner with a week ago told me seriously that the people liked and trusted them, but didn't like the regular police. When I ask my *Mengguzu* (Mongolian) friends about this, do they trust the *Wujing*, they say "Maybe...", neither agreeing or disagreeing.

2003

January 13

<u>Guangzhou</u>: I saw my lovely Japanese friend, Miyuki (now a Japanese language teacher at a major university here) last Saturday. She was robbed last fall; it has scrambled her life and her feelings for China. About five months ago she had gone to <u>Zhuhai</u> to stay with friends for two weeks, until her new place at the university was ready. They had an empty house and Miyuki was staying there. She had sent most of her things there by mail from her former city, all packaged up. She came back to the house one evening and noticed the door felt funny when she put the key in the lock. One of the robbers was still inside.

The frightened thief rushed out when she opened the door, knocking her aside with something in his hand, she thought a book. This terrified her but she wasn't hurt. She immediately called 110 (the emergency line to police) and three policemen arrived in only a few minutes. The police were kind to her and careful. More cops arrived and started searching the neighborhood. They took fingerprints, photos, and collected evidence. They caught the robbers a few weeks later, contacted her and told her they were professionals. They tied them to her robbery by fingerprints but didn't recover anything belonging to her.

She lost her laptop computer and all her disks (no other backups for two or three years). She lost her mobile phone, address book, clothes, papers, money, credit cards. Only a few books and clothes were left. She lost three or four years of work that was in her computer, and they took the box of disks because it was packed with the laptop. She canceled the credit cards, no problem. And one of them had insurance, 30% of original purchase cost, for the computer, phone, and a couple of other things. All the original receipts were in Japan, and her parents sent them to her. She was carrying her passport so didn't lose that.

She is making better backups now, anyway, and makes two sets, one for her office and one for her flat. Miyuki thinks this is her last year here. She doesn't want to stay in China any more. I understand her feeling, as two robberies I experienced nearly thirty years ago have left scars lasting to this day. And mine weren't so devastating as hers.

March 7

I was in China for all of the first Gulf War, here for the spy plane incident, and here on September 11. During the spy plane incident, and in the aftermath of the "mistaken" bombing of the Chinese embassy, I never had any Chinese person direct anger at me. Many told me that they were angry at the American government, but over and over again I was told "We are not angry with American people".

Why is it that so many US citizens seem to equate people with their governments, and Chinese citizens seem able to be so generous?

March 20

<u>Baise</u>: Walking around last night, I got picked up. Four little girls spotted me and ran up to try their English. (My name is____, what's yours? How are you? This is eraser, that is desk.) Three of them were ten, and one was twelve. I said good night to them, and walked on. Half a block later they caught up with me, grabbed my hands from both sides and walked with me for half an hour practicing their English, and me, my Chinese. Most adults smiled at us warmly as we walked down the dark streets. The *fuwuyuan* at my hotel seemed a little worried when we all showed up at 10:00 P.M., but the little girls wanted to see where I lived even though I had said good night to them several times. I said goodbye to them in the lobby. They were disappointed as they really wanted to see my room, but the manager looked worried. So I gave each of them my name card and said good night. 10:00 P.M. seemed pretty late to be out wandering around with a stranger and I was worried that their parents might be worried.

First time that's happened to me on this trip. I felt a bit strange and uncomfortable, as though people would be suspicious of me with four little girls. I'm Americanized. I hope they don't get in any trouble for disappearing with me until so late.

March 23

Yesterday afternoon while I was trying to take a nap, all four little girls came back and crowded into my room, wanting me to go out and play, walk around, whatever. The *fuwuyuan* came with them as she was worried that the girls were a nuisance, unwelcome, and she might need to send them away. I really didn't want to see them right then, just wanted to sleep. Oh well, some things cannot be denied. So I stood there in my underpants and visited with them. The *fuwuyuan* wandered away, having decided they weren't bothering me. The girls didn't care that I was only wearing underpants, and the *fuwuyuan* didn't care. I begged off going out right then, made a date to go to the park with them today and went back to bed. So they are going to an English corner with me this morning.

One of the things I enjoy in China is being around children with nobody worrying about it. In the USA, somebody might call the cops, and the kids probably wouldn't even smile at me anyway. Much less come up to speak with me. And having four little girls in my hotel room: unacceptable. The kids I have contact with in the USA are the children of friends.

The little girls showed up almost on time, pretty early for them on a Saturday morning. We went off in motor *sanlunche* to the park. The littlest girl was in a bad mood and left us before we found our ride. Don't know about her, she was sour the other evening too.

At the park, the three girls led me around from bench to bench. Each one consisting of a pair of carved stone animals holding the stone slab seat of the bench between them. Many different kinds of stone, and many kinds of animals: cats, squirrels, bear, deer, ducks, horses, mice, camels, pandas, all nicely done. As the girls towed me around, they named the different creatures for me in Chinese. The park has a huge fountain at the entrance, very loud when gushing, a great mass and mist of water and white sound. These new public places are very nice, human, human scale, and very popular with the local people. The girls knew all the benches, and where to find the different animals.

A lot is being invested in these kinds of public places around China, everywhere I've been the last few years. Big cities, such as Beijing; small cities like Baise; and the county-sized places (*xian*). I don't see these parks in the really small towns (*cun*), but they don't have much of anything in the way of dedicated public spaces, maybe because the countryside is all around. More and more of these parks have nice public exercise machines that are popular and free. The first time I visited Baise in 1998, this park was a miserable place with an entrance fee. Now it is free, popular, and nice, with the big fountain and the wonderful carved stone benches. Baise is a little famous for all the different colors and kinds of stone quarried in the mountains nearby, so the benches represent something local.

When the English corner started, a special public event run by the English club of the local medical college, the little girls got bored. The two ten-year-olds went home, but the twelve-year-old sat on the ground and waited. The English club took me to a nice lunch afterward and included her. She was delighted. Then I took her to her home and went back to my hotel for a nap.

Kids in China seem a protected species. They run around everywhere by themselves, talk to me, follow me around, and adults mostly smile warmly, "Look at the children having fun!" I like this freedom, it's wonderful. They, the same as American kids, are taught not to talk to strangers, but they are given rules to judge by. Strangers are fine, it's the dangerous strangers they are supposed to avoid. And all the adults seem to watch all the children.

Hotels

1988

April 6

Guiping, Guangxi: Last night when I got off the boat, I was confused. We came in at a different dock than the one I spotted on the tiny map I found in Wuzhou, so I got lost trying to follow the map by counting intersections. The streets were dimly lit and muddy so I was spending most of my attention dodging mud holes. When it got a lot darker (street lights further apart), I retraced my steps to the dock and showed the name of the hotel, written in Chinese by a student from Guiping whom I had met in Wuzhou, to a pedestrian who pointed the opposite direction.

I wisely decided to follow the pointing, and soon found myself on a slightly busier street. Still confused, I stopped under a street lamp and hailed a couple of young men walking the same direction. They looked at my notes, also pointed on down the street the way I was heading and indicated they would walk with me to the hotel. By the time we arrived at the hotel a half mile later, we were a group of eight or ten excited and happy young men, all talking loudly, with me saying regularly "*Wo budong*" (I don't understand), the approximate limit of my Chinese. The young man I had hailed on the street filled out my hotel registration forms for me, seeming to enjoy himself greatly, both amused by me and truly helpful. Very helpful they were, and I needed it.

The room is clean, the nicest I've had, with blankets, sheets, towel, soap, tea, cups, and thermos of hot water. The bed is the usual, a thin ≈1/2 inch cotton pad over boards (which is ideal for my back, just like my bed at home), two chairs and an end table. In bed, I watched Chinese TV for a half hour. *Gongfu* (Kung Fu), cowboys and Indians Chinese-style. I'm sure Ronnie Reagan didn't act in any worse films. No wonder everyone likes to watch foreigners — it's more entertaining than TV.

April 24

Guiyang, Guizhou: Looking for a hotel — first one at 50元, next

33, then 30, finally one for 9元 FEC. For the first time I am sharing a room with Chinese people. The hotel didn't want to accept me, but with the help of an engineer I met, a Mr. Zen, I got admitted. I'm a poor student at Beijing University, by the fiction he evolved for me.

I share the room with two men who are nice, friendly, and have no English. One is from Tianjin, the other from Shanghai (they pointed out their homes on my map). Both are a long way from home. They like the TV full volume, offer me everything they have, almost won't accept any refusals, smoke steadily, and spit sunflower seed hulls all over the floor, along with matches, cigarette butts, and other assorted litter. Just how it is. Good thing it doesn't bother me too much or I'd find myself in a 30-50元 room. I watched a TV commercial for steel Georgia buggies with a trip dump box. Then an ad for a dual-spindle lathe. A bit different from prime time commercials in the US.

I watched, with my roommates, the *Gongfu* series that seems to have everyone around here hooked. It takes place sometime in the past. One standard part has the old master doing exercises to keep his fingers tough. He makes many fast passes in the air, with impressive whistling sound effects, and then, punch, punch, punch, jabs his fingers in a pot of sand. When he stops and turns away, the sand quietly smokes. The heroine is a beautiful girl, whose hair and dress is always perfect and undisturbed. She also does her exercises with amazing sound effects. She regularly stands off whole hordes of enemies who come at her from all sides, with all kinds of weapons. She tosses them every which direction, and never is her hair so much as disturbed. She regularly rescues the hero, a young master. He's tied up with huge ropes, and as soon as she vanquishes the hordes, she cuts him free and then acts demure and helpless. She seems to love him dearly, and he's a little scared of her. She beats everybody up, including him every once in a while. He doesn't seem very bright. *Gongfu* cowboys and Indians, good guys and bad guys.

June 8

<u>Gongxian, Henan</u>: This is a "sort of" hotel. It's sort of reasonable, sort of clean, sort of cheap. I have a single room with a double bed and a mirrored wardrobe (my first on all counts in China, and none of them important, compared to a cleaner toilet), almost the nicest room here. The best ones across the hall have TV, but are otherwise the same. When I checked in, I was offered a room for 20元, said too much, was offered one for 10元, and accepted. I wonder if the next step would have been 5元.

When I arrived here a few days ago, they (almost everyone in the hotel all together) took me to a different room, a double. I showed them my picture book of home. Four of us sat around on both beds having great fun, and then in walked the man. My album was closed and given back with thanks. Everyone sat on their hands and looked at the floor while the man read them what I think was the riot act. About fraternizing with guests, I guess.

So I handed him the book. He couldn't resist it and everything calmed down. He wanted me to take a better room, I said too much money. The young girl who had a little written English found "same," and "a bargain" in my dictionary. So off we went to the fourth floor, this room. 10元 is too much, this is the poorest, smelliest hotel I've been in yet, but the room is relatively clean. No showers or washroom of any sort in the hotel. There is a tap on the floor below me, where I can fill a basin to take to my room for washing. No provisions for heat that I see, this place must be cold in the winter, but it sure is hot now. There is a ceiling fan in every room and it helps to have some air movement.

June 15

I made it to <u>Luoyang</u> long after dark, checked my pack at the station, and carrying only a small bag, set out to look for a hotel. I hired a man with a three-wheel motorbike sidecar to run me around. First hotel, 27元, second *meiyou* (don't have), third 120元, fourth 25元, and the fifth, 10元. So here I am.

Writing this just now, a guy from another room interrupted me. He burst into my room and turned on my TV, very excited. He tuned in a boxing match saying *"Meiguo ren, Meiguo ren!"* (American, American!). My TV set thankfully didn't work well, so he ran back to his room to watch the rest of the match. Earlier, he had dropped in to watch me writing.

1991

January 31

<u>Beijing</u>: This hotel is the pits. It has a dispirited staff, bad morale, bad housekeeping, and the plumbing is lousy. My bed is only US$2.05 a night, so perhaps I'm being too critical. I got in late last night, long after curfew[1], and found the hotel locked up. I pounded on the gate until a young man let me in.

---

[1] There was a street curfew in Beijing in early 1991, left over from 6/4, the Tian'anmen incident. It's the only time I've experienced a curfew in China.

He was curious about me, so I gave him my card. He saw the line about precision explosives work (a past career of mine), pointed at the line and then at me. I said, yes, I did that. Ha, he is a blaster too. (Working in a hotel because he has some English.) We talked shop for half an hour before I went to bed, mostly in English. He wanted me to blow up the hotel, both the old and new buildings. I'm to let him know first, so he can get out safely. I don't think he's too fond of his job.

February 15

Luoyang: Last night, Yang (a young middle school English teacher who's been helping me with my business) told me I should stay in a better class of hotel next time. He says the businessmen I deal with would have more respect for me, be more favorably impressed. Staying at the *Youyi Binguan* (Friendship Hotel) would have cost me about US$200 more for the two weeks I've been here. Mohammed, a small businessman from Bangladesh, says a penny saved... if you earn $1000 and spend it, it is nothing. However, Yang is smart, and he's trying to teach me about China. He has what he laughingly calls a "smooth mouth". He has a brain and is a good negotiator as well.

December 9

Dapeng, Guangdong: Not too bad, this hotel. The worst bit is the lumpy mattress. 10元 seems high, but I'm in Shenzhen County, and near a big construction site. The toughie bikers, *liumang, wulai,* are always trying to pimp for me and when I don't respond, they mince around fluttering their eyes, flipping their wrists, and speaking in falsetto. Not fun.

Their motorcycles are mostly Honda 125s. Helmets are standard, so they must be required by law, and the law enforced. With a *motuo* (motor, motorcycle) they are in business. A bus pulls in, 2元 fare, and the door is mobbed by a dozen *motuo*, all yelling, all trying to pick up riders, the people getting off the bus, for a short trip somewhere for which they expect 5元. This is not "pick up the tourist" (because there aren't any) but picking up Chinese riders. It seems to be macho to have a *motuo*, macho to be the most insistent, loudest, first to crowd around the door. All this makes it difficult and unpleasant to get off a bus.

One toughie offered to procure me a girl, complete with graphic finger gestures so there was no chance I misunderstood the great thing he was offering. Two old ladies came up right then, briefly negotiated with him, and climbed aboard his *motuo* for a ride somewhere. He was polite and respectful to them; very different from the way he had been behaving with me.

At least most of the Hondas have good mufflers and are quieter than their drivers.

This is a rather unpleasant town. A thousand or so foreign workers, plus all of the Chinese temporary workers from other parts of China, most of whom mix little with the local community, at a major construction project — plus, it's a part of Shenzhen, that weird economic swamp, an SEZ (Special Economic Zone). All this creates an unpleasant atmosphere, but it is certainly beautiful country around here, and it has been fun and interesting, meeting some of the temporary workers in the evenings when they are off work.

1992

January 6

Wenling, Zhejiang: I've been rousted by the police. When I got here, a young man guided me to a budget hotel. I got a room and went out walking for a while, but felt a bit intimidated by the size of the crowd I drew. I've been too long in Guangzhou, a big city used to foreigners.

So I went back to the hotel, and then came the knocks: first, a man from the hotel. He looked at my passport and asked many questions I couldn't understand or answer. He was wearing a jeans jacket with a plastic brand tag on the front, "WORKER – Your Brand". He left and came back later with a police cadre (ranking officer) who insisted I move to the Wenling *Binguan*, a fancier hotel. I said *"taigui"* (too expensive), he said *"buxing"*. I said *"wo budong"* (I don't understand). We fooled around for almost an hour, he telling me I had to leave and me saying either I liked it here, or that I lacked the ability to understand.

An hour and a half later I was awakened by another policeman who let himself into my room. He was upset and worried, with much shouting and arm waving. He didn't seem well-educated, as he couldn't use my Chinese-English dictionary. But he still managed to make it clear that I was to leave, and I made it clear to him that I liked it here. The hotel staff who had followed him seemed worried. He had a bunch of registration forms in English. I have no idea where he found them. After about an hour of him frowning loudly and me smiling stupidly (I'm sorry, I can't understand, I'm a stupid but polite foreigner), and two more visits to my room with other people who didn't help any, he finally let me go back to bed after he told me firmly that I was to be packed and ready to leave the next morning at 8:00 A.M., that he would come for me at 8:15. He made the times clear by repeatedly setting my alarm clock and showing it to me.

The police cadre (the first guy) returned later, but finally relented and allowed me to sleep here. He will meet me at 8:15 A.M. tomorrow and put me on a bus to somewhere else. To sleep.

January 7

Waiting for the chief, the cadre from yesterday: the hotel was upset when I went out to find breakfast. They wanted me to stay in my room and wait. I assured them I only wanted to eat and would be right back. They were sure relieved when I returned. The chief arrived right on the minute. I was packed and ready like a good boy, and he made it clear that he was going to set me on my path. We marched off at a brisk pace. He tried to lead me like a docile prisoner and I tried to walk abreast or a little ahead of him, like an equal. We dodged around bikes and pedestrians, gaining and losing ground by adroit maneuvers. He turned into a courtyard, which I assumed was the police station. We went up a few flights of stairs and into an office. I sat and was given tea, always the first thing. People started coming in, presenting me their cards, and I gave them mine. What do you know, I was in an FTC (foreign trade company)! Finally, a young man appeared who spoke a little English, very rough. The chief was gone, I hadn't noticed when he left. The English speaker, Hu, told me they'll take me in a car to the factory that makes the patcher sewing machines I'm here to buy.

January 8

Yesterday, Hu took me to a different hotel. It's a jumble of old creaking two story buildings with wooden floors. I got a huge (12' x 16') room with a nice hard bed, three chairs, a desk, two end table cabinets, a dresser, a black and white TV, and a wash stand with basin. And of course thermoses of hot water, cups, and tea. All this for less than I was paying at the other place. Everybody kept telling me the other hotel wasn't safe. It seemed fine but this one is even cheaper, so, okay! I thought they were trying to ram me into a more expensive hotel. I don't really know what was going on, so what's new?

Hu, the interpreter at the FTC, tells me Wenling is a closed county, an area closed to foreigners. That's why the policeman was upset, how about that? And the hotel I'm in now is owned by the government. All problems solved. What does an FTC do in an area where foreigners aren't allowed? Often, when officials are worried about me, I don't know why and can't find out. I apologize and forget about it.

February 21

Guangzhou: After dinner, Lai took me walking. He's a mechanical engineer and a sales representative for a Japanese excavator manufacturer. We walked through a red light district west of the train station. There were heavily made up girls standing around everywhere, and many small hotels.

In the same area a bit farther down the street were many country people who come to Guangzhou seeking riches. He called them the "Blind Flow", and said this was a literal translation of the Chinese words used commonly to talk about this urban migration. One person comes from a village to Guangzhou, makes some money and goes home, telling what he did. Then all of his friends go to Guangzhou, hoping to do exactly the same thing. No changes are made, it's done by formula. Get to Guangzhou, stand in exactly the same spot the friend stood in, and wait for someone to come and offer a job, or however it worked.

For blocks around the station, there were people sleeping under bridges or on the street, or standing and walking aimlessly. We passed a flop house. I assumed it was cheap and run by the government. Lai said, "Let's go see", so we went in for a few minutes. It consisted of beds side by side, as many as could be crammed into a large room, with narrow aisles between. Lai looked around and spoke to a few people. We walked on and he told me a bed there cost 10元. The flop house was private and not trying to help people, but only to get as much of their money as possible quickly, before someone else got it. Pretty bleak.

He said that if one person got a bed, others follow and also get beds, the "Blind Flow". I said that hotels were much cheaper only a little way from here, that private rooms were available for 10元. Not near the station, said Lai. And the formula, always the formula: stay near the station and riches will come to you.

November 13

Hangzhou, Zhejiang: At my hotel I couldn't find the *fuwuyuan*, the woman with the keys. The other girls looked for her, but they weren't able to find her either. This gets old. She's never around and I can't have my own room key. I came back again after ten minutes, still no keys. So I quietly slipped the room's lock with my American driver's license, and started my laundry. About that time, the *fuwuyuan* showed up. She was angry and demanding to know how I got into my room. I played stupid and pretended I didn't understand her. She angrily insisted so finally I showed her my license, and mimed a demonstration on a door. She looked unhappy, a bit puzzled and huffy.

I finished my laundry in the bathroom down the hall, and found my door locked, again. So I found her and asked her to unlock it. She came with me but refused to take out her keys. She wanted me to show her how I opened it. I did, and then she wanted to try it. I showed her the problems, such as catching the edge of the card on the screws, and she finally managed to get it to work herself. I showed her some simple things easily done to make it difficult to unlock the door this way. She went off a bit stiffly, but seemed pleased. Later, I asked her if I was *liumang*, a hoodlum. She replied, *"bushi"* (no). I guess I'm okay. And she seems to be around now when I want the door unlocked. More than one way to skin a cat.

1998

March 6

In <u>Guigang</u>, I found a promising looking hotel and went in to register. They refused and tried to send me on up the street. A lot of small hotels unused to dealing with foreign visitors will say "no rooms". So I waited politely a bit and asked, <u>could</u> they give me a bed? Yes, so they eventually showed me a room for 80元, I said too much, so up to the forth floor, a room a bit smaller, 50元, okay. That's a bit over $6 per night.

I've got a nice bathroom and shower with hot water for four hours in the evening. Two rooms, a big color TV, four thermoses of hot water, fifteen cups, six padded chairs, a couch, double bed, a bar, and several assorted tables and pieces of furniture. Oh, and a balcony and air conditioner in each room. I could have a party or small reception here, it's big enough. The room could handle twenty people, but there wouldn't be enough cups.

On my way back after supper, I looked up at the front of my hotel from the other side of the street. There, in English, "Rich Gentleman's Night Club" in huge neon outlined letters. And I picked up (got picked up by) a girl who grabbed my wrist and asked me if I wanted to eat. I said I already had and was full. She asked where I was going and I indicated the hotel. She said "Okay!" and started into the hotel at a fast clip, still holding my wrist. I dragged my feet, stopping her, and tried to explain I didn't need or want whatever. She shrugged and trotted off. I guess I can reach my own conclusions. It's definitely not an ordinary hotel.

March 12

Yulin: I got back to my hotel after midnight. The place was locked up, but the staff wasn't in bed yet. I think they were waiting for me to come in. This morning I got kicked out. The PSB (Public Security Bureau) had told them they could not house a foreign visitor. I told them the PSB could talk directly to me if they wanted me to move and that I was happy there. They said this would make trouble for them. So a friend (a Mongolian businessman I met in the hotel who speaks English) helped me find a new hotel and negotiated the price down for me.

My new hotel, the *Yulin Shi Ying Binguan*, had the room price posted at 100元 but I'm paying 50元. I'll have to try to learn how to do that. I'm in an older building (but not the oldest) and it's quiet. The new building was built to house Deng Xiaoping when he visited the south about ten years ago, I'm told.

I told the first hotel when I left that I liked them and the hotel, and wanted to stay. They appreciated that and said, "See you next time", when I said goodbye.

March 22

Nanning: Last night, the *fuwuyuan* (floor woman at the hotel) decided to take care of me. At 7:30, she burst in and found me typing at my computer, as I had been for several hours. She read me the riot act (in Chinese, of course), said I needed to go eat dinner and had been taking too much cold medicine. She made me put on a jacket before she herded me out the door. When I got back, she made sure I knew where the padded quilt was (it's been much too hot to need it but it's suddenly turned colder, and I needed the jacket she had made me put on). She wasn't satisfied that I knew where the quilt was; she stood there and watched until I put it on the bed. Then she shut the window, smiled, bid me good night, and left.

She was right, it was past time for dinner and the way I'm feeling (a bad cold), it's easy to forget. I don't have the energy to deal with finding a place to eat, and ordering, and that makes it take longer to get better.

April 11

I arrived back in Nanning last night, and checked back into the Nanning *Tiedao Binguan*, the same floor but a different room. Immediately the *fuwuyuan* brought me a cup I had abandoned when I was here before, and asked me if I had forgotten it. I thanked her and told her I didn't want it. My new room doesn't have a balcony, but she told me I could have my old one with the balcony today, if I wanted it.

2000

January 22

I'm settled in a hotel in <u>Wuzhou</u>, <u>Guangxi</u>. A bit fancy for my taste, 40元, but the hotel I've stayed in before, the "Yuan Jing", seems to be gone, taken out by the ramp and road construction for a new bridge. Work was starting on the new bridge across the mouth of the Guijiang (the river branch to the north) when I was here two years ago. Now, it is nearly finished, a fine beautiful concrete arch bridge with a suspended concrete deck. I went across it with my bicycle at dusk, after the work had slowed down. I stopped to talk to a man, maybe a worker or engineer, but probably a local stroller. He kept asking me about "*Jiu Jin Shan*", a term I recognized, knew I had learned but couldn't remember. Finally, it clicked: "Old Gold Hills", an old name for San Francisco. He was asking me with a lot of pride if this new bridge was as fine as the Golden Gate. This one is smaller, but as fine. It will be a nice centerpiece for the city.

2001

May 7

<u>Beijing</u>: This is a funny hotel, the Underground Hotel of the Geosciences Institute. It's a converted and redecorated bomb shelter and I'm on the top level, above all the heavy sealed doors. I have a room with three beds and a window, about six inches of it above grade. It's a private room because I'm paying for all the beds. Certainly not a tourist spot, but it's great for me, 40元, about $5 a night, a bargain in Beijing. A drawback is no shower; I must wash out of a basin. Foreigners aren't allowed to stay here but the manager doesn't seem to care, he refused to look at my passport. Ignorance is bliss; I guess he could argue he didn't know I was a foreigner. Most of the guests are Chinese students in short term language classes (six weeks to six months) in various universities nearby, sort of a dormitory. I have an English corner in my room every evening. With the two extra beds, ten can sit.

May 29

<u>Wuyuan, Nei Menggu</u>: There was a bus into town, which is about thirty km from the train station. Some others who got off the train guided me through ranks of taxis with pushy drivers. Half a block behind the taxis was a small local bus, cheap. I wouldn't have found it

213

without help. In town, an especially helpful woman, one of the ones who had guided me to the bus, walked me to the door of a hotel and waited long enough to be sure I got a bed.

May 31

Today, a young policewoman came to the hotel with alien registration forms. She didn't understand anything about them and wanted my name in Chinese. I tried to explain I didn't have a Chinese name and in any case, my name had to be the same as on my passport. She panicked and panicked everyone else. She wouldn't read my visa, which is in Chinese and the most important thing. It was a stupid encounter. I finally left to go buy some tissue and detergent. When I came back a few minutes later she was gone, but everyone else in the hotel was still panicked. I had a headache, which made me impatient with the whole game. I'm usually polite, and say sorry, sorry, sorry, I don't walk out.

This hotel is a funny place. It's clean, with many employees. A Shanghai man in a nearby business asked me if I knew the police were watching me. He said my hotel wasn't allowed to take foreigners. He thought it would be okay if I were doing business, but traveling and writing: not okay. Maybe I'm the talk of the town.

Anyway, the hotel: my large and comfortable room has two beds, 10-foot ceilings, and 7 1/2 ft. door openings. It's bright, 2/3 of the west wall is window, almost to the ceiling. Good ventilation. Hot water (plenty) is from a coal-fired boiler next to the showers down the hall. A friendly old man tends it, and cleans the toilets and showers. The room has fake (contact paper with wooden moldings) plywood wainscoting, and a nice ceramic tile floor that is fake parquet. A few minutes' study allowed me to find a repeat of the grain pattern in the fake plywood. Fooled me at first, it even has fake water stains. I may be the first foreign guest the hotel has had. Even with the police trouble, they want to take photographs with me. It's arranged for tomorrow morning, 10:00 AM, when the light is just right. A professional photographer is coming, we'll move many chairs out onto the sidewalk in front, and the whole staff will pose with me. The manager says they want to redecorate the lobby and will use the photos. It was the boiler-tender's idea, and he's arranging it all. Hard to say what the pecking order is in a place like this.

June 8

<u>Linhe</u>, 5:00 P.M.: I got ready to take a shower and wash my hair,

but the shower, located on a different floor, was occupied. There is only one shower for two huge floors, thirty to fifty rooms, but better than no shower, like the underground hotel in Beijing. They have serious water pressure problems. The fifth time I went down, the shower was free but there was no water. They say "this evening". Darn. And I thought it was the perfect time, dinnertime and not too busy.

9:45 P.M., I've had my shower, washed my hair, and done my laundry. There is not a single hook or wire to hang anything on, not even in the shower. What are you supposed to do with your clothes? Where do you hang your towel to dry? The staff is nice, the hotel is reasonably clean, but it's like nobody ever tried to live in it.

July 9

<u>Erlian</u>: Last night, passing the restaurant where I've been having dinner, I saw two pretty *laowai* (foreign) girls. I backed up and went in to speak to them. They were young English women on their way to a few weeks' volunteer job in a Mongolian orphanage. They weren't happy with their hotel so I showed them mine. An hour later, the *fuwuyuan* came knocking, asking me to come to the lobby. They were there, trying to check in. They had got scared at their hotel and jumped ship, abandoning 100元 they had paid. I helped them get checked in.

Another knock at my door, a man this time, insisting I go up with him to the girls' room. So up I went, with him and the *fuwuyuan*. The man was upset and the young women told me he was the man who had frightened them. I told him they were afraid of him, and he seemed dumbfounded. I finally worked out that he wanted their copy of the *fapiao* (receipt) for his hotel. They dug it out, gave it to him, and he left. The *fuwuyuan* stayed through all of this. She knew there was possible trouble brewing. After the man left, I spent an hour talking to them, getting their minds into a different track. I sure didn't know what was going on. They seemed practical and levelheaded, but very young and scared.

August 1

<u>Huhhot</u>: I'm having an argument with my hotel, the *Beiyuan*. They want 50元 per night for my crappy room, even after a drain pipe leaked all over my bed, waking me by dripping stinky water on me. The total is 300元 this morning, but I'm only willing to pay them 180元. The *fuwuyuan* work hard and are nice, but the management stinks like the drain water. They certainly don't spend anything on maintenance, such as fixing the clogged drains that make the place stink, and make life

miserable for the *fuwuyuan*. This place raises my blood pressure, makes me angry for the same reasons I dislike the "hole" in <u>Guangzhou</u>, a "youth hostel".

I'll try the tourist administration with a complaint, and will plan on paying when I leave. I'll give them what I think is fair, but be prepared to pay what they are demanding and forget about it. Difficult, I'm angry, but it's not worth spoiling my week. So, some theatrics: I made the mess on the other bed (I changed beds after the pipe leaked on me) a bit worse, made it fresh again with a touch of pee for smell and tea for color. The *fuwuyuan*, who have been nice through all this, tell me I ought to pay only 25元 and have called downstairs. I'll see. I made sure they understood I wasn't mad at them, only the people at reception.

August 2

Last night, I resolved the argument. Ulan, a *Mengguzu* (Mongolian minority) friend, called Mr. Baier, also a *Mengguzu*, at the tourist board. She says he is a kind man and that he will call or come to my room. I waited for an hour, and then the desk called me to come down. They wanted me to pay the full amount and were implacable. I said I would pay a fair price, but not 300元. The manager came out and I told them Mr. Baier was coming, just wait. The manager pretended he didn't know whom I was talking about. Then he told me they would accept 200元, and I said again I will pay a fair price, but not that much. We finally agreed on 175元, shortly before Mr. Baier was to arrive. We also agreed I would move to a single room tomorrow, 30元, 60% of what they had originally wanted. So it's settled, 50元 for the first night, and 29元 since then. I wanted the single room when I arrived, but they said "*meiyou*". I've now got what I wanted and have paid what I should have paid, but I sure used up a lot of emotional energy.

Wow, for two days of fighting and passionate arguments, I saved about US$15. I guess it was worth it for the principle of the matter. And, if I stay here for another week or two, I'll save a bit. Actually, the $2.50/day I argued for is 20% of my total daily cost in China, including travel.

August 5

The girls on my floor, the *fuwuyuan*, were delighted when I won my argument with the management and reception, but sorry I moved to a different floor.

Boy, do I get ugly looks now if the woman at reception catches sight of me. She and the manager (jerks, and probably skimming any overcharges they get from foreign visitors) are angry they lost the argument and face. It's a crappy hotel and nearly as expensive as any place I stay in China, even in the large expensive cities. I should still talk to the tourist board man, as the hotel makes it hard for backpackers. They have budget-priced small single rooms such as the one I have now, but they tell foreign visitors *meiyou* (don't have). Perhaps I have adjusted that a little, but I think I only made them mad. I did make the *fuwuyuan* happy.

The single rooms are a little strange: go to the seventh floor by elevator, down a corridor into a different wing, and up stairs to the eighth floor, toilet on seven, and shower on six. Inconvenient, but it smells better and they have many rooms. They ought to offer travelers the choice.

August 29

Lanzhou, Gansu: At 7:00 A.M. this morning, two unconnected Americans arrived in my three-bed room and confused my packing a bit. The first was a young man from Boston, been in China for a week or two. He had studied a couple of semesters of Chinese in a college in Ohio. An okay guy. Next a young woman arrived, bubbly, full of crap, wanting to know about Lhasa. I said I had been to Ge'ermu, and she said "Is it as shitty a place as I've heard and read?" I said it was an ordinary Chinese city, full of foreign visitors on their way to Lhasa, all with the idea it was a lousy place. Whew, glad I was leaving in minutes. I don't think I could have put up with her for very long.

September 15

Nanning, Guangxi: It was hot last night so, since I had the three-bed room to myself I went to sleep naked on the bamboo mat, something I almost never do in China, but it was comfortable. Sure enough, about 11:00 P.M. the *fuwuyuan* opened the door and turned on the lights to let in two new roommates. At least they were guys.

2002

June 25

Nearly to Beijing and the struggle to get off the train and into a hotel. I hope the hostel has a bed, and I remember how to find it. It's late and I just want a bed. The underground hotel is halfway across the city.

The youth hostel (there are a few branches of the International Youth Hostel in China now) was where I remembered and the same price as last year, 60元 w/o card for a bed in a six-bed room. Showers are as bad as I remembered them. The drains still don't work, so you must stand ankle-deep in dirty water. The hostel is attached to a big hotel, and used as training for new workers, I think.

June 26

After one night, I moved to the underground hotel at *Dizhi Daxue*, again 40元 for a three-bed room, all mine. Same room as last year, 007, I like the number. The hotel is filled with students from many parts of China, most studying English in short courses, also the same.

July 7

I see "Adam and Eve" sex boutiques all around, although I haven't seen one in *Haidian* (the university district). They feature displays of vibrators and fancy condoms in the windows, with sexy pictures and an opaque partition that gives shy customers privacy while they look at the goods. Mei Chan, a European-born Chinese working in Beijing, says the Chinese people she has asked consider the shops and products natural.

July 12

Huhhot: I spent more than an hour making the rounds of other hotels. This one is near perfect, just what I want, the third place in three days. I've finally got a keeper. I have a north-facing room (no direct sun), fourth floor, phone in the hall, shower and toilet down the hall, 50 元. If it was 30-35元, it would be perfect. It's all *Mengguzu*, Mongolian folks running it. They were friendly and didn't want to see my passport but said they could have foreign guests. Nice hard bed, shower with hot water all the time, clean and friendly and is located on a little side street near *Neida* (Inner Mongolia University).

July 13

The hotel is run by the government of a prefecture NE of here. I'm sure they don't really have a license to have foreign guests, as they weren't interested in my passport. It's the cleanest place I've ever stayed in in China, with the possible exception of some private homes. The floor is so clean I could eat off it, clear to the back corners under the bed. And it's friendly. Yesterday, one of the young girls wanted to finish my laundry for me. I said I could do it, and finished my Levi's, turning them inside out to dry. I came back later and they were gone. When I returned late in the evening, she brought them to me dry, turned right side out and neatly folded, maybe even pressed.

August 16

Urumqi, Xinjiang: This hotel is owned by the army and has big tour groups, mostly Chinese, with suites of rooms, tour buses, set meals, fruit in the rooms, and other goodies. No fruit in my room though, a shared five-bed room. It has nothing except rotating people.

The toilets and wash rooms are clean, but on different floors and some distance away. The closest one is usually busy with the hotel girls washing and doing laundry. The shower is in the basement of a different building and costs 5元. This is the first place I've stayed where the shower costs extra. It seems to be located in the brothel of the hotel, and comes complete with a room that has a bed and pictures of naked ladies on the walls. I take my shower in midmorning when it's quiet, only a few tired girls lounging around. There is plenty of hot water, good pressure, and a good shower head.

2003

March 18

Baise: I have a huge room with toilet and shower complete with a demand hot water heater. It has a big window and is fairly quiet, except for a clutch of pool tables under the window. So far, they have been quiet by about 11:30 P.M.. I'll see how that goes. There are two beds, they asked 25元 for the room, but I gave the manager 100元 for five days. It's a new *zhaodaisuo*, I'd guess it's been open less than six months. The building is barely finished.

April 9

This *zhaodaisuo* is mostly okay, but little things irritate me. The owner is trying to save money. They only make hot water for the thermoses once a day, and many people staying here complain. Only the owner can make the phone available for calls out, for pay with a meter. The girls aren't trusted to do it. I don't think she (the owner) will keep good workers; it's too embarrassing for them.

April 13

Guangzhou: I bargained the price down with reception at the hostel. They let me pay for another day at 150元, but insisted there was no discount from the posted 320元 after the big trade fair starts. And how much would I be willing to pay, they asked?

I said I'd give them 200元, 1000元 for five days. They said "Impossible!" and "Maybe you can talk with the manager". The price is up because of the Guangzhou Export Commodities Fair. All prices in Guangzhou go up, but since it is also the time of SARS, there are few foreigners here and little business. We eventually agreed on 200元 /night for a week's stay. The place is mostly empty. I'm renting a big double room as I'm going to be helping an American friend who is coming for the show. It's well outside my range.

April 27

Jun, an old friend, thinks the hostel may be closed the next time I come. Their business is sure bad; the stupid greedy manager treats the workers badly and also treats the guests badly. He irritates regular customers and doesn't get rid of bad workers. They are mostly family of his friends, I think. I've disliked him since I first met him a dozen years or more ago. The hostel has gotten fancier and more expensive and has at the same time become a less desirable place to stay. The parts that were good are gone. I've called it the "pit", or the "hole" for years, and Dingri, from Nepal and another regular calls it the "refugee camp".

2004

January 19

Wuzhou, Guangxi: It was funny the other evening: Wei and I were in my room looking at pictures when there was a knock at the door. I opened it, and a pretty girl asked "*Anmo, haobuhao?*" (how about a massage). I said no thanks, and she said "*Weishenme?*" (why), then craned to look past me and saw Wei. She said "Oh!" with her eyes and mouth wide, and disappeared. Wei, busy with my computer, didn't notice.

March 26

Kunming: The *Chahua* now has a youth hostel section, 30元 for a bed in an eight-bed dorm. Their next cheapest bed is a double for 120 元, which they say is a steep off-season discount. If I planned to stay in Kunming more than a few days, I'd want to find another hotel. The first night I shared the dorm with Uri, a young man from Israel. He had just finished five years in the army and thought Bush was the greatest thing since sliced bread. He said he had been indoctrinated since he was three (my words, not a direct quote). He's very military and in China to study some kind of *wushu* (martial arts).

April 28

Nanjing: The hotel I eventually found yesterday morning, the

Hehai *Binguan*, costs 176元/night for a big two-room and toilet, two-bed *fangjian* (room). It's hard to find anything budget-priced in many cities near the coast. It has too many things, some of which don't work, and beds that are too soft. The curtains, carpets, upholstery, pillows and blankets, and even the towels reek of cigarette smoke. I hate fancy rooms with all the crap that soaks up this stink.

October 15

Beijing: The Dida underground hotel where I've stayed the last couple of years is not open to foreigners anymore, so I'm booked into a hostel near Wudaokou in the university district, 75元 for a tiny private room with a phone and broadband Ethernet access. There is a decent shower and toilet down the hall, but it serves a lot of rooms. The place isn't full, no problem this morning. It's a basement room with no window, so I have no sense of day or night, but is has powerful, efficient ventilation and modern card-lock doors.

The room is tiny, a bunk-type bed above a small desk and chair. I had them remove the TV so I had a place to put my pack. There's room to turn around alongside the bed if I don't have my pack on. A bargain for Beijing at about US$8/night. Be nice to be able to sense daylight, I don't like not knowing if it is night or day without looking at my watch. One friend said with admiration "This place was designed by a real businessman."

November 20

Kuqar, Xinjiang: This hotel, steeply discounted to 120元 for *shuangren fangjian* (twin room), stinks. Like every "nice" hotel with carpets, drapes, and bedspreads, everything in it is saturated with cigarette smoke, including the pillows.

A *zhaodaisuo* is better for me, simpler, has less to soak up the stink, and costs one third. The simple rooms have everything I need. Having a toilet in the room is nice, but many *zhaodaisuo* have that, too. And often the room toilets stink. If the toilet is down the hall, it doesn't matter if it smells like a toilet.

December 22

Xining, Qinghai: When I checked into the hotel, I was recognized and welcomed, no discount. After I had been here eight days, the *fuwutai* told me the tenth day was free, for customers who stayed so long. A few days later, the hotel went into redecorating mode: starting on the top floor, workers stripped out the rooms and started painting, a crew of at least ten. Yesterday, while I was having a shower, they arrived on my floor, the third. I got switched to a room on the fourth, a big double room, freshly painted. The smell is pretty bad from the water-base paint, cleaners, and solvents. And I'm now on the street-side of the building, a lot noisier.

2005

September 24

<u>Xiamen</u> is a coastal city with clean air like San Francisco. My friend Liu took me to a small hotel out by the university, a place I never would have found by myself. The sign says it's an International Youth Hostel, the "Anywhere Inn". I got a bed in a dorm, 50元.

It's hot, but this four-bed room has a powerful air conditioner and good ventilation. It's a funny little hotel, a new business, with a small kitchen, three common rooms, piles of CDs, a music system, and a courtyard with tables. The showers are set up badly, the single control valve installed upside down so the flexible pipe to the shower head is bent repeatedly and breaks quickly, a big maintenance problem. In the room, there are not enough hooks for one person, much less for four. There are badly designed wooden chairs that are uncomfortable, and most are already broken. The place is clean, all the furniture is natural-finish pine, and the room has four big cupboards, one for each bed, lockable with key supplied.

While cleaning, the *fuwuyuan* asked me how about the room? I told her it needed more hooks to hang clothes, and showed her the problem with the shower. But she's just the cleaning lady, I think she has no power to make improvements or even suggestions.

September 27

The basic rate in this hostel is fine as Xiamen's an expensive city (I checked the IYH [International Youth Hostel] web site, this place is unlisted so probably not a member, their sign is unofficial) and I've mostly had the room to myself. They overcharge for everything else, as much as they think they can get. Most of the guests are young Chinese travelers who found the place by searching in Chinese on the Internet for budget accommodation in Xiamen. First local phone call I made, they charged me 1元/minute. The second call several days later, the same. I complained bitterly and the *fuwutai* tried to look surprised, but only looked embarrassed, and said "To Xiamen? Oh, 0.5元/minute." That's still high but better; on the street it is 0.2元. When I inquired about Internet the first day I was there, they told me 15元/hour, but they tell the Chinese customers 5元, and it's mostly 2.5元 at *wangba* in the neighborhood. I think one of the rules of IYH is that they charge locals and foreign visitors the same rates for everything.

October 24

Made it <u>Huhhot</u> this morning, put my bike together and rode off in search of a hotel. I bought a map and found my way across the city with little trouble. I went straight to the tiny place on Ulan *Xixiang* (alley or small street) where I had stayed four years ago and got a room, SW facing window, fifth floor walk up, toilet and bath, no phone or TV. 35 元, a big step down from the 100元 I was paying for a very nice room in the Beiwai foreigner's residence, with phone, TV, bath, and elevator. This place is more in line with my budget, but the other place was a bargain for Beijing and had windows, which the Huaqingyuan didn't.

It's cold, I need to wear everything I've got, there won't be much street food while I'm here. I found *malatang* across from the south gate of *Neida* (Inner Mongolia University), and have a beer, 7.5元. For lunch, I had a couple of roasted sweet potatoes. I've come way down in cost. This is my first US$6 day on this trip, Beijing was costing me about US$25/day.

October 26

Had a good shower. The electric water heater took about an hour to heat after I plugged it in. The toilet is Western-style low-flush, and there is a good sink. Both the sink and shower valves are single control style of reasonable quality. The room has a twin bed with a mattress which was too soft for my back, so I took it off and stood it against the wall. It was on a wooden pallet on a steel frame, and had a thick cotton pad, just fine. Two quilts, plenty warm. There's a hot water radiator in the room, big double glazed windows almost to the ceiling, deep windowsill the full width of the room, and a small table/cabinet, plenty of room to spread out my stuff, but no hooks or lines of any sort to hang my clothes on, nothing in the bathroom or main room. There was an unused TV cable which I washed and rigged to the window, so now I have a reasonable line to hang clothes. The floor is tile, pretty clean, the walls have been painted recently, and the door has a nice latch/dead bolt. There are a couple of framed pictures on the walls and drapes on the window.

I think this place has changed hands, is no longer *Mengguzu*-owned and run.

December 25

<u>Chengdu</u>: My room at the Jiaotong *Binguan* is an "economical double", no "economical singles" available, although they promise me one would be available soon. I bargained the price down to 70元 from 90元, still too expensive, and they told me 90元 was a big low season discount. It is unheated, they tried to get me to take a room for 30元 more, heated. Today, the *fuwuyuan* brought in an electric pad for the top of the mattress, a big improvement, and I bought and smuggled in a small radiant electric heater, 30元. The old man who sold it to me happily helped me wrap it after I explained the reason, that it wasn't allowed by the hotel. We found the box and turned it inside out so all the printing was on the inside and tied it up with string. There were no questions when I carried it into the hotel. With the pad and the heater, it is warm enough to work for hours in my room.

February 27

<u>Bajie, Guizhou</u>: Rode my bike here from Xingyi yesterday, less than 50 km, not too many hills, light rain part of the way. I had several maps, none were very detailed, and they disagreed with each other. I expected to find a bridge across the river to Guangxi, but the reservoir behind the Tianshengqiao power station is huge and nearly 100 km long. I looked at the ferry landing, and then went to look for a hotel. By then, I had picked up a retinue of kids, led by a girl about ten years old. At the landing, she had been drawing with chalk on the pavement. By the way she kept glancing at me, I was sure she was drawing my picture. I went to look, she ran off, and sure enough, there I was, a stick figure with glasses, beard, and ponytail. Some adults walked over to see what I was looking at and the little girl came back when she saw I wasn't angry. Bajie is small, little more than a village, a *Buyizu* minority community, possibly the smallest place I've ever looked for a hotel.

I asked a young man sorting shrimp on the side of the street about a *zhaodaisuo*, and he pointed up the street. So I pushed my loaded bike up the hill, a dozen kids trailing along behind. I didn't see anything that looked like a hotel, but the kids stopped and a boy pointed at an unpromising place and said "*lüshe*" (private hotel). I went into the open front room, was offered a chair, sat, and asked about a bed. They said yes, 5元, and showed me to a room with four beds, me the only guest. I got my bags, cleaned up a little, and drank some tea. Then out to the waiting kids, about twenty now, to go off on a guided exploration of the town. A boy of fifteen had joined the group, and he knew a little English. The youngest was four years old.

Back to the hotel for dinner, a good sleep (no shower in the place), and breakfast in the morning. I asked how much I owed them for the room, dinner, and breakfast. The woman was hesitant, didn't want any money, finally said 10元, and then tried to refuse my money because I had made the kids so happy. I think it was the lowest priced room I've had in China. As I loaded my bags on my bike, the kids arrived with bags of food and fruit, gifts from their families. I tried to refuse but wasn't allowed, went off to the ferry with bags of food hanging off my handlebars. And I forgot to return the room key, in the confusion with the kids. I feel bad about that.

Food

1988

March 25

Hong Kong: Back to a vegetarian restaurant for dinner — fried *doufu* (tofu) in brown sauce with steamed rice. I sure wish it was brown rice. This vegetarian place is serious and has a sign out front warning customers not to bring any meat onto the premises. The waiter recognized me from yesterday so he didn't spend any time yelling "Nomee, nomee," at me, which I had eventually understood as "no meat".

March 27

Sitting in a noodle shop waiting for oat & egg — I don't know exactly what that will be. Ah, looks like hot oatmeal with a raw egg broken in. Not bad, in fact a good idea, although I could do without the sugar they added. This place has a sort of ice cream parlor attached. A man has been beating frost off the refrigerator coils with a huge metal spoon: bang. Bang, bang. Looks hard on the plumbing.

April 1

Wuzhou, Guangxi: I made eating the first order of business. Went right into the kitchen, a first. It made things easy. I pointed at everything that looked good, and got a dish with lima beans, peas, green onions, mushrooms, pork. Good!

April 2

I stopped to watch food being cooked at a street stall. They asked with gestures if I wanted to eat. I refused, just watching, but I liked what

I saw so I decided to eat there. I was invited to eat what I had watched being cooked, and to sit down at the table with everyone. Everybody ate and when the food ran out more was cooked. I showed my album about home. After half an hour, I got up to pay and my money was refused. When I insisted on paying, the cook, who had had a big chef's knife in his hand most of the time, made a final chopping motion with his hand between us. I gracefully (I hope) retreated, very full, a first class feed.

April 9

Guiping: Sitting at a table in a small restaurant eating, I refuse offers of rice spirits. Good food, and much laughter. One of the offerers of spirits points to my long hair and cups his hands over his breasts, looks at me inquiringly. All laugh, men, women, and children. A pretty girl of about eight is fascinated by me, but shy. I try to catch one of her pigtails to compare the length of her hair with mine. She runs, hides, and comes back. I measure my hair with my tape measure and try to measure hers. She runs, again comes back, I offer her the tape, and she runs. Her mother takes the tape, and with help from others catches the laughing girl and measures her pigtail. It's two cm longer than mine. Much laughter, and the girl is very pleased.

April 28

Huangguoshu, Guizhou: Reminded myself I'm a slow learner; after a good breakfast at a reasonable price, I was overcharged again for lunch. I better remember to ask the price when I order. I can't bargain after I've eaten. Oh well, it was a good lunch.

June 19

Luoyang: What a dinner! Five of us around a tiny table in my friend's small two-room apartment, the table piled high with huge shrimp, eggplant, mushrooms and eggs, frog legs with peppers, eel and vegetables, several plates of raw vegetables, two different kinds of preserved eggs, and beer and wine, wow.

1991

December 4

Guangzhou: I'm eating in a little cafe to the tune of "Unchained Melody". The old woman (mother?) runs everything with a sharp tongue and eye. She sits, cleaning bean sprouts and vegetables while barking out orders, or she stands over the others and tells them what to do. She mostly sits behind a little desk with a *suanpan* (Chinese abacus) and collects the money. I wouldn't like to work for her but perhaps she has a pleasant side. She runs a tight ship, and this is the lowest cost clean place to eat near the hotel.

1993

January 29

Guangzhou: I'm engaged in what is too common a behavior for me in China, wandering around hungry with too little energy or gumption to go get food. When I actually go into a place, I have little or no problem, but in this mood, I often get cheated. Of course, getting cheated is relative: overcharged is a more reasonable term, usually only 10-20% higher than normal.

February 1

I was told Chinese work to live; that Westerners live to work, and don't know how to spend their money. There may be a difference in the idea of pleasure. I don't enjoy eating a meal in a hot, noisy, crowded restaurant, whatever it costs. I wouldn't enjoy it if it was free, and I certainly don't enjoy it when it's expensive and I can get as good or better food on the street for less money. May be an irresolvable cultural difference.

1998

February 16

Guangzhou: Lunch at the *Liqian* — It's still there, the old lady is still there, and she looks fairly good. She remembers me, and even smiled! She was sick and looked terrible last time I was here, nearly four years ago. I assumed she'd be out of it by now. Tough old bird. The waitresses don't seem to pay much attention to her anymore when she rails at them; they smile and keep on with their work. They all used to duck.

February 21

Wuzhou, Guangxi: I've ordered dinner, and have a beer in front of me. The *Zhujiang* beer from Guangzhou is good. These are big bottles, 640 ml. They offered me the Chinese version of Pabst, but the lower priced *Zhujiang* is better.

February 22

Out for breakfast, sitting in a small restaurant waiting for *jidan xifan (zhou)*, my favorite rice porridge with egg. The food's great, the girl who seems in charge has been over to check on me several times, and even to sit and talk for a few minutes.

Mostly, we talk about how little I understand, how little I speak, and how much I don't understand. My ability is improving. I can talk a lot now about how I can't understand. Truly though, to be able to walk into a place such as this and order easily what I want is great. I can manage that, at least simple food, so some assume I understand and speak Chinese.

February 24

<u>Guiping</u>: At a street restaurant west of the hotel, the men at the next table sent me a bowl of soup, with greetings and welcome.

March 11

<u>Yulin</u>: Out for breakfast, *meiyou xifan, you mifen* (don't have *xifan*, have *mifen*). I don't know what that is, but I said okay... Rice-flour noodles.

Dinner with Wang and her husband, her brother and his wife. We ate dog as promised. Her husband explained Yulin's dog dish is flavored much the same as in Guangzhou, but that other places had their own taste. It was quite a feed.

Dog meat is fine, tastes great. I've eaten it many times but it costs more than most other kinds of meat. It's special. Dog is another kind of meat, the dogs are raised for meat, the same as chickens or sheep. In the south of China, when the weather gets cold, suddenly there are restaurants specializing in dog meat everywhere. People seem to believe eating dog meat makes you warm, something from Chinese medicine. Eating dog is most popular in the south, but I think you can find it anywhere in China. There is no attempt to hide eating dog from Westerners' eyes. In fact, many Chinese think it's funny Americans get upset about it. So they sometimes go out of their way to show it: "Do you know what you're eating?...."

March 16

<u>Nanning</u>, on a street of street food, Zhongshan *Lu* (Road): I've got a plate of snow peas and liver, a plate of greens, and a beer in front of me, will have rice soon.... Looks good, okay! I had some trouble trying to get a firm price, but I think it should be 14元 with the beer. *Wa*! The bill is 23元.

That's a problem with having so many friends. They feed me and take me out to eat and I forget how to order food. I'm not complaining; I could have no friends.

March 29

Kunming: At an expat restaurant, I ordered cashew chicken, snow peas, rice, and beer. The place seemed to be run by a shaggy Brit, or maybe he's Dutch. There were a couple of foreign guys at another table who rolled and lit a joint. The conversation I overheard had it to be local weed from Dali.

The dinner was okay but a bit expensive. It was easy as the menu was in English and Chinese, and in my low energy state, easy was important or I wouldn't eat. I may come back, although there seem to be many places in this area with translated menus. This particular place goes farther than most, offering Western and Chinese food, hamburgers, French fries, and other stuff I don't want.

2000

January 7

Xiamen, Fujian: I came across a phrase on the Internet a few days ago: "China is undergoing a transition from life under communism to life under communist-sanctioned consumerism." There are five McDonald's, four Kentucky Fried Chicken, and two Pizza Huts here (that I've seen), ugh. America exports such wonderful stuff.

I was out last night with a local newspaper editor and a bunch of reporters. The editor told me that the third word Chinese babies learn to say is "*Maidanglao*" (McDonald's), right after they learn "Baba", and "Mama". It's a popular joke. The power of advertising.

January 9

In a Chinese restaurant, I met the foreign manager for all the McDonald's in Fujian Province. He told me there are 252 in China now, not counting Hong Kong, and fifteen of them are in Fujian, including the five in Xiamen. This guy is American, stressed out, pudgy, gray-faced, and speaks corporate-talk. I mentioned the baby's third word: he was proud it was a popular joke, it showed their marketing worked.

January 11

On the sidewalk in front of a McDonald's, loudspeakers play their music and jingles. Little kids are laughing, dancing, singing along, and slapping their mamas (*Mama, Mama, Mama! Maidanglao, Maidanglao, Maidanglao!*). Ugh, the power of TV advertising. Works here, too.

January 15

At breakfast half an hour earlier than usual. The girl smiled at me and looked over her shoulder at the clock. I've been watching her prepare my breakfast for the past several days. She cuts up the vegetables with scissors.

January 25

<u>Wuzhou, Guangxi</u>: I like the place where I've eaten dinner every night since I arrived. With the cold weather, one of the dishes I have is a wonderful hot soup. The cook is a master, a tall thin man who cooks beautifully. The bottle of beer is 640 ml, so I'm slightly drunk at the end of dinner. I stagger away, barely able to walk. All his vegetables come out crisp, everything perfect. It's in a bad location beyond the end of a market on a dark street. The first night, my dinner cost me 20元 with a beer, and it has stayed the same price every night, although I've ordered quite different foods.

The restaurant's chickens run loose in the street out front, but have a cage; sometimes they run into their cage. When a customer orders chicken, one of them promptly loses its head. Now that's fresh meat! The chickens hurry around under the cook's feet picking over all the dropped bits, but they are picky about what they will eat.

February 21

<u>Yulin</u>: Something new that seems popular in restaurants at the moment: there are pictures of Western meals and foods, hamburgers, forks, spoons, pitchers of orange juice, salads. These foods unavailable, only for decoration.

February 22

<u>Nanning</u>: I find riding a bicycle is a wonderful way to bargain for food on a food street such as Zhongshan *Lu*. I go from *dapaidang* to *dapaidang* staying straddle of my bike while I ask prices, ready to move on. The prices I'm being given that way are about half what I remember from two years ago, when I was on foot. I'll see when I pay. Eating in *dapaidang* is interesting, sitting on the street, watching the street passby, and watching the competing places trying to pull in customers. Everyone passing is assessed and the locals are ignored. Before my dinner arrived, a woman wanted to polish my shoes. I eventually let her,

1元 agreed, and a small boy selling flowers came in to watch. He was looking over my shoulder as I wrote, and then started giving me a shoulder massage. He had all the moves down, but not enough strength in his hands and arms to do it well. When my food came, I asked him to stop, and asked him how many years he had. He said seven. I gave him 0.7元 (seven *mao*) and he pretended to be very disappointed and stared at the money in his outstretched hand for a long time. Finally he went off when he saw he wasn't getting any more, and gave me a very nice shy smile as he left. The woman, still polishing my shoes, also gave me a nice smile. She was earning less, working harder and longer, and using some supplies. These are proud but very poor people on the street, unwilling to beg but making a meager living.

2001

March 12

Qinzhou, Guangxi: I visited some English classes in a middle school. After refusing a big meal with the school leaders, I ate with the students in their dining room. The school leader sat with us and ate the same food. I think it was the first time for him to eat there. It both amused the students and made them nervous. We joked about cleaning your plate, so the leader carefully cleaned his although he had earlier pushed some bits aside. Pretty funny, and none of the students missed it. The women cooking the food were worried and also pleased. I'm happy I made it happen.

April 11

Yulin, at dinner in a place around the corner from my hotel where I often ate last year. They certainly recognized and welcomed me. The daughters of the restaurant owner leaned on me hard for help with their English lessons. I wasn't sure I was going to get to eat. At 7:00 P.M., a TV show came on, and they leaped up to watch it. Much more interesting than me or English lessons, and anyway, their father and brother had been telling them to leave me alone and let me eat.

April 22

Xiamen, Fujian fast food: There are many Chinese knockoffs of the McD-KFC style fast food places. This fast food influence may make a big change: reduce the quality of diet, increase obesity, and improve general service levels and public area cleanliness. A mixed bag. The dozens of Chinese fast food knockoffs are all trying to meet the same

Western service standards. Most of the knockoffs have English names, such as JolliBee, Chicken Mcbits, Miss D's, Dicos, Little Pretty, New One Race, and Quick and Pretty Food.

Looking at the McDonald's: they have relatively high Western standards of service and training. The workers are all trained and required to smile, be polite, give good and fast service, and keep the places as clean as possible. They have more trash cans, I think, including out front on the sidewalk, than any other place in China. The staff even clean the sidewalk regularly. They have clean toilets, with soap, toilet paper, and hot-air hand driers.

April 23

I've been eating breakfast in a small place where the cook is a nicely dressed elderly man who looks like a prosperous retired professor in his nicely fitted suit. He fixes me what I want, my standard *jidan zhugan zhou* (rice porridge with pig liver and egg) and a bit of greens and chopped green onion added for color and flavor.

June 5

<u>Wuyuan, Nei Menggu</u>: This place where I've been eating an unappetizing breakfast of noodles each day reminds me of Duarte's Restaurant in the '70s in Pescadero, California: each morning, a bunch of old men hold down a couple of tables, and solve the problems of the empire. Some wear straw hats with carefully turned brims, some wear dark glasses even inside, and a few drink beer with breakfast. Sounds like they tell dirty jokes. They cackle....

For some reason, it takes a long time to fix my simple noodles. It should take only a few minutes, but takes fifteen minutes. Everything is slow, except the tea, which comes immediately. It is a social place, a place to come and chat leisurely over food. Lots of waiting for a bowl of noodles that fills my belly but provides little satisfaction, much less pleasure. Most of the clientele look retired, many long retired.

Meanwhile, the old codger in the straw hat who's here every morning has made his rounds of the tables, explaining about me for the umpteenth time. What I understand is "American", and "Washington State". He has it clearly, state, not DC. He always emphasizes the "*zhou*", state.

June 29

<u>Erlian</u>: Everywhere here, *naicha*, (salty milk tea) is served in a bowl. Okay with me, I like it.

July 2

Pai huanggua: smashed cucumber. Cut it into big pieces and whacked with the back or side of a big knife, it shatters nicely. Sprinkle it with a bit of salt, or a bit of vinegar....

Yogurt is excellent here. A small shop has it, and local cheese and butter. Smells great.

July 4

Breakfast: they put thin plastic film over the tablecloth, several layers. Just pull off a layer and throw it away when dirty. So there's this film floating up around you in the breeze and the static electricity in the dry air, while you try to eat. Some places put clips or clothespins on the corners to control it. I weight down the corners with the sugar dish, toothpick holder, and whatever. The plastic film has become popular at the same time the government is urging everyone to cut down on plastic disposables, to reduce "white pollution" (plastic bags).

Xiaomi zhou, *xifan*, is made with millet. Called *xiaomi*, lit. small rice.

August 7

I was given a hunk of dried Mongolian cheese that was like a piece of stone, although I was told it got harder if it was really dry. By scoring it with my knife, I can break off a corner. What I really need is a claw hammer, to bust off pieces. Soak the piece in hot water or milk tea for a few minutes and it's possible to gnaw it, or at least scrape off a bit of the surface with my teeth. It's excellent cheese, but hard to eat. After a piece has been in my mouth for awhile, enzymes start to soften it.

August 12

At dinner, I was made an honorary Mongolian — Since I like *naicha* (milk tea) I must be a Mongolian, they said. An awful lot of the *Han* here also drink *naicha*....

Green Food: a big campaign, the words are on signs and in restaurants. I'm unsure of the exact meaning or purpose here, but I think it means eating meat raised on the grasslands, free range instead of feedlot.

August 14

Lanzhou, Gansu: I like the sanitation at this *dapaidang*. They pull a plastic bag over the bowl or plate, to provide a clean surface, and later strip it off, leaving the bowl reusable without washing. This uses a lot of plastic bags that end up in the compostable food waste, and thus into the fields, but I don't get sick.

August 19

Ge'ermu (Golmud), Qinghai: At dinner last night, I wanted a beer. The Muslim place where I was eating didn't serve it, so I went walking after I finished my supper. I didn't want to sit and drink, and was about to head back to the hotel when three men in their thirties stopped me and asked me to have a beer with them. We squatted on the sidewalk and drank the beer they were carrying. They were middle school teachers, two *Hanzu* teaching Chinese and math, and the other *Zangzu* (Tibetan), an art teacher.

I ate breakfast in the ridiculous sterile dining room of the hotel. The only customer was me. Fake Doric columns, a big buffet, actually a fair meal with egg, vegetable, meat, peanuts, and so forth, but no fun. 6元.

September 2

Nanning: Zhongshan *Lu*, the food street. I could see the place where I've eaten on three different trips, most recently six months ago. I wheeled my bike over and without any hint of recognition, the girl pointed to a spot to park it. An older woman, possibly her mother, came out while I was looking over the available food. She said *"Fuzhu, youyu"*, what I've often ordered in the past. I told her she had a good memory, added to the order from the produce on display, and sat down at a table. I didn't order a beer, hadn't gotten around to it. A man, maybe the husband and father, promptly brought me a bottle of *Li Quan* beer, the brand I prefer here, and opened it without looking at me for a confirmation. Good memories.

Being remembered, recognized as an old customer is an aspect of traveling in China I enjoy a lot. So I go out of my way to go back to places I have enjoyed in the past. And my shoes which were getting shabby have been beautifully polished by a roving shoe shiner, while I was waiting for my food. It sure wasn't my bike they recognized.

It's nice to be back in the south, where I easily get exactly the kind of food I like best. A perfect breakfast, and lots of vegetables for dinner. I've been missing southern food, especially the vegetables. In much of the south, three or four crops can be grown each year so vegetables are a major part of the diet.

2002

June 12

Changsha, Hunan: Miyuki (a Japanese teacher in the university) and I had a wonderful dinner of crawdads, fresh tomatoes, cucumbers, and long green beans, and we shared a beer. So much food we didn't eat any rice. Of course, sitting across from Miyuki made it better. She has cut off all her long beautiful hair, alas. Cheap, 26元, about $3.25 for the two of us.

June 14

Chenglingji: I walked over toward the restaurant of a guy who helped me find a hotel last night, and found it not yet open. He came running across the huge open parking area above the dock calling to me and took me in, while his wife was still folding up their bedding. I've been writing this while she whipped up a breakfast for me, egg soup, rice, and fried onion and meat. Not the *xifan* I wanted, but much more, and good. He'll make something off me, but he was truly helpful yesterday. Business looks bleak for them. River traffic is way down, this isn't a good location any more.

The guy vastly overcharged me, maybe three times normal price. Oh well... The worst part, his wife didn't want to charge me so much and the two of them had an argument which left her feeling bad. Me too, feeling bad. They didn't realize I understood much of it.

June 30

Beijing: I took Lian, an English major I've known since she was a middle school student, to a fancy place, the "All Sages" bookshop and coffee house, and we shared a huge banana split. She's an ice cream lover but she'd never had anything like that before, and me not for more than thirty years. It had chocolate, strawberry, and peach ice cream in it. How about that.

Supper by myself in the new student restaurant in *Dizhi Daxue* (Geosciences University). This place will seat 500 and is designed to be easy to keep clean. There are nine food preparation places down one side, each offering a different regional cuisine. Students pay with a prepaid card, swiped through a card reader. Non-students such as me select our food, ask the price and pay a central cashier, getting a ticket to take back. Cheap, and surprisingly good. The place is airy and bright, with well-designed fluorescent fixtures, much nicer than the common bare tubes. There are several big screen TVs down one side, each on a different channel. At the crowded end of the hall, the TV is showing the World Cup finals. China is soccer-crazy, their first year in the World Cup, and tonight is the final game.

July 13

Huhhot: I met Sarna for lunch and ended up carrying off the

remnants. I've chewed all the mutton off a shoulder blade after trimming away most of the fat. Good. And now I'm eating a soft crumbly cheese, *nai doufu* (milk tofu), and *gan naiyou*, dried cream. They are rich and excellent. I've also got some spicy dried camel meat, with bread. And *suan nai doufu*, a good and new-to-me sour cheese made from yogurt or sour milk. *Wa*, I'm stuffed.

July 14

At dinner in the little hotel restaurant, the neighboring diners are singing, men only, mostly solo with no body or face movement as they sing loudly, melancholy. It's funny sitting here, only *Mengwen* (Mongolian language) to be heard.

A new (to me) traditional Mongolian vegetable, *sha cong*, desert onion (lit. sand onion) grows wild. People and sheep eat it. It looks a bit like grass, very mild, tender and good.

August 2

Shanshan, Xinjiang: Went walking out into the desert and ate a sweet and wonderful *Hamigua* (Hami melon), while sitting in the sand dunes. The grapes will be ripe in about a week. There are only a few now, but lots of melons, cheap. The sand was burning hot and many people were burying themselves in it, for its traditional curative properties. It's said to be especially good for arthritis and other aches and pains.

August 18

Urumqi: I stopped for a lunch of kebab and *nang*. While eating, I was writing in my journal as I often do. A bunch of the restaurant workers gathered around to watch. Then a slightly older and pretty Uyghur girl I had been discreetly watching came over and sat down next to me.

She asked me (in English, to my surprise) where I was from, said she was from Turpan, had studied English one year, and will study this fall at *Xinda* (Xinjiang University). I told her I was happy to have her practice her English with me if she had time. So she made a date to meet me as soon as she got off work, at 5:30. Aanisa, *wa*, very pretty. I better go take a nap. See what happens to travelers!

August 20

Eating kebab and *nang* again, I'm remembering watching a butcher in Bugur cutting up meat for kebab. He striped all the meat off a skinned and gutted sheep carcass in about five minutes, leaving a clean skeleton.

The skill with which he parted the meat from the vertebrae and ribs was impressive.

August 26

Seric, a Kazakh friend, arranges things for Chinese tour groups. He tells me many of the Chinese tourists spend 15,000元 for a weeks' vacation here, including hotel, food, transportation, and some mini-tours. That's more than ten times what I spend per week for my entire trip in China, including round-trip airfare. The people in these groups spend a couple hundred per night for a bed and maybe a couple hundred more for dinner.

September 8

Guangzhou, Shamian Dao (Shamian Island): The place is gentrified. I miss the *Liqian* restaurant and the old lady who ran it. Nice and low class, famous in Lonely Planet, and perfect for me. I usually don't find the recommended places to be to my liking, but the *Liqian* was a delightful exception. It's now long gone, but the tree that grew up through the roof is still there, with a disfigured place on the trunk from contact with the building. Otherwise, there's no sign a building was ever there.

2003

January 22

Guangzhou, breakfast at same place: Today the servers told me what kind of tea I wanted and asked me if I wanted the same food. The price has varied by the day, up and down from 6.5元 to 8.5元, although I've eaten exactly the same thing. This morning, I greeted and sat with an old man I had greeted several times before. An old woman at another table caught my eye and pointed under my stool. There was a neatly folded plastic bag on the floor; she thought it was something I had dropped.

Walking through the new Qingping Chinese Medicinal Herbs Market every morning on my way to and from breakfast is wonderful. It's better than the old market because it's clean, designed to be a market, and the herbal smells aren't mixed with street smells of the old alley. I love the odors, but my Chinese friends say "It smells like medicine." I expect the rent's a lot higher for the sellers.

February 4

Guiping, Guangxi: With Lian, I went to dinner in an old courtyard style house (called "*si he yuan*" in the *hutong* in Beijing, but no special name here). A large extended family lives in the place, fairly traditional with a room devoted to a family altar. Lian is a third-year student at a good university in Beijing, a girl I've know since she was in middle school here. We made *jiaozi* (dumplings) in the large kitchen, eight or ten people working together. I made some too but I'm unskilled. Then off to sit in a room with TV, where Lian and three others played *majiang* (mahjong) with many changing players. Then a good dinner with five or six different dishes and soup, eighteen people around a big table. A nice evening, interesting and unlike what I'd expected.

When we left, I took a dark back way, carrying Lian on my bike. We passed a small medicine shop where some men were playing *erhu*, *gaohu*, *bahu* (three sizes of Chinese two-string fiddles including a big one I'd never seen before), banjo, and something like a small guitar with three strings. I stopped to listen for a moment and Lian asked "Why?" An old man, the oldest of the group, hurried out to grab my arm and pull me into the shop. He told the others that he knew me (I had spoken to him by chance on the street the day before, wishing him good fortune in the new year.) They began playing again rather badly, out of time and tune with each other, and then asked Lian what to play next so she suggested a song. One man asked her if she could sing it. So we had a songfest, Lian singing many songs with them. It was fun and the men were pleased to have a foreign visitor listening, but especially pleased to have a girl singing traditional songs with them. She knew a lot of songs to my surprise, a side of her I had not guessed.

February 12

Nanning: Gao told me that in Nanning (all Guangxi?) now, small restaurants and *dapaidang* must get their dishes from a central washing and sterilization place, and must pay for this. At breakfast at a *dapaidang* this morning, I watched the owner take an enameled steel dish for me out of a small steel box packed full of identical dishes. The dish had a small paper tag on the rim attesting to its cleanliness. The clean dishes, delivered, cost 0.2元 each. A guy delivers them and picks up the dirty ones on *sanlunche* (tricycle truck). It ups costs for the *dapaidang*, and creates a new kind of business, while improving public health. Or more cynically, puts some money in somebody's pocket.

These centrally sterilized bowls have paper tags, and most small restaurants have a sign on the wall instructing customers to remove the tag: "Be responsible, do your civic duty!". Another friend says there have been articles in the papers telling people to remove the tags so the bowls can't be reused by unscrupulous places, and to refuse food served in bowels without the tags.

March 21

<u>Baise</u>: At dinner in the same place I had breakfast today. I saw the place and they saw me when I was out walking with some little girls last night. Not a bad introduction. I didn't ask the price, just sat down and told them what I wanted. This usually works, and I come back to the places that give me good food and a fair price the first time.

Dinner was a bit expensive. While I was playing with their kids, the mother and father had a talk, wondering about what to charge me. I ignored it as though I didn't understand anything they were talking about. In any case, it's less than I was paying in Nanning. And they are trying to put a couple of kids through school. They overcharged me about 10%, 2元.

April 25

<u>Guangzhou</u>: I was joined at my table in a tiny back-street *dapaidang* across the river by a man with a serious speech impediment or mental disability. He wanted to pay for my dinner. I managed to deflect him, paying for myself and I hope not insulting him. Some of the regulars were worried he would scare me. They were signing behind his back that I needn't be afraid of him. And when I paid while he was trying to pay for me, the old lady took my money and ignored his, so he put his money away.

April 30

<u>Beijing</u>: Ilyas's biggest problem is food. He's a Uyghur postdoc researcher in super conducting applications and a friend. He isn't allowed to leave his institute because of SARS (during the latter half of the SARS time, many people were quarantined inside their institutes to reduce any chance of contagion, and this quarantine had just started). He hasn't had a good meal in three or four days, due to his Muslim food rules. There is a Muslim restaurant in *Linda* (Forestry University) nearby, not great but it's good enough. He has talked to his advisor about this problem, and thinks they will work out a solution. He says he isn't eating enough for his body, much less his soul. I offered to carry proper Halal food to the gate, if he could find a way to meet me there. I'm outside and free, but can't enter any schools or institutes.

May 7

Talked with Ilyas on the phone. He now has a "license", his word, to go to the Muslim restaurant in *Linda* for lunch and dinner. He says it's okay, but not tasty. The manager and workers are *Han*, he thinks, but they follow Halal rules. Maybe he'll get permission to go out to dinner with me. I promised a good Uyghur dinner, if it is possible.

I've been buying nice prickly cucumbers and wonderful cherry tomatoes, to wash and eat fresh. They are delicious and I've been eating about a pound of each every day. Other than breakfast, I've been eating in my room a lot, buying part of a roasted chicken or duck, hot bread, and a beer. Few restaurants are open, in fact most public places are closed, due to SARS. (More about SARS in the chapter, "Sick on the Road".)

2004

January 20

Wuzhou, Guangxi: Had dinner last night with three students from a private English night school: Liang, a nurse, and an older woman, Chen, who works as a typist at the *Wuzhou Ribao* (daily newspaper), and a guy, thirty, who teaches truck and car driving. Zheng, an engineer at a hydro plant on the river joined us later. We were supposed to go to an English party at the school, but had a great dinner (Which I managed to pay for by sneaking off to the toilet. I got back to the table to be met with a disgusted "You paid, didn't you?" Maybe it was also a little admiring).

April 3

Chengdu: Bon, Bot, But, or Boot (the pronunciation is somewhere between) is a traditional name for the country west of here. TBot is a name for the people who live in high places (in one Tibetan dialect). This has become the foreign name "Tibet". Some Tibetan factions like the Chinese name, *Xizang*, which is a transliteration or attempt to replicate the sound of the traditional name from another dialect; others call it by their own dialect's name. Most use the name "Tibet" only when speaking to foreigners. Lasang, a Tibetan postgraduate student at a university here, referred in English to *Xizang* as "T.R.", for the Tibet Autonomous Region. And he used "Tibet" to refer to the greater area traditionally populated by *Zangzu* (Tibetans), which includes a bit of Xinjiang, a good chunk of Qinghai and Gansu, and parts of Sichuan and Yunnan.

About *Zangzu* manners (Lasang's group, anyway, he's from a nomadic family in southern Gansu), if I drop food on the floor, pick it up and put it aside on the table. Never kick it away or step on it. If food falls on the table, pick it up and eat it if the table is clean. And if the floor or ground is clean, picking up what was dropped and eating it is okay and proper. It is most polite to drink a bowl of tea with two hands, but one hand is okay. When food or tea is set in front of me, it is polite to pull it slightly toward me with both hands, especially if an older person is serving. Never put my feet on the table. Never step over, across, or stand over books. These things are a lot different from common Chinese manners.

A major division of Tibetan people: farmer or nomad (herders). Farmers live in houses and eat with *kuaizi* (chopsticks). Nomads carry their own bowl, don't eat out of others' dishes, and use a spoon or fingers (traditionally). They can eat out of others' dishes, but usually only with family or close friends.

On the subject of Tibetan schools, he wants so much more than what has so impressed me about *shaoshu minzu* (minority) education in China: the huge effort toward language preservation. He questions the value of studying in your own language, if the content of the curriculum is poor. He says the students learn everything that was bad about the old Tibet, but very little about the parts that were good. Most students care little about Tibetan culture, religion, or language. He told me that if I want to do something for Tibetan students, I should encourage them to learn about the good things from their culture, especially compassion.

He spoke about Christian missionaries in the Tibetan areas and used a coffee metaphor: Westerners drink coffee, but he drank milk as a child and drinks milk now. It's OK if they drink coffee, but that's no reason for him to drink it, or for them to try to make him drink it....

April 9

<u>Xining, Qinghai</u>: We ate in a *Hui* or *Salar* (Muslim minorities) place. Tserang said it was no problem for her, but many Tibetans didn't and wouldn't eat in such places. A year or two ago, a rumor spread that the *Hui* put something secret into the food that turned people into Muslims. She said this was a stupid idea, nothing could do that. However, most Tibetans in this area stopped eating in *Hui* places, so many went broke and had to close. In her hometown, near where Sichuan, Xizang, and Qinghai touch, there are many recently opened Tibetan restaurants, and only a few *Hui* places left. Now, as the rumor fades, many Tibetans are again eating in them.

241

This distrust seems to have root in recent historical differences, when there were some *Hui* warlords (*Guomindang* (Nationalist) supported?). The *Hui* these days are commonly businessmen but few Tibetans are, adding a modern reason for suspicion and distrust. Tibetans seem to have few *Hui* friends, but they commonly have *Han* friends.

2005

November 5

Huhhot: The modern little restaurant where I've been eating breakfast is a popular fast breakfast and lunch place specializing in *doujiang* (soybean milk) and *doufu*. They have a crew of eight to ten efficient and busy yellow aproned and hatted workers, serving, cleaning, washing dishes, and running the *doujiang* and *doufu* machines constantly. The place is sleekly modern, all stainless steel and clean plastic. I think it is a chain, I've seen some similar places elsewhere. Seems like good wholesome food, but a little more expensive than on the street. My standard breakfast of a bowl of *hei mizhou* with beans, *roubao* (a bun stuffed with donkey meat), and a hard-boiled egg costs 6元. I get a miserable little throwaway plastic spoon, too small and with many sharp edges.

Today, the girl taking my order put the *roubao* in a dish with tongs, and turning to hand it to another girl to shove into the microwave, dumped it on the floor. Yet another girl snatched it up and dumped it into the waste bucket under the counter without missing a beat, never even glanced up, and went on with her work.

The positions seem to rotate: the guy who was running the *doujiang* machine yesterday is mopping the floor and entryway today. All the girls do everything, take orders, clear tables, take money, make change. The boys seem to run the machines.

December 25

Chengdu: Night before last, I met Lasang and two friends at a small Tibetan restaurant for *naicha* and *shandih*. Yesterday afternoon, I met Licheng and Meijia again, both young doctors doing postgraduate work in gynecology. I took them to dinner there, a first for them. They are both *Hanzu*, from the north and west.

Shandih (a sort of stew made with rice and yak meat) is very different here from that in Xining, more like a mild curry. Lasang says in this area there is a bit of a mix of flavoring from Nepal and India, and also China mixed into Tibetan food. In Xining, the *shandih* had little seasoning and I liked it better. At this restaurant, it has less meat and more chunks of potato. Three nights in a row I've come here, I really like the *naicha*, very similar to the Mongolian *naicha*. While eating my supper tonight, a young monk, 21, and his sister, 26, from Lhasa sat down with me. He knew a little English and she was studying English in Lhasa. Their mother is in a hospital here. I gave her my card, he took it to read and pocketed it as though I had given it to him. *Hanzu* men rarely do that, I wonder if it is common behavior with *Zangzu*?

Internet

2001

March 27

Guiping, Guangxi: I find *wangba* (Internet bars) everywhere in great profusion. There must be at least twenty in this small city now. A year ago, there was one, in the telephone office. The ones I've been in so far all charge 2-2.5元/hour, 25-30¢.

March 30

I was in Guiping's newest *wangba* (opened a couple of days ago) when a bunch of men came in. I was busy online and didn't look up, just heard them talking. One man came over, sat close behind me, and started reading over my shoulder. Kind of rude, I didn't like it, but I ignored him. Then another man came over and said in English "We are police, stop now!". I looked up and saw there were six or seven black uniformed cops in the bar. I asked if I could finish the email I was writing to my sister. He said okay, but do it fast. I typed "Gotta go", hit send, and logged off.

The one who spoke English told me there was something wrong with the bar, and I must go outside. So I went out front and sat on my bike and watched while the cops talked to the young man who ran the place. Finally, the cop came out and told me in good English that I couldn't use this bar any more. I told him it was a good place, the best I'd found in Guiping and asked him if I could pay for the time I had used. He looked at me as though I was a little crazy but said okay, so I paid the owner for half an hour. The young cop seemed to want to practice his English. He told me as soon as a few things were taken care of I could use the bar again, probably in a couple of months. I guess the owner had neglected to register or pay some license fees or something.

He didn't look happy. I think he was facing some fines, plus being shut down while he went through the proper steps. Oh well, kind of exciting to be caught in a raid.

I went back later that evening. The *wangba* was open, but the owner wasn't there. His friend said there was no trouble. The police had taken away two of their computers and told them they could pick them up in a few days. He said the cops hadn't told them I wasn't to use the bar any more.

April 30

Xiamen: To Burnt Sugar, a little coffee house, to talk with Xiao Liu and Yaya. Liu had a CD map of Beijing, an up-to-date *dianzi ditu*, electric map. He wanted to show it to Yaya who is a real Beijinger. It cost him 6元, a copy (pirate) CD. It had amazing satellite and aerial photos with great scaling and search functions, but no *pinyin* display, only *pinyin* entry. At least Liu didn't find how to display *pinyin*. Useless for me as I can't read anywhere near enough Chinese to use it.

May 15

Beijing: A *wangba* down the street offers English, Chinese, Japanese, and Korean operating systems. The computers are shut down when a customer leaves. At startup, the new customer chooses the language. I didn't like the required startup, I thought it a waste of time but now I see I get to choose. With English, I get a full suite of software and Windows Server 2000, Word and everything, menus in English.

June 17

Huhhot Internet cafes: No change on the ground here. The widely reported (outside of China) "crackdowns" are often local events. Most of my friends from other areas report little activity, all the places still open. I had one report from Nanning two weeks ago that about half of the cafes had been closed, but it was business as usual at the rest, just a little more crowded. These "crackdowns" may be controlling measures, fairly normal procedure for the Chinese government in many areas. Slap a few whatevers down, kill a chicken to scare the monkeys, and let the rest continue, maybe a bit more cautiously.

Here in Inner Mongolia, the best *wangba* have been open about a month, the same as other places I've been. New places open all the time. There have been widely reported new rules (mid-May) banning children (under eighteen) from *wangba*. This place I'm using, 103 nice computers, DDN connection (very fast), open one month and in space rented from

244

the main public library, is full of kids. There are three kids within an arm's length of me right now who can't be more than fifteen.

August 23

<u>Ge'ermu, Qinghai</u>: *Wa*! At *wangba*, a foreigner came in and sat at the next computer. His body odor almost knocked me over. Something I learned fairly early in China, make an effort to keep clean. Later a smoker ran me out of the *wangba* – That's been happening a lot, especially as it turns colder and the doors are kept shut more.

September 12

I was in China when the Gulf War started, and for the duration. The news I listened to then was on short-wave radio. There are many small short-wave radios available, and I used to buy a good little one for less than US$10. These days, I get most of my news on the Internet and no longer carry a radio. I can use the Internet for forty hours for US$10, and do it at any time of the day. I'm no longer tied to broadcasting schedules, but inexpensive short-wave radios are still easy to find.

2002

June 28

Here in <u>Beijing</u> after the terrible arson fire where more than twentyt students died, yes, the *wangba* are all closed, and I've done some serious searching. I've gone to most of the fifty or so I visited last year when I was doing research for an article, all are closed. Most have the doors chained, but their computers are all still visible. In a few, the computers have been removed. Some have the doors open with somebody sitting there minding the shop, telling everyone they are closed.

However, I easily get online at the university libraries. The cost is about the same, and the two I've tried don't care I'm not a student. The wait isn't long because game-playing is forbidden, the activity that keeps most of the computers in *wangba* occupied.

July 4

Bei, a well-known professor and friend, feels the crackdown on *wangba* immediately after the arson fire was at least partially inspired by the Beijing government's fear of the students. They had to do something fast or the students might have hit the streets. He believes the *wangba* in Beijing won't be allowed to reopen until after the Peoples' Congress in September, at the earliest. He believes the reason the government reacted so quickly was because they were scared of student rage if they didn't respond. So the first *wangba* to be closed were the ones immediately around the universities. All the rest in the city were closed within a day or two.

July 26

After the <u>Beijing</u> *wangba* fire, there has been a spate of sensational, wildly inaccurate and outdated pieces in the US press on *wangba* in China. A particularly good example of this kind of story appeared in *The Los Angeles Times*.[1]

August 18

<u>Urumqi</u>: I'm about ready to leave this *wangba*. I've got a bunch of giggling teenage girls all around me, shouting at each other as they do their chat on the Internet. They're driving me nuts, but at least they don't smoke.

2003

February 5

<u>Jiangkou, Guangxi</u>: Gao hadn't been to his hometown since we went there together about three years ago. To his surprise, there were four *wangba*. In <u>Jintian</u>, a smaller town on the way, we saw two. On the way home we ate lunch in a village, <u>Nanmu</u>, and saw one *wangba* in a tent. Gao told me before we started that there were none in any of those places. He spotted the last place while we were eating.

In <u>Jiangkou</u>, the *wangba* were above electronic games places which themselves were behind curtains. Most had signs out if I looked in the right place, if my eye spotted them. Neither Gao nor I spotted any of the signs the first time down the street, even though we were both looking, but the locals know where they are, and strangers don't come here for Internet.

March 20

<u>Baise</u>: Trading English and Chinese with some little girls, I pointed at a *wangba* we passed. The oldest, twelve, said with a shrug "*Buhao de difang*" (not a good place).

---

[1] *The Los Angeles Times*, June 28, 2002, <u>Dens of the Cyber Addicts</u>.

May 11

<u>Beijing</u>: SARS is no fun. All the universities are under tight quarantine and all the Internet cafes are closed, as are most public entertainment and gathering places. Hard to do my email. And I can't get into the universities to use their libraries, as they are quarantined.

2004

April 3

<u>Chengdu</u>: The *wangba* I found and used most often had about 200 computers and a fast connection, maybe the fastest I've ever used. 1 元/hour from 8:00 A.M. to noon. I'd stay about 1 1/2 hours, they'd charge me 1元. Noon to midnight, 2元/hour. I wasn't sure about the midnight to 8:00 A.M. rate, but I think it was eight hours for 4元. The *wangba* was a ten-minute walk from my hotel. Inside the hotel was a ten computer *wangba* with a miserably slow connection for 10元/hour. It pays to look around for better service and better price.

April 19

<u>Xining, Qinghai</u>: I've been having a problem accessing my email at *wangba*. Some students called it the "Internet Police", special software on the computers at *wangba*. They showed me how to get around the "police". Instead of using Internet Explorer, I can use Tencent Explorer, an alternate browser. No problem when I used it, although I don't like the interface as well.

October 10

On the plane to <u>Hong Kong</u>, I sat next to a Microsoft engineer. He got out his beautiful new IBM ThinkPad computer. I, being a smart ass, said "I see you've got one of those new Chinese computers." He said "No! This is an IBM, three months old, made in America." We turned it over and sure enough, "Made in China". He was dumbfounded, and yet he was a computer engineer, doing Microsoft business in China. Isn't it reasonable to expect he would know?

December 15

Lenovo, a major Chinese computer company, has bought IBM's entire PC division (or a controlling stake), for $1.25 billion. With the purchase, Lenovo became the third largest PC maker in the world, behind only Dell and Hewlett-Packard.

2005

September 27

<u>Xiamen</u>: Spent the evening with my friend Xiao Liu, who works at Dell. We ate noodles and then went to the new Brown Sugar coffee shop. It and most others around Xiamen University have free WiFi for customers (he helped set it up). I'm told this is common in coffee shops in Beijing, probably also in many other cities. I don't have a wireless card in my computer, so I can't research it. I'm behind the curve.

Sick

1988

April 19

I have a bad cold and I'm feeling sorry for myself. Right now, fifty people watching closely as I blow my nose is more than I can face. Everywhere I go, anything I do attracts large crowds of friendly but curious people.

May 10

<u>Kunming</u>: Zhuang is a drug researcher who works in drug inspection and control. He says his work unit, the Yunnan Provincial Drug Quality Control Institute, is something like the FDA (Food and Drug Administration) in the USA. He travels around the province two months of the year in plain clothes acting like an ordinary customer, buying samples of both TCM and Western medicines from pharmacies, markets, manufacturers, and suppliers. Back at his lab, he does qualitative and quantitative analysis.

He told me most drugs bought packaged and sealed, and most raw products bought in pharmacies (as opposed to those bought on the street) are of high quality.

I had hoped to visit his lab, but the leader of his *danwei* (work unit) was out of town. The second in command, an army man, took the easy course and made no decision, neither letting me in nor telling me I couldn't come in, so I wasn't able to enter. No one can criticize his decision, as he didn't make one.

June 11

<u>Gongxian, Henan</u>: I badly messed up my back. A combination of a rough train ride, eleven hours hard-seat from Beijing to Zhengzhou (about my endurance limit for hard seat); three nights in <u>Zhengzhou</u> in

one of the worst beds I think I've ever slept on; a four-hour bus ride with my feet up on a wheel-well and my chin on my knees; and then clumsily stumbling on some stairs. My back went into spasms that night (a few days ago), something that's never happened to me before. I was very frightened and needed help. I found the word for help in my phrase book but didn't call out, stuck in my hotel room in a small town. I was both embarrassed, and afraid of someone trying to move me, hurting me worse, and that I wouldn't be able to stop them. I decided I had to try to get up, get dressed, and under my own power, get to a hospital. The pain was so bad I was imagining surgery.

I started by preparing a simple, carefully printed description of my trouble in English, starting with the train, bad bed, bus, and stumble, ending in muscle spasms. And I found all the key words in my small English-Chinese dictionary (I had to choose words that were in the dictionary). In my phrase book, I found phrases in Chinese for "I want to see a doctor," "pain," "backache," and "please, will you take me." I pissed in my washbasin. It was either that or on the floor, as the toilet was on the floor below and I didn't think I could manage the stairs twice.

I made it down the stairs and found the hotel woman, the one who unlocks my door for me, mopping the floor. I showed her the phrases. I'm sure I reeked of sweat and fear. She expressed immediate concern, yelled at everybody, and tossed down her mop. Off we went slowly, me with little mincing steps, and she pacing me, letting me use her for support on my Long March, about a quarter mile.

I took a small bag with what I would need immediately if I stayed in the hospital, and had roughly arranged things in my room so other stuff could be brought to me. The woman was good; she didn't try to help me but let me move at my own pace. She explained what was going on to people along the way to the hospital, and there was much sympathetic laughter from everyone. She stopped a man she knew and took his money, all he had, I think. It was sort of hidden. I wasn't asked for money or given a chance to produce any.

At the hospital entrance, she paid a registration fee for me, and we went to a doctor's office that had a steady stream of patients pouring through. A doctor in his late thirties studied my paper but clearly couldn't read any English. I pointed out key words in my dictionary.

He had me lie on the examining table, assisting me in just the right way. He had good hands and immediately inspired my confidence. He knew just how and when to help, offering only support and letting me do all the moving. He quickly felt my spine and the corded muscles, poked, tapped, hammered, and flexed my legs, put me through various

249

movements, checking at what point the pain started. All this was happening with the whole line of patients as an interested audience. He abandoned me on the examining table and went off to deal with other patients.

After a while two young doctors came in, a man and a woman in their mid-twenties. They were able to read some English, but were rusty and embarrassed. With effort and dictionaries (they had brought two more) they worked out what I had written. The three doctors consulted, came to a decision, and explained through the same dictionary process that X-rays were unnecessary, and that they'd give me muscle relaxant drugs, both pills, and injections directly into the muscles in my back. After the injections and a rough massage, I went off with the hotel woman (who had waited with me through all this) on my Long March back to the hotel. It seemed at least four times as far going back as it had been coming. The pills they gave me turned me into a dishrag. I slept and ate, and was not in pain the next day. They gave me five days worth of the "relax muscles" pills. The hotel people brought food to my room for me.

The hospital visit and pills cost less than US$2.00, and the woman tried to refuse my money when I wanted to pay back what she had spent. I had to push the money into her pocket. Then she went off to get me precise change, and brought back more food for me to eat.

June 12

The hotel staff is friendly, and concerned. The young people here at the hotel who can read and write a bit of English came to visit me. I think they are children of the staff. I was eating instant noodles when they came in. The boy pointed to some Chinese characters painted on the door. He explained that they said "No food or eating in the room". He took care of the matter by pulling the curtains. Of course the staff have been in and out, no fuss, and have brought me the food. Perhaps I could be more discreet but since I'm paying a few *kuai* too much for the room (foreigner price), I feel I have special privileges. And I'm pretty sick, I can't go out.

Foreign friend, special privileges: everywhere, people treat me better than they seem to treat most other Chinese. If the others are family, that's a special relationship. It gets extended at a reduced level to friends, then to people from your home town, to people who speak the same dialect, and on down. I feel I'm accorded the "friend" status: lower than family, but a lot higher than someone who doesn't speak the local dialect.

The government directs the people to treat foreign visitors as "foreign friends" so it's policy, but it feels real. I think it's the way most people truly view me. And I'm polite in return and curious about everybody and everything. I'm interested in the people. Even if I was a jerk, I'd be treated as a "foreign friend" on the surface but I don't think it would go very deep.

1991

December 6

<u>Guangzhou</u>: I visited the USA Consulate Citizen Services yesterday, looking for information on malaria and appropriate prophylactic medicine. I wasn't able to talk to a "white man", as some Nigerians I met put it. The consulate gave me absolutely no information beyond a bunch of useless printed travel advisories about the dangers of traveling in China.

December 18

Yesterday, I made telephone contact with a nurse at the consulate, one Mary Brown. She was a big fat help. In answer to my questions about malaria, she told me they advise all Americans to seek medical care and medicine outside of China if at all possible. For instance, go to Hong Kong. She didn't know anything about Maloprim (a malarial prophylactic) but said if a pharmacy in Hong Kong recommended it, it's fine.

But do I need to take anything? I told her I planned to be in rural areas, and asked what she could tell me of the risks. She said she knew nothing about this, but knew it was safe in Guangzhou. She was no help at all, and was clearly relieved when I said goodbye. I guess being semi-polite to people such as me is a part of her job she doesn't like. I got the distinct impression she viewed China as a dirty and dangerous place where no good Americans travel.

1992

January 17

I'm missing four days, but today I'm going to live. It's a beautiful day, and I'm weak but over it. I've been seriously sick with fever, vomiting, diarrhea, and headache. At a farewell dinner for me earlier that evening, Hu (my FTC interpreter) and friends were eating some uncooked small clams, a local delicacy, and they wanted me to try some. I was reluctant, as they were raw. At their urging I foolishly ate one, only one.

251

The next morning when I was supposed to leave, Hu found me still in bed, so sick I was unable to get up. He got me dressed and took me by pedicab to a hospital near the hotel. They gave me a pint or more of intravenous fluids with antibiotics. The IV took more than two hours, and I was also given pills and other medicine. I had violent diarrhea several times while at the hospital, and Hu would carry the IV bottle to the toilet and hold it while I shook and shit and moaned. Some interpreter, what a job! Yesterday, I was better but didn't eat anything all day. Today I've actually been out for breakfast and am sitting in the sun.

Hu was apologetic about his part in urging me to eat the clams. He said they all knew that sometimes Chinese people from outside the local area get sick from eating them, and they ought to have thought about that before they insisted.

January 21

This part of <u>Zhejiang</u> is closed to foreigners. I was absolutely to leave a week ago, under explicit orders from the police, but I foiled that by getting sick. There was no question of my leaving right then anymore, as I was much too sick. By the time I had recovered, the police seemed to have forgotten they had ordered me to leave, and instead followed me everywhere for the rest of my stay. I felt fine a few days ago, but then relapsed, so back to the hospital for a repeat of the IV. It's not a way I'd recommend trying to get an extension on an expulsion order. I think I'm over it now....

October 18

<u>Guangzhou</u>: I've started two weeks of daily *zhenjiu* (acupuncture) treatments, to try to control severe migraines I've had for the past few years. Each treatment lasts an hour to an hour and a half. Yang *Yisheng* (doctor), a young woman, seems especially knowledgeable and speaks fair English. The idea of a cervical spinal fusion (suggested in the US) to fix my problems horrifies her (me too). She says two weeks is enough to see if *zhenjiu* helps, and that there is no point in continuing if there is not a definite improvement by then.

October 20

Dr. Yang asked me to pay for a few days in advance and then got into a long and complicated explanation about the receipt, and to bring it back up after I paid. Turned out an old woman had lost her receipt and could not get reimbursed for a treatment. Yang put the old woman's name on the bill and gave her the receipt after I had paid. I told her she was a doctor who fixed many things!

December 15

Hangzhou: At the TCM hospital, I again saw the doctor/interpreter, Lihua. I like her, and hope I have a chance to talk with her outside the hospital. Xu *Yisheng*, the head doctor, is good but I don't think I'd want to work under him. He's officious with his staff although he treats me well, with special treatment I sometimes receive as a foreign visitor.

Some of this "special" treatment I don't especially like, such as being pushed to the front of a line ahead of Chinese patients who are waiting patiently. He also sees that I pay a "special" foreigner price, four times what I've paid elsewhere. I hope the extra money supports some of the patients who have to wait longer.

1993

February 10

Yang, a brilliant doctor of 29, warned me in advance the *zhenjiu* treatments would vary; each doctor would give me his own treatment, and this didn't matter much. Continuing the treatments as close to daily as possible was what was important. She wrote a paper for me in Chinese, explaining my problems and describing her treatment. I used this paper to get treatment from more than a dozen doctors in other places, only one of whom spoke any English. Each doctor added to the paper, writing their own treatments and observations. One doctor in a small town at a hospital that had never before had a foreign patient told me through an interpreter "Many paths, one goal".

At any rate, it's been an interesting experiment. I've learned a lot about traditional Chinese medicine, Chinese hospitals, and Chinese culture. Most of all, it has been a blessing not having the regular migraines. The results are hard to evaluate, but any time I managed to get daily treatments, I had no migraines. When I stop the treatments, in just a few days the migraines come back nearly the same as before. I've been spending less time on the treatments than I usually spend sick with migraines; the treatments are interesting, and I've seen the insides of a lot of different Chinese hospitals.

When I first met Dr. Yang, she said traditional Chinese medicine was not much better at treating migraines than Western medicine, but that it has had some success.

1994

February 21

<u>Guangzhou</u>: I'm at a hospital, hoping to get a painful hemorrhoid looked at. It's been a problem for a couple of weeks, the worst I've ever had. I'm registered now, and waiting to see the proper specialist, maybe get ointment or something.

Change plans; the doctor wants to do a small operation right now, to remove the blood clots. When I protested the idea of surgery, another doctor who spoke English and was helping me got right in my face: "Do you just like pain?" she asked emphatically. I put my objections on the back burner. I'm afraid of the surgery, but I went to the doctor for help because I'm in pain and miserable.

An hour later, I'd been tested for penicillin allergy, and had my pants down around my knees, huddled on my side on an operating table. The surgeon, who didn't speak any English, went to work. He picked out the clots, put them on a piece of gauze and stuck them under my nose for me to admire. Not exactly what I wanted to see. Now my hind end is bandaged up and I'm supposed to stay in bed for a day. I go back tomorrow morning for a checkup. Plus take a bunch of medicine, some Western, some Chinese, three times a day for three days. I was told the actual surgery was the same as is done in the West, but that the whole treatment is better here because of the added Chinese medicine.

February 22

I'm less uncomfortable this morning, with no pain. I'll head back to the hospital to have a checkup shortly. Although I was unhappy and apprehensive about the surgery, the relief was nearly instantaneous. I'm to go back again on Saturday for a final check.

I had some difficulty getting home after the surgery. I was told flatly not to ride my bike, but I couldn't leave it at the hospital. And the taxis didn't want to stop for me and my bike. I put the bike on the other side of the sidewalk and pretended it wasn't mine, until I got a taxi to stop. The driver was annoyed but let me load the bike in his trunk. The cab ride cost more than a tenth the cost of the surgery. It's not far, I can get home in an easy half-hour by bike.

1998

April 6

<u>Kunming</u>: I went with a water company engineer to the home of

his parents and grandfather. His father is an electrical engineer and his mother, who has excellent English, is a doctor, gynecology and family planning. His younger brother, who also knows English, is a dentist doing his residency. The grandfather, 88 years old, is a retired doctor, a malarial specialist. He was educated in Shanghai (graduated 1938), has excellent English, and fled from the Japanese to Yunnan in 1942.

The old doctor told me the only real risk from chloroquine resistant malaria is along the border regions with Laos, Cambodia, Myanmar, and a little along the border with Viet Nam. In Kunming, malarial risk is insignificant during the winter, and only a small risk during the months of July through November.

Mefloquine is expensive, and not made in China. *Qing hao su* is a Chinese medicine from an Artimisia species, used only for treatment, not for prevention. It is the only good drug available now, and must be used carefully so as to avoid creating resistance to it. It works fast, very well, is metabolized quickly, and is short-acting. He said Walter Reed (in the USA) synthesized the drug about ten years ago, and CDC (Centers for Disease Control) works with it. It is a traditional drug in China but its use for malaria is relatively new, only discovered about twenty years ago. He says currently there are two American researchers working with it in Thailand. He's an interesting old man with a clear mind, although if I asked him any questions, he lost track of what he was telling me. Before his grandson brought me to meet him, he had instructed me to ask few questions, told me his grandfather was impatient with his slowing mind and would leave the room if he lost track.

2001

March 27

Guiping, Guangxi: It's one week since I felt this cold coming on. I'm still rough today, but this is the first time in several days I can go up stairs without feeling like stopping every ten steps. Don't know what I had, it hit me hard and I certainly ended up with a bad bacterial secondary infection. When I'm this sick, it's hard to remember ever having been sicker.

I'm in the hospital writing this, all plumbed up again to the IV, the way I'm getting the antibiotics. Today, no penicillin reaction test. Had a test the first time and again yesterday, as Su (the nurse) got into a new batch of penicillin, but today is the same batch as yesterday. The whole IV rig is one use, disposable. I'm watched carefully, an alert glance by a nurse or doctor every few minutes while I'm hooked up. They won't let me leave until a half hour after each treatment, watching for any adverse reaction.

There are six hospitals in this small (for China) city. Last year, a girl died from a penicillin reaction in one of the other hospitals. I'm told the nurses had followed all the rules in that case. Now the rules are even more stringent, and rigorously followed.

Here on the edge of the tropics in late winter, colds are a big problem for me. One day it's so hot I can barely stand it, then it rains, and a week later I'm wrapped up in my long underwear and every bit of clothing I've got and still cold. Flu and colds are common here. When the wet and hot monsoon starts around June, many people with lingering colds and secondary infections end up with pneumonia. I've been told the hospitals fill up, and often beds are set up in the corridors for the overflow.

August 7

<u>Huhhot</u>: Had dinner with a Mongolian friend at her aunt's restaurant the night before last. I had serious diarrhea yesterday morning that started the night before. I took the berberine pills yesterday. Sanitation is not great at her aunt's place. I watched the dishes and cups being washed in a bucket of cold water on the floor, and being handed wet to the customers. I'm paying the price. Last night, I had a fever and a bad headache, in addition to the diarrhea. This morning, I felt OK but still a little weak. Thanks to the berberine pills.

August 22

<u>Ge'ermu, Qinghai</u>: Ugh, I feel a cold coming on, so I'm drinking a lot of *Banlangen*. It's a Chinese medicine that comes in small bags, dissolves in hot water, neutral taste although some brands have a lot of sugar added. It's supposed to boost resistance, best taken at the first hint of a cold. I like it and think it helps. In any case it doesn't cost much and certainly doesn't hurt me.

September 5

<u>Nanning, Guangxi</u>: The dentist's name is Chen. Dr. Xia, a CET specialist I met a couple of years ago introduced me to him, saying "Fred, this is Dr. Chen. Dr. Chen, take care of my friend Fred", and then she hurried back to her work, stethoscope dangling out of the pocket of her white coat. Boy, she's pretty! I registered and Chen went to work. He sent me off for X-rays, and I'm waiting for them to be developed. He has already replaced several fractured fillings, and

wants to cap one or two of the teeth he filled. I told him to use his judgment, to do the best work he could and to do what needed doing the most.

Chen's English is plenty good enough for necessary communication, discussing problems and options, and talking about other things. He's a pediatric dentist, just right for me: good, skillful, and gentle.

He told me he could do either amalgam or resin. He said resin is better, but many people prefer amalgam because it is quicker and more economical. He also said there is no evidence to support worry about health risks from the mercury in amalgam, and dentists who remove amalgam only to replace it with resin are unethical. That matches my understanding.

September 6

Dr. Chen transferred me to a prosthedontist, Lai, who wanted to know what kind of work I wanted. I told him to do the best quality. He expressed concern, saying that would be expensive. I told him it was a bargain compared to USA prices, so he recommended porcelain for the crowns and bridge.

Lai, like Chen, is also a teaching dentist in the medical university. He worked on me for 2.5 hours, preparing to make four crowns and a two-tooth bridge. What I save on this dental work, compared to having it done in the USA, easily pays for my whole six-month trip.

September 9

Jinguang: Vivi is only twenty, an English major at Guangxi University, and exceptionally pretty. She's a singer, has performed all over China, has been on TV many times, and probably has been to more places in China than me.

She was in Lanzhou a couple of weeks ago at the same time I was there, but we didn't know it and hadn't met yet anyway, except in email. While there she got bitten by a monkey because she was feeding peanuts to the wrong one. The one she was ignoring took exception to her favoritism and bit her on the leg. She is finishing up a series of rabies shots now. This seems a standard precaution in this part of China, after any kind of animal bite. No tests were done to see if the monkey was rabid.

When I heard the story, I told her she needed to be more careful and feed all the monkeys. She's been buying me peanuts ever since. When we got on the bus to head for Song's village, she had four bags for me, all different kinds.

September 14

At the hospital today getting my crowns fitted, Lai asked me if the US would make war on the Muslim world. I had no answer for him. I wonder if that is a common perception or worry among the Chinese? Most people say the attack was terrible, and they are sorry, sorry it happened, sorry that it happened to the US, sorry for me. Many Chinese people stop me on the street to say "I'm sorry."

2002

June 23

<u>Nanjing, Jiangsu</u>: Many of the negatives Jasper Becker describes in his recent book, <u>The Chinese</u> (2000), are true but could equally well apply to many other countries including the USA. He is writing about China, but even so, I don't find it balanced. Talking about medical care and health insurance, he paints a grim picture. He never mentions that nearly a quarter of all Americans are in the same boat, simply can't afford medical care and don't have insurance. Not so hot, for the richest country in the world. Describing street markets, the farmer's vegetable and meat markets, he sees Chinese as afraid of being cheated by other Chinese. His example is the official scale-tester: most street markets have an overseeing office somewhere, and if a customer suspects a seller's scale, he can quietly go down to the office and come back in a few minutes with an official and standard weights, and actually watch the scale tested. Seeing this many times over the years, I've thought "How great, so fast!". Becker sees people afraid of being cheated; I see people who, like me, want to get fair value for their money.

Becker finds the cup half-empty, and I see it as half-full. I like to think of myself as an educated optimist, and he seems an unreconstructed pessimist.

2003

February 13

<u>Nanning, Guangxi</u>: (The beginning of SARS) Southern China is gripped with a small health hysteria: Influenza, or some kind of respiratory infection. It's said several hundred people in Guangzhou are hospitalized and a few have died. Before I picked up on this, I had tried to buy some *Banlangen*. The first shop asked 15元. I squawked and walked out, and the price dropped to 10元. 2元 is the normal price here. Another place asked 20元, several others 7-10元, and a couple of

shops said "*Meiyoula*" (don't have). I finally got a bag for 6元. I later heard people were paying as much as 50元.

Who knows? Anyway, I'm eating my *Banlangen*.

February 24

I'm getting more work done on my teeth, continuing from where I left off on my last trip. Chen is an excellent dentist. It was my plan to do more, and I've told him I'll stay here as long as necessary. I figure top quality dental care costs me about 5% of USA prices for middle quality treatment. Not the most exciting thing to do while traveling, but it more than pays for the trip.

As in most Chinese hospitals, patients wander in and out of the treatment and examining rooms. A girl of about seven or eight has been watching Chen working on a woman's teeth. Neither pay any attention to her. The little girl stays carefully out of the way, while looking into the woman's mouth and watching the work. The kids here have a much better idea of what to expect, and are consequently less afraid and more cooperative. Chen tells me there is still dental phobia.

March 7

So far, I have had no anesthetics this time or last, and only a few twinges of pain. I am constantly nervous and expecting pain. I'm used to receiving anesthetics for any dental work and always have in the USA, but Chen is good. He has discussed injections with me, offered them if I want, but says he thinks I can endure. He says injections are more painful than the work he is doing and tells me to raise a finger if I feel any pain. If I do, he immediately stops and shuts off his equipment for a few minutes. He says much of the pain is caused by heat buildup. The worst pain has been sharp twinges that fade quickly. It takes hours to recover from the anesthetics.

March 11

I had my tenth dental appointment this morning, two to go to finish all I wanted, more than I had hoped to get done. The total bill will be about US$240.

March 15

Baise, SARS: Reports of this virus caused a bit of a panic in Guangxi in early February. My educated friends laughed it off. When the panic struck, the medicine shops made a killing for a few days by doubling or quadrupling the price of *Banlangen*. After a few days, the government forbid this profiteering and told the shops they could not raise the price of medicines, only allowing the shops to sell out what they had, at normal price.

A few people in Guangzhou have died from this virus, but fewer have died than from any other common cause. I read on the Internet that there is concern in medical circles, as hospital workers have been infected, and there is concern the virus could spread. But the numbers are tiny, no cause for panic or even much concern, for ordinary people.

I'm glad to see the Western media has picked it up, with their usual talent for covering unimportant stories while ignoring all the real news their corporate sponsors and owners want people to ignore.

April 2

SARS! It reminds me of when Tyan, an American engineer and old friend, was in DR Congo (then Zaire) and the Ebola panic was in full spate. I had asked him about his safety by email; his response was angry. He said many more people died every day from cholera on the streets of Kinshasa than the total number of deaths worldwide from Ebola. He thought the amount of money spent on only the media hype about Ebola could have easily completely eliminated cholera in Kinshasa.

SARS makes a lurid story, something new, and distracts Americans from Iraq and domestic problems. Maybe the focus on SARS is <u>for</u> distraction: Saddam is to distract us from Enron; SARS is to distract us from undercutting the United Nations. Media hype; new news, it's exciting. We've never seen it before. *Wa*! Bushit! (A nice expletive, invented by my Chinese friend Song).

April 8

The hype about SARS is something: in reality, 4% infected die, about the same rate as for pneumonia. 103 people have died so far worldwide, compared to 36,000 deaths related to influenza every year in the USA alone. Perhaps ten times that number die from influenza each year in China, as the population is nearly six times that of the USA, and people live closer together resulting in faster spread.

April 30

Beijing, SARS: The state of panic is extreme. In a city that is said to have a population of more than twelve million (the reality, if you count the transient workers and visitors, is probably at least half again larger), there are 800 confirmed cases of SARS, and 42 deaths. The total worldwide yesterday, 4510 confirmed, 276 dead.

For comparison, malaria infects 300-500 million worldwide, and kills 500,000 yearly: 3000 die daily. The USA alone has about 43,000 traffic fatalities each year, and far greater numbers of serious injuries.

Most of the panic in China seems to stem from the Western media and charges that the Chinese government is hiding something. If the Western media wasn't focused on this story, I don't think there'd be any panic here. Is that good or bad? From what I read on the Internet, SARS appears to be a nasty bug that if uncontained could be big, but containment efforts here seem overly aggressive.

I'm careful but not afraid. I don't want to catch a cold, as that would make everybody afraid of me. I am worried my friends will be afraid of me, a traveler. I've been keeping informed about SARS, and I look at the CDC (USA Center for Disease Control) and WHO (World Health Organization) web sites daily for any advisories. I think my chance of being killed by a taxi is hundreds of times greater than my chance of getting SARS, and I'm unafraid of taxis, although I do keep my eye on them. I was knocked down by one once....

May 3

Beijing is the center of the SARS panic in China: I arrived here six days ago to see what was going on. My Beijing friends warned me sternly not to come, except for one who said "Come if you want to see what is happening". The city is virtually under martial law. The streets are empty. Most of my friends cannot see me, because they are locked in their institutes and universities. I can't go in, they can't go out. And some of them are afraid to see me.

I'm riding my bike daily and enjoying the empty streets. Tomorrow, I plan to go to the Summer Palace; it's probably beautiful with everything in bloom. And no people. I'm told it's full of photographers, making the most of their chance to take pictures of the flowers without hordes of people spoiling their shots.

I don't know if I can leave Beijing, and I don't know if another place would accept me, anyway. My air ticket is booked to go home on May 21, but I'll see what happens. Rumors are rife, I have no way to tell what to believe. Many places inside China, perhaps most places, would place me in quarantine for two weeks if I arrived from Beijing, according to reports I hear. And I fly out of Hong Kong.

This morning on the street, I watched a paranoid man wearing a face mask. He was clearly afraid of touching anything, or getting near any other people. His eyes were darting around as he walked down the sidewalk. He avoided others, staying as far from them as possible. He found a clear spot and after glancing both ways, pulled down his face mask to light a cigarette: fear of the new vs. no fear of the known.

2004

November 9

Urumqi: Last night, a Uyghur friend's wife gave birth to a girl. I visited her this evening at the hospital and saw the new baby. I didn't want to go as I was feeling a catch in my chest, maybe a cold coming on, but my friend insisted, saying it was important for me to go, Uyghur custom. She had had a c-section and will stay in the hospital for five to seven days. Her nice private (ordinary) room with two beds is large and modern. Her sister sleeps in the other bed, to be near her. The room costs 40元/day, the same as my budget hotel. The total cost, including the surgery and room, everything, is 5,000元, about US$600. Without the c-section, the total cost would have been less than 2,000元. The surgery was her choice and probably unnecessary, but she opted for it after twenty hours of labor. This is common in China these days, c-section rates are much higher than in the US, I'm told.

2005

December 26

Chongqing: I met Dr. Chen this morning. She helped me find the office that gives vaccines and get a flu shot (*Da Liu Gan Yu Fang Zhen,* 打流感预防针), and we had breakfast together. The flu shot was the latest batch and cost 79.5元, a little more expensive in China than in America compared to income, but a good price for me. I've never gotten a flu shot in China before, but had left the US before the new vaccine was ready. Then we biked out to her lab. It's very new, just open this term, a key laboratory in China. She is working on gynecological tumors and cancer, using mice in her experiments. She has fifty 'nude' mice, and says they eat better than she does. If she could choose again, she says she might choose heart rather than GYN (gynecology).

For her degree in Chinese medicine, she studied about 40% Western, 60% Chinese medicine. A Western medicine doctor in China usually studies less than 10% Chinese medicine, while a Chinese medicine doctor often studies more than 20% Western. She had a higher mix. Her postgraduate research is in Western medicine GYN.

She told me that Western and Chinese medicines have different roles to play in treating diseases. For example, Chinese medicine is good at chronic infections while Western does well in acute infections. And Western GYN can't find good ways to settle problems about menstruation while traditional Chinese medicine can. It is a reason for her to study both Chinese medicine and Western GYN. And most important she said, nowadays graduates in Western medicine have better chances to find good jobs and earn more money.

Money

1988

March 31

<u>Guangzhou</u>: There are many moneychangers around the train station. Changing goes like this: a Chinese person approaches and says "change money." I ask the rate, we dicker and come to an agreement. I state the amount of FEC I want to change, and the changer produces the money, counts it, then hands it to me and backs off. I count it carefully, beckon the changer back and hand him the FEC, which he counts. We thank each other and go our own ways. The transactions are quite open on the street. No one can miss seeing what is happening.

1991

January 20

<u>Guangzhou</u>: When I'm offered a higher rate than usual on the street, it is a rip-off. The changer counts out the *RMB*, hands it to me, I count and find it is short. He expresses dismay and indignation, takes the *RMB* back and counts it, Oh my God! it's short. All the while folding a bill off the bottom while adding one to the top. So no more money changing on the street for me. I'll stick with small shops where I know the same people will still be there tomorrow.

1998

March 20

<u>Nanning</u>: Matti, a Finnish engineer working here, introduced me to his bank. It is a black market for Hong Kong and US dollars, paying about 2 1/2% more than the official rate. I was unaware of this market. The code is "dollar, dollar", with a US or Hong Kong dollar shown. The code I remember from the bad old FEC–*RMB* trading days was "change money". The Bank of China pays the official rate minus about 2% for currency. So the street market gives 4 1/2% more than the bank.

2000

January 4

<u>Xiamen</u>: After lunch we visited the moneychangers. Chen, a businessman, said the changers operate on about a 1% margin (the difference between buying and selling) and are tied into Taiwan, Macao, and Hong Kong. They check and change their rates daily, based on Hong Kong.

The changers supply hard currency to people leaving China for various reasons, and to businesses, here primarily smuggling. The smugglers must pay in hard currency for goods bought outside China, whatever it is they are smuggling in.

At the second money changer, a man was leaving as we entered. He was stuffing a six-inch high stack of US$100 bills into a plastic shopping bag as he walked out. No personal security guard, very casual.

2001

July 8

<u>Erlian, Nei Menggu</u>: Changing money, Narsu had me use the mother of a student of hers. She said the family was poor, the father drove *sanlunche* (pedicab), and their son was a good student. I got a reasonable rate, plus I put my business in the right place.

2002

June 17

<u>Nanjing</u>: A new thing, there are 24-hour banking centers everywhere here. They are brightly lit places with a row of ATMs, all shiny new. (**N.B.** — By 2005, these 24-hour banking centers are common everywhere in China. I don't use them; I don't use plastic.)

2003

April 3

<u>Baise</u>: I went to the bank at 11:40 AM (posted closing time 12:00), and they told me to return after 2:30. Wish I knew the black market here, it's always more efficient and less maddening than the Bank of China.

May 10

<u>Beijing</u>: I spent an hour and a half pedaling around starting at 11:00 A.M., trying to cash a couple of traveler's checks. I got sent from bank to bank, and told to come back after 1:00 P.M. So I finally tried a

US$100 bill at a bank that had a big sign saying "24-hour foreign exchange". They also told me to come back after 1:00 P.M. One of the places I had tried was the big old Friendship Hotel. Their exchange window was closed. All this before noon.

I get 820-821元 for a US$100 traveler's check at a bank, and about 2% less for cash. Frustrated, I went to the black market by the west gate of Beijing University. There I got 824元 for cash and was finished in about one minute. I should have started with the black market, saving time and frustration. I'd been thinking there was no reason to carry cash, but it sure was better this time.

2004

January 16

<u>Guangzhou</u>: Cashed a couple of traveler's checks at the Bank of China branch outside the White Swan Hotel. They were fast, the fastest I've ever experienced. Perhaps the bank is finally serious about stamping out the black market, or maybe this is a special "hurry up" speed for tourists. This branch is for the hotel's clientele.

November 3

<u>Urumqi, Xinjiang</u>: There are many Russian, Pakistani, and other central Asian businessmen here. Maryamgul, a Uyghur student, described the common Pakistani businessmen as shopkeepers, small importers. The big Russian Business Center has a thriving currency black market in front, and there is another in front of the Bank of China at *Nanmen*. That one is safer, she thinks. I had tried to cash a traveler's check at the Bank of China, using a photocopy of my passport (my passport is at the *Gong'anju*, for a visa extension). The bank wouldn't do it, said I had to have my passport, that otherwise it was illegal for them. Black market again....

2005

January 4

<u>Chengdu</u>: The main branch of the Bank of China was covered with scaffolding, but still open. Many people were loitering around the entrance. A young woman standing in a prime position caught my eye. We dickered and completed the transaction in about three minutes, with a bank guard watching and policemen wandering past.

As I started to move away, she called me back and gave me a business card. It had the flags of twelve different countries on it (I assume currencies she traded), her name, and her mobile telephone number.

<u>Beijing</u>: The black market is in the same place by the west gate of the university. They gave me 803元 and would sell me US$100 for 810元, less than a 1% margin. So I got 2元 more than the bank gives me for traveler's checks, only 1/10 of 1%, but fast. The whole transaction took minutes, and the same woman as two years ago. Makes me feel confident.

Queues

1988

<u>Hong Kong</u>: In line for the express train to the border at <u>Lowu</u>. In the queue, some people stand politely while others crowd. There is a low-key argument in Chinese as a polite person gives a crowder hell. The crowder heatedly and self-righteously defends his right to crowd, holding his place or advantage with an out thrust chin, stiff back and loud sniff, sure of his rights or at least his place in the line.

1992

<u>Guiping, Guangxi</u>: Gao arrived to take me to Jintian on another family outing. We had two jeeps, brothers, wives, nephews, and friends, a big crowd. We went to a landing for the ferry across the river. It was crowded, with a long line of vehicles waiting on the road. But his younger brother's pretty wife has *guanxi* (connections), so we got to go the head of the line fast. She works in the county road department and is also responsible for getting the jeeps.

The countryside was beautiful. Beyond Jintian, we went to a village at the end of a dirt road and had a noodle lunch at a small restaurant. I attracted a lot of attention. Gao said that probably no foreigners had ever been to this village before. I expressed disbelief, and said I didn't think many places like that existed. About then a tiny, very old lady pushed her way through the crowd. She was fearless and bright eyed, came straight over, sat down beside me, and started talking directly to me in the local dialect. Gao interpreted. She wanted to know how old I was, how many children, all the standard questions, and told me she had five great-grandchildren. Testing what Gao had told me, I had him ask her if she'd ever seen a foreigner in her village before. She answered, "Only on TV!", and doubled over in laughter.

Gao told me he used to carry 80 kg of vegetables 24 km with a shoulder pole to sell at that village. He said it was a four-hour fast walk. That was during the Cultural Revolution, a part of his life after he and his family had been sent to the countryside. He hadn't been back until today.

1999

January 25

What my great-aunt Ruby called the "pee-rade": on the train, rise and shine at 6:00 A.M. in the hard sleeper; that's when music starts loudly on the speakers. It's 6:30 now, and I've learned to be prompt. The line at the toilets and washbasins gets long fast. I've already washed my face, brushed my teeth, and answered the call. There will be a line for another hour. It's important to stand close to the door of the toilet or someone can pretend they think you are waiting to wash, and crowd in when the door is opened.

Sometime I've got to get somebody to try to explain the "rise early" policy to me. In many places, loudspeakers blare music beginning at 5:30 or 6:00 A.M.

2001

June 28

Erlian, Nei Menggu: I showered and washed my hair this morning, after waiting fifty minutes while four young women took showers together. After fifteen minutes, I got rude and started knocking on the door every five minutes. After forty minutes, I started pounding on the door. I got pretty angry, raised my blood pressure. I could have gone back to my room, but I wanted to wash my hair and knew the water would be turned off soon.

July 5

Washed a few clothes and waited forty minutes for the shower, two pigs hogging it the whole time; it's not easy with the current water situation in the midst of a serious drought. I left when the hot water was finished. I didn't want to wash my hair in cold water. The routine yesterday was the same (I think the same women): one woman went into the shower and locked the door before the water came on about 7:00 A.M. When the water came on, she started a leisurely shower.

Twenty minutes later, another woman, a friend of the first, showed up and was let in to start her leisurely shower (there are three shower heads in the shower room). This morning, the hot water was finished at 7:40, so I did a quick upper body wash in cold water.

While I was waiting in line for the shower, a man came to check three times, and a woman came with her bag once, sighed, and went on her way. This kind of piggishness sure raises my blood pressure. I only knocked on the door twice this time, asking please hurry politely. I got an angry self-centered response both times. I guess if I really want to wash my hair with hot water, I need to lock myself in before 7:00 A.M. and wait for the water to come on.

August 28

Lanzhou, Gansu: Spent an hour in a tight scrum at the train station, trying to get a ticket for today. It's the back-to-school rush.

There was a sixtyish man in the line behind me. Working together we drew a hard line against the crowders and queue jumpers, as far as we could reach. Sometimes this involved grabbing, shirt-pulling, and long hard staring contests, but together we always won. I've never done this before, and he probably hadn't either. It started when I stuck my arm in front of a crowder who then tried to stare me down. The older man grabbed his arm and joined the staring contest, two against one. The crowder left and we shook hands. We really went to work then, our partnership formed. It was exhilarating, but perhaps not worth it. No tickets for either of us, and I went back to the hotel with my legs shaking from the tension and strain.

2002

July 19

Huhhot: I'm at breakfast early, 6:30 A.M.; they're not set up yet. This place where I've been eating breakfast is a big restaurant. For breakfast, they set up the *baozi* and egg cooking, and ordering and paying outside the front door. The noodle and *zhou* cooking is set up just inside the door. It's a busy place.

Everything jams up at the girl who takes the orders and money and makes change. She gives small tickets showing what you've paid for. She has a big plastic organizer that holds the little plastic-covered tickets, about twenty different kinds. And she has a smaller box holding the money, crumbs, bicycle keys, odd bits of paper, lighters, and other junk. When I tell her what I want, she pulls out the proper tickets, adds up the price in her head, and tells me the total. I pay and she tries to find the correct change in her box. There are often four to eight people all trying to order and pay at the same time, some crowding, some waiting patiently, and some yelling "*Kuai dian! Kuai dian!*" (hurry, hurry). The girl is completely overwhelmed, although she manages to stay calm and polite. Either she is not very bright and can't make it work, or she has an impossible system imposed on her from above that can't work.

2004

November 9

Urumqi, waiting for a visa extension: Boy, people are lazy at the PSB (Public Security Bureau) passport and visa office here. This morning, the pregnant young woman who took my money could barely be troubled. She ran my two 100元 notes through an automatic counter several times, counted out my change (two 20元 notes), then added 20+20 twice on a calculator to be sure it made 40元. Now, having returned to pick up my passport ten minutes after the office opened, I watch her wandering around with her tea cup. Fifty people are waiting in lines at various windows and none of the staff are doing anything. Nobody who works here is taking care of business yet, as far as I can tell. I had been told sternly to return exactly when the office opened. The people who work here have POWER over everyone who is waiting. Maybe not as bad as going to the US-INS (Immigration and Naturalization Service) office in Seattle....

December 27

Xining, Qinghai: At the train station waiting, an hour ahead of departure. Before the gates were opened, the station officers made everybody line up single-file, in two lines. Many officers were patrolling, keeping order.

I watched one cool jerk evade this by casually watching the cops, grabbing any chance to move up ten or twenty people, and pushing back into the line. Every time he saw an opportunity he'd move again. He didn't make eye contact with anyone, acted casual, relaxed, and nonchalant. He completely evaded the monitors, and as far as I saw, no one objected directly to him. Most ignored him even when he pushed in directly front of them.

December 28

Chengdu in an hour and a half. This is an older train, with only one toilet per car. I won a small confrontation, waiting to use the toilet. The worst part of waiting is breathing smoke, because the waiting area for the toilet is next to the smoking area at the end of the car. I was waiting near the door but not blocking the aisle, when a guy pushed in front of me and stood smoking in my face. When the toilet door opened, I pushed in front of him. He backed down, and there was never any eye contact.

Phones

1993

November 1?

<u>Zhejiang</u>: Pagers, called BBG (*bibiji*, beeper) are much more common in Guangzhou and in Jiaojiang, a small city in Zhejiang, than in the USA. The pagers cost about 2,000元, I'm not sure of the monthly cost. I guess this is one way of expanding phone communications faster. It's simply not possible for everyone to have phones quickly.

Chen, an agricultural research scientist in Guangzhou, told me he missed his chance to get a home phone for 1,000元; now he must wait and it will cost more.

1998

February 2?

<u>Guangxi</u>: Gao has a phone now, and tells me you can get one installed in two weeks, paying a 1,200元 installation charge and 19元 per month, plus a charge per three minutes for all calls including local calls. Long distance of course costs more. There is no charge for receiving calls. He cannot dial international calls, only domestic and to Hong Kong. An IDD (international direct dialing) phone costs more. He's unsure of the price but says many phones on the street are IDD and can call anywhere. The phone line he has can have a fax or computer connected with no further charge, only the per-three-minute charge.

March 12

Xige's mobile "freewalk" (what he calls it) phone is paid for by his company. The bill can run 20,000-30,000元 a month. As a traveling salesman and motorcycle factory representative, the phone is his office, and he can receive and make calls to and from anywhere. I think his company pays the long-distance charges both ways, so calls made to him are billed to the customer as a local call, no matter where they are or where he is. An important thing for a traveling salesman.

2001

June 18

Huhhot: Mobile phones are everywhere. China already has become the second largest user of mobile phones in the world, behind the USA. Forecasts predict China will become the first in three or four years. I think that is pessimistic, as mobile phone use here seems uncountable. It is common for people to register a phone with a false ID, and I don't think those get counted. I expect China to become number one sooner. People use their phones everywhere, while riding bicycles, in buses, trains, elevators, restaurants. It is common to watch people sit down to eat and carefully line up their pager and phone next to their chopsticks. A few kinds of phones double as pagers.

I saw a "poor" man working hard delivering coal on his *sanlunche*. He was filthy with coal dust and using a mobile phone to talk with his customers to arrange deliveries, saving a lot of time and energy. A little shocking to me to see someone like him with a mobile phone.

China uses a single standard system across the entire country. Service and reliability seem much better than in the USA and there are no problems with compatibility. I've read Motorola has paid billions over the past five years for licenses to build and operate part of the system in China.

2002

June 25

Anhui Province, on the train between Nanjing and Beijing: The guy in the berth opposite me used his cell phone for SMS for about half an hour after the lights went out last night. There must be at least ten mobile phones obviously in use in this car and it's an ordinary hard sleeper on a long-distance train. There are sixty passengers in a car so around 20% obviously have phones, and the coverage seems nearly seamless along the rail line.

July 24

A report on the Internet says China's mobile phone users are up to nearly 180 million now. It's predicted the number will exceed fixed landline phones in a year or two.

Soon China will have more Internet users than any other country.

Now they are #3. Last year, the number of mobile phones passed the USA and China became the world's biggest mobile phone market. By now they have nearly half again more cell phones than the USA.

July 27

So many people with mobile phones. The coverage seems seamless along this rail line in <u>Nei Menggu</u> (Inner Mongolia). How good the coverage is up in the mountains or out in the desert, I don't know. It seems as if nearly every other person in this hard sleeper has one. There's no status any more, it's just a utility. There are some new local wireless phones, called *Xiaolingtong*, that are as cheap per minute as a landline home phone. They are not as good as the regular mobile phones that can roam. Mobile phones that work any place in China are common.

September 7

<u>Guangzhou</u>: I wandered through a maze of shops selling mobile phones, parts, tools, and accessories, just west of the *Nanfang* department store. Wow. Gives me another view of the mobile phone phenomenon. It would take hours to quickly explore all these shops.

2003

January 14

The old bomb shelter north of the *Nanfang* department store is now an enormous mobile phone mall. Twice as big as last fall. Phones, parts, cases, cards....

February 11

I'm interested in the *Xiaolingtong* phone service in China. I saw it for the first time last year in Nei Menggu, and understood it only as a local area variant on the mobile phones. I've now learned that it is an entirely separate system and growing very rapidly.

MII (China Ministry of Information Industry) announced last November that China mobile phone users had reached 200 million, a penetration of 15%. And those numbers don't include *Xiaolingtong*, which I think is counted as a landline phone. I haven't been able to find any numbers for it. Many are carrying *Xiaolingtong* now. The numbers must be huge, but I haven't been able to learn the extent of areas offering the service as that is also growing and changing quickly.

Xiaolingtong means "little smart". The *Xiaolingtong* handset looks the same as a cell phone but is much lower-cost, and the service is also much cheaper. I haven't seen any reports of use of this telephone technology in the USA, but it is used a little in Japan, and some other countries are interested. Most English language reports I see describe it as a low-tech and antiquated system, but that sure isn't what I see: its phones seem to do nearly everything mobile phones do, but the price is a lot lower.

A *Xiaolingtong* handset costs as little as $35 and can have a working number in less than an hour. Most handset purchases come with a credit that will pay the monthly and call charges for about two months for a heavy user, and up to six months for a light user.

Signal quality is not as good as a mobile phone. The landline phone system provides the backbone. The base stations are economical and quick to install, requiring only phone and power lines and a spot on the roof of a building, but the system may require 50-100 or more in a mobile phone cell, the area covered by four towers. In Japan, it had poor acceptance as it was priced too high for low-end users. I've read it is now being marketed there to high-end users as a data connection for notebook computers.

March 7

Xiaolingtong is also called WLL (Wireless Local Loop). Voice quality is poor, but my Chinese friends say "Good enough, you can understand it". As far as I know, nothing similar has ever been tried in the USA. It is growing very fast here in China, at the expense of the mobile (cell) phone network.

According to a report I read on the net, mobile phones in China gained six million new subscribers (5% of the USA total) in the month of January, but the mobile phone companies are complaining that *Xiaolingtong* has reduced their growth by 60%. This report pegged *Xiaolingtong* subscribers at twenty million at the end of January, probably a great underestimate as no official numbers are being published (that I can find) because *Xiaolingtong* has no permanent operating license for all of China yet. I first saw a phone of this type last summer.

April 2

<u>Baise</u>: Along the road to the big reservoir following the Nankun railway, there are big signs (China Telecom) and along the tracks (China Railcom) showing pictures and drawings of fiber optics cables explaining the cables have no salvage value. The China Telecom signs show a huge and handsome serious policeman with drawn gun tripping

a small dark peasant, his shears and a coil of stolen cable flying.

I had never thought about the problems caused to the communications networks by poor thieves stealing cable to salvage the copper or aluminum. If this is a big problem, it may change; the fiber has little or no salvage value so if the thieves are educated it will get much less damage.

2004

March 10

Mobile phones: I've been using VV's old one, a nice simple Nokia a couple of years old. It's convenient to have in my pocket, but I can sure waste a lot of time on SMS. I used to think email was a fast way to communicate, but compared to SMS, it's slow. The messages can only be 160 letters, including spaces. Costs one *mao* each to send SMS, and here in <u>Guangxi</u>, it's free to receive with some contracts. Making or receiving voice calls costs two *mao*/minute, plus long distances charges. The service I've got costs 20元/month, and the SIM card cost 20元. This is the cheapest plan and only works in Nanning, no roaming. Used phones similar to this one are easily available for around 400元 with a warrantee.

Want a landline phone? The installation cost for new service is now around 60元, and one can be installed in a few days. A few years ago, it took months and cost more than 1,000元.

April 11

He didn't want to talk about it in his apartment. We went out to lunch and he took the battery out of his mobile phone, fearing it could be used as a listening device. Then talked... Is this necessary?

Suggested Reading

There are thousands of books about China. These are some that stick in my mind for one reason or another. They can provide some background and understanding.

General

<u>Nineteen Ways of Looking at Wang Wei</u>, Eliot Weinberger & Casio Paz, 1987, Omar Bell Ltd.

A beautiful small book exploring the difficulties of making Chinese to English translations. The example used is a famous short poem, with nineteen different reputable translations.

<u>Legacies: A Chinese Mosaic</u>, Bette Bao Lord, 1990, Alfred A. Knopf.

This book was finished in the aftermath of 6/4, the Tian'anmen Square incident. In it, many different Chinese people tell their stories, bits they chose to tell. Most of the stories revolve around the time of the Cultural Revolution, and are used to set a background for the events leading up to 6/4. She puts a very human face on a tragedy that turned a generation of students from "This is my country", to "I'm working for me".

<u>God's Chinese Son</u>, Jonathan Spence, 1996, WW Norton.

Chinese history, about *Taiping Tianguo*, the Taiping uprising of the mid-1800s, perhaps the greatest peasant uprising in history. Eminently readable.

<u>The Chan's Great Continent</u>, Jonathan Spence, 1998, WW Norton.

China in the Western mind, beginning with Marco Polo.

<u>400 Million Customers</u>, Carl Crow, 1937.

An excellent old book, written by an American advertising agent who had spent 25 years in China. Many things he describes are unchanged. The last few chapters about business were uninteresting to me.

China, Inc., How the Rise of the Next Superpower Challenges America and the World, Ted C. Fishman, 2005, Scribner.
A current and glassy-eyed view, quite good.

Notes From China, Barbara W. Tuchman, 1972, Collier.
A small collection of articles by Tuchman that were based on a 1972 visit to China, including an essay, "If Mao Had Come to Washington in 1945". She writes with sensitivity about staring, control of foreigners, and other still-current topics.

Coming Home Crazy, Bill Holm, 1990, 2000, Milkweed Editions.
A collection of essays resulting from a year spent teaching in China in the late '80s. The physical descriptions are dated; the cultural observations are not. A theme replayed throughout the book is his difficulty reentering USA culture and society.

Boats

Sail and Sweep in China, by G.R.G.Worcester, 1966, 146 pp., Her Majesty's Stationery Office, London.

The Junks and Sampans of the Yangtze River, by G.R.G.Worcester. 1971, Naval Institute Press.
If you just like boats, or are particularly interested in Chinese boats, Worcester's two books are extraordinary. Most of the materials were recorded in the 1920s and 30s. I have found little other information on this subject. It's wonderful to have his beautiful and detailed sketches and observations, when there is so little recorded. Many of the different boat types he describes can still be seen on the back waters, although most have engines now.

USA-China Politics

Thread of the Silkworm, Iris Chang, 1995, Basic Books (Harper Collins).
This is the story of Qian Xuesen, famous as the father of China's missile and space program. In the '50s McCarthy craziness, he was deported from the USA and sent back to China, arguably one of the worst mistakes the USA made during that period of "Red" hunting.

Well researched and documented.

(Jasper Becker, a knowledgeable commentator on China, remarks on Qian's "defection" in his recent book, <u>The Chinese</u>. However, according to Chang and what I've read elsewhere, Qian Xuesen, who by the early '50s, had been in the US for more than twenty years, was cut off from his work, research, and students, as was J. Robert Oppenheimer, and finally held in detention before being deported. In no way was that a "defection". How history gets rewritten.)

<u>A Convenient Spy</u>, Dan Stober and Ian Hoffman, 2001, Simon and Schuster.

A detailed look at the Wen Ho Lee/Los Alamos "spy" scandal and the Cox Report of the late '90s, a more recent episode following in the footsteps of Qian Xuesen's story, above. Also well researched and documented.

These two books provide some background, a way to understand something of the history of current political attitudes in the USA toward China. For more depth, try <u>Owen Lattimore and the "Loss" of China</u>, Robert P. Newman, 1992, UC Press.

Newman quotes from Lattimore's introduction to a 1970 reprinting of <u>China Shakes the World</u>, by Jack Belden: "Page after page is a reminder that the stupid, obvious, unnecessary mistakes made by the American political and military establishments in China have been made over again, and are still being made, in Vietnam." The United States had in the late 1940s, and still had, a "bewitched belief that the incantation of words like "freedom" and "democracy" (accompanied by the spending of lots of money) could somehow conjure up an Ohio-like or New England-like regime capable of reversing a revolution already in being." America was still a "society blinded by imperialistic preconceptions".

Business

<u>One Billion Customers</u>, James McGregor, 2005, Wall Street Journal Books (Simon & Schuster).

Culturally sensitive, with interesting and valuable observations about doing business in China. He gives credit to Carl Crow's "Four Hundred Million Customers", for the title.

<u>The Chinese Century</u>, Oded Shenkar, 2006, Wharton School Publishing.

Excellent, perceptive and up-to-date, full of mixed metaphors. I liked it.

<u>Mr. China</u>, Tim Clissold, 2004, Harper Business.

This guy first visited China in 1988, the same year as me. His perspective is from the world of investment banking, but he is entertaining, and sensitive to many issues in China.

Fiction

Death of a Red Heroine;
A Loyal Character Dance;
When Red is Black, Qiu Xiaolong, 1999-2004.
These three novels were written in the USA, but are set in the world of Shanghai police in the early '90s. They are fun, and provide lots of Chinese background, a bit outdated but useful and interesting. I think the political workings of the job place in China haven't changed much.
The Laughing Sutra, Mark Salzman, 1992, Vintage Books.
Perhaps this book should be first on my list. Salzman's wonderful little fable gives a nice feel for various Chinese/American cultural differences.

Practical Travel Skills

Bugs, Bites & Bowels, Dr. Jane Wilson-Howarth, 2002, Cadogan Guides.
Basic information on staying healthy while traveling. Not specific to China.
Europe Through the Back Door, Rick Steves (Updated regularly).
General information and practical advice about how to travel and how to think about traveling, what to carry, how to use guidebooks, choices in appropriate shoes, luggage, and clothing, and many other topics. It is specific to Europe, but much of his advice can equally well apply to China.

Glossary

(Most Chinese words and phrases have multiple meanings; the 198 terms given here fit this book.)

Ànmó	按摩	Massage
Báijiǔ	白酒	A colorless distilled spirit (like vodka or gin)
Bǎnlángēn	板蓝根	A cold medicine
Bāozi	包子	Steamed stuffed bun
Bīnguǎn	宾馆	Guesthouse; hotel
Bù	不	"*Bu*" is a negative form, also used as "no"
Bùdǒng	不懂	Don't understand
Bùhǎo	不好	Not good
Bǔpiào	补票	Upgrade ticket
Búshì	不是	Not so; not true
Bùxíng	不行	Won't work; no
Chāi	拆	Pull down; demolish
Chéngpiào	乘票	"Ride ticket", no seat reservation (also **Zhànpiào** 站票)
Chūnjié	春节	"Spring Festival", Chinese New Year
Chūnyùn	春运	"Spring Transportation", the travel crunch around *Chunjie*
Cūn	村	Village (an administrative division: "small town" is a better description)
Dānwèi	单位	Unit; work unit; employer, or place of employment
Dà	大	Big; large; great

279

Dà bízi	大鼻子	Big nose, an old name for foreigners
Dàdào	大道	Avenue; broad road
Dǎo	岛	Island
Dàpáidàng	大排档	Small street restaurant
Dà tǔdòu	大土豆	Big potato, important person
Dàxué	大学	University
Diànzǐ dìtú	电子地图	"Electric map", a map on a CD
Dìfāng	地方	Place
Dìtú	地图	Map
Dìyī	第一	First
Dōngfēng	东风	*East Wind*, name of a major truck manufacturer
Dòufu	豆腐	Tofu, bean curd
Fángjiān	房间	Room
Fúwùtái	服务台	Service desk; reception
Fúwùyuán	服务员	Service person; floor person
Fǔzhú	腐竹	A kind of dried tofu
Gǎnmào	感冒	Cold; flu
Gōngfu	功夫	A martial art; gung-fu
Gōngshè	公社	Commune (Still found in place names, but obsolete as a political devision; now *xiang* or *zhen*, *zhen* being a little richer)
Gòule	够了	Enough
Guānxi	关系	Connections; relationship
Guòlái	过来	Come over; come here; come up
Guō	锅	Wok; pot; pan; cooker
Hàn, Hànzú	汉，汉族	The dominant Chinese ethnic group, *Han* nationality
Hànyǔ	汉语	Chinese language
Hǎidiàn	海淀	The main university district in Beijing
Hǎo	好	Good
Hǎobùhǎo	好不好	Is it good or bad? How is it?
Hòumén	后门	Back door; the "unofficial" way
Hóngqí	红旗	Red flag

280

Huángjīnzhōu	黄金周	Golden weeks, week-long national holidays
Huángliánsù	黄连素	Berberine Hydrochloride (a Chinese medicine), also **Yánsuān Xiǎobòjiǎn** 盐酸小檗碱
Huáshèngdùn	华盛顿	Washington
Huí, Huímín	回，回民	Hui ethnic group or people, a Chinese-Muslim minority
Huǒchē	火车	Railroad train, lit. "fire vehicle"
Huǒchē shíkèbiǎo	火车时刻表	Train schedule or timetable (common oral use)
Huǒtǒng	火桶	Fire bucket, used for heat in some areas
Hútong	胡同	Alley; lane. Usually refers to old residential streets in Beijing
Jiāng	江	River (also a surname, i.e. Jiāng Zemin)
Jiǎozi	饺子	Chinese dumplings
Jīdàn zhōu	鸡蛋粥	Chicken-egg and rice porridge
Jièguāng	借光	Excuse me, lit. "lend some light"
Jīn	斤	Traditional unit of weight, now 0.5 kg
Kǎlā OK	卡拉 OK	Karaoke; KTV; singing in bars to music on TV
Kēlì	颗粒	Small pellets; preparation (usu. medicine)
Kělián	可怜	Pity; have pity; pitiful
Kōngtiáo	空调	Air-conditioning; air-conditioned
Kuài	块	Basic unit of money: *kuai, yuan*
Kuài	快	Fast
Kuài diǎn	快点	A little faster; hurry up
Kuàikè, Kuàibā, Kuàibān, Kuàichē	快客，快巴，快班，快车	Express bus; express
Kuàizi	筷子	Chopsticks
Lǎowài	老外	Foreigner, lit. "old outside", old being a term of respect

Lǐ	里	Traditional unit of distance, now 0.5 km
Liǎng lǐ	两里	Two *li*, sometimes an indeterminate distance, as in "Not far". Commonly, *liang li di*, or *er li di*.
Lièchē shíkèbiǎo	列车时刻表	Train schedule or timetable (written, more formal)
Língqián	零钱	Small money; change
Liúmáng	流氓	Hoodlum; gangster
Lìzhī	荔枝	Litchi
Lù	路	Road; path
Lǚguǎn	旅馆	Private hotel (also **Lǚshè** 旅社)
Mǎidān	买单，埋单	Bring the bill (in a restaurant), formerly Cantonese
Màidāngláo	麦当劳	McDonald's
Májiàng	麻将	Mahjong, a game played with small hard tiles
Mǎmahūhū	马马虎虎	So-so, lit. "horse horse, tiger tiger"
Máo	毛	Dime, a tenth of a *yuan*. Also **Jiǎo** 角
Méibànfǎ, méibànfǎla	没办法，没办法啦	No way; no means; nothing to be done about it
Méiyǒu, méiyǒula	没有，没有啦	Don't have, a universal "no"
Méiyǒuwèntí	没有问题	No problem
Měiguó	美国	United States of America, a short form of 美利坚合众国
Měiguórén	美国人	American
Měnggǔzú	蒙古族	Mongolian person, preferred and official. Also **Měngzú** 蒙族
Mǐfěn	米粉	Rice-flour noodles
Mínzú	民族	Nationality, ethnic group
Mótuō	摩托	Motor; motorcycle
Nǎichá	奶茶	Milk tea, popular in Mongolian and Tibetan regions
Náng	馕	Flat bread made by Uyghur and Kazakh people

282

Nèibù	内部	Inside; internal; restricted or classified
Nǐhǎo	你好	How are you; hello; how do you do
Pāi huángguā	拍黄瓜	Smashed cucumber salad
Piàn	片	Tablet; pill; piece
Piào	票	Ticket
Píngzi	瓶子	Jar; bottle; traveling tea cup
Pīnyīn	拼音	Official Romanization of *Putonghua*, giving phonetic spelling
Pùbù	瀑布	Waterfall
Pǔtōnghuà	普通话	Modern Standard Chinese language; common speech; Mandarin
Qiáo	桥	Bridge
Qìgōng	气功	Breathing exercises; mystical power
Quánguó	全国	Whole country; all China
Quánguó lièchē shíkèbiǎo	全国列车时刻表	Whole country train schedule book
Rénmínbì	人民币	The Chinese currency, *RMB*
Ruǎnwò	软卧	Soft sleeper (on the train)
Ruǎnzuò	软座	Soft seat (on the train). Sometimes **Ruǎnxí** 软席
Sānlúnchē	三轮车	Pedicab (pedal-powered tricycle taxi); tricycle truck
Shàng	上	Upper; on top
Shàngwǎng	上网	On the net; using Internet
Shǎoshù mínzú	少数民族	Minority ethnic group or nationality
Shūdiàn	书店	Bookstore
Shǒufàn	手饭	Rice pilau or pilaf; also called **Zhuāfàn** 抓饭
Shǒujī	手机	Mobile or cell phone, lit. "hand machine"
Sìhéyuàn	四合院	Traditional courtyard house
Suànpán	算盘	Chinese abacus
Suānnǎi	酸奶	Yogurt

Tàiguì, tàiguìle	太贵，太贵了	Too expensive
Tiānzhīdào	天知道	Heaven knows
Tiělù	铁路	Railroad, lit. "iron road"
Tuōchuán	拖船	Tugboat
Wàidìrén	外地人	Outside person, not a local
Wàiguórén	外国人	Foreigner, lit. "outside country person"
Wān	湾	Gulf or bay, as in "San Francisco Bay"
Wǎn'ān	晚安	Good night
Wángbādàn	王八蛋	Bastard, lit. "Tortoise egg"
Wǎngbā	网吧	Internet cafe
Wèi	喂	Hey; hello (answering telephone)
Wèi shénme	为什么	Why?
Wǒ bùdǒng	我不懂	I don't understand
Wú	无	Nothing; nil; not have
Wúlài	无赖	Rascal; scoundrel
Wǔjǐng	武警	Armed Police, the civil arm of the PLA
Wǔshù	武术	Martial arts
Wúzuò	无座	No seat (printed on a ticket)
Xià	下	Lower; below; down
Xiàn	县	County; county seat
Xiǎojiě	小姐	Miss (**Xiǎomèi 小妹** is now preferred by many)
Xiǎolíngtōng	小灵通	"Little Smart", a wireless telephone system; Also called PAS or WLL
Xiǎomǐ	小米	Millet
Xiǎotōu	小偷	Thief (sneak thief, not a robber)
Xīfàn	稀饭	Rice porridge, congee
Xīnhuá	新华	The government bookstore; New China
Xīyào	西药	Western medicine
Yánggǒu	洋狗	Foreign dog, a pejorative (lit. "ocean dog", dog from across the ocean)

Yángguǐzi	洋鬼子	Foreign devil, a pejorative
Yánsuān Xiǎobòjiǎn	盐酸小檗碱	Berberine Hydrochloride (a Chinese medicine, also **Huángliánsù 黄连素**)
Yáolǔ	摇橹	Sculling oar, yuloh
Yīdiǎndiǎn	一点点	A little; a few
Yīdiǎndiǎn qián	一点点钱	Only a little money
Yīgèrén	一个人	One person; alone; by yourself
Yīngwén	英文	English language
Yìngwò	硬卧	Hard sleeper (on the train)
Yìngzuò	硬座	Hard seat (on the train)
Yīshēng	医生	Doctor
Yīyuàn	医院	Hospital
Yǒu	有	Have; possess; exist
Yóutiáo	油条	Fried bread sticks
Yóuyú	鱿鱼	Squid
Yuán	元	The unit of *RMB*, Chinese currency
Zhànpiào	站票	Standing ticket (no seat or berth)
Zhàntáipiào	站台票	Platform ticket (at the train station)
Zàngzú	藏族	Tibetan person
Zhāodàisuǒ	招待所	Hostel; a simple hotel, usually government-run
Zhēnjiǔ	针灸	Acupuncture
Zhōng	中	Center; middle
Zhōngguó	中国	The country of China (short name)
Zhōngguórén	中国人	Person or citizen of China
Zhōngpù	中铺	Middle berth (on ticket)
Zhōngwén	中文	The Chinese language
Zhōngyào	中药	Traditional Chinese Medicine, TCM
Zhōu	州	State; prefecture
Zhuāfàn	抓饭	Rice pilau or pilaf; also called **Shǒufàn 手饭**
Zhuàngzú	壮族	*Zhuang* nationality person; Zhuang
Zhūgān	猪肝	Pig liver
Zòngzi	粽子	Glutinous rice wrapped in a palm or banana leaf and steamed
Zǒu	走	Walk; go
Zuò	坐	Sit

About the Author

Who am I, what am I doing in China, and what are my qualifications for writing this book? Well, I've spent a lot of time in China wandering around. I first visited China in 1988 for half a year and have returned thirteen more times for several months each time. My first visit came about because my late sister and her partner were teaching English in Beijing, and she invited me to visit. Going to China was beyond my imagination, as I knew absolutely no Chinese, but somehow I managed. As it turned out, I was in China on my own for more than a month before I got to Beijing. I spent 23 days of that first month without seeing another foreign visitor, something that is still easy to do anywhere off the beaten track.

The next several times I visited China I did some small business: in 1988, I had spotted and purchased a small hand-powered shoe repair sewing machine that looked useful. It was common on the streets in China then and you can still find them today. I saw how it could be used in the USA and developed a niche market, importing and selling it for harness repair to North American farmers working with draft horses. I also imported other common items that were not copies of Western products. This business now seems to have been an excuse, something to justify the time I already wanted to spend in China, and a way to pay for my trips. I'm not much of a businessman and have little business background or real interest, but my practical and technical skills caused me to see uses for common and simple tools. I quit when I got bored, but the sewing machines are still being sold in the USA and many farmers use them.

I've survived the confusions of an ultimately unsuccessful marriage to a Chinese woman who had been a big city police officer. It was a five-year crash-course in culture shock and sensitivity, and increased my respect for the martial arts (she never actually hurt me). I've traveled in diverse parts of China, met people from various sub- and minority cultures, picked up bits of their languages and seen something of China through their eyes. I've learned scraps of different cultural standards, often through embarrassing experiences. Maybe some of my stories will save your face from being as red as mine is sometimes. I've sorted out complex dental care for myself and saved a lot of money (see the chapter, "Sick"). And while doing that, I've become friends with doctors, dentists, and professors, and learned about their work in China.

I brought a Chinese friend to Washington State in the USA for half a year as a visiting teacher, arranging funding, school contacts, and an official invitation from the state. He visited about thirty schools, teaching something of China and observing different US educational techniques. I've assisted many Chinese friends going abroad for research or study, and often assist others going to China. Working with Chinese friends, I've helped polish the English in applications, reports, and research papers. I've assisted with English textbooks, including an English grammar in Mongolian language, a Uyghur/Chinese/English text, and two Uyghur language English texts. I'm credited in some of them as "English Editor".

Professionally, I'm a working technician and engineer, mostly electrical and civil. I worked on the Whole Earth Catalog 37 years ago. I've always liked to build things; I can weld, and I ran a machine shop for a few years. I fix my own computer. In the '70s, I had a business doing precision explosives work. I do road construction and maintenance, and some selective logging. I like to mess around in boats. I'm a nuts and bolts kind of guy, and I love to collect details. I'm largely self-employed and sixty years old.

In the last five years, watching China change has become the most important thing in my life. I've now spent nearly 8% of my life there, yet I've barely scratched the surface of that huge country. I spend some time in the cities, but I like to get out to small places in the countryside, as I'm a rural kind of guy. My Chinese language skills are still pretty minimal: I can get by, but my Chinese friends all speak English.